:60 Second Bluesbusters

:60 Second Bluesbusters

Quick Pick-Me-Up Techniques

Joyce Quick, M.A., M.S.W. and Lexie Pfetzing, M.A.

New Horizon Press
Far Hills, New Jersey

Quick, Joyce and Lexie Pfetzing:
    :60 Second Bluesbusters: Quick Pick-Me-Up Techniques

Cover Design: Norma Erhler Rahn
Interior Design: Susan M. Sanderson

Library of Congress Control Number: 2004108082

ISBN: 0-88282-249-7
New Horizon Press

Manufactured in the U.S.A.

2009   2008   2007   2006   2005   /   5   4   3   2   1

Dedication

To my mother, Ruth, who had more than her share of reasons to be blue, but gave only love and kindness to her family. To Lorna, Dan, and Stephanie, who make my heart glad and my house noisy. And to Henry Ruth, newest member of the clan: on you, our genes look golden.

J.Q.

To Javier, whose caring and support kept me going. To Jeff and Jennifer, my light/dark, happy/sad, up/down offspring, with all my love. And to my amazing grandchildren, Sam, Zack, and Hannah, the sunshine and joy of my life.

L.P.

Contents

Everybody Gets the Blues

The color blue can be pale and powdery or dark as midnight. Blue moods come in many shades, too. Not only that, they invade every life at one time or another. Ranging from "a bit low" to "life is pointless," these blue moods often sneak up on us when we're not looking, Sometimes they hit us when we have every reason to be happy and they may stop us cold when we're just getting warmed up.

There are almost always reasons for these low feelings, most often linked to beliefs, body chemistry or behavior. You may not know the particular reason for your blues, but that's okay, you don't have to recognize it. With some effort and perhaps some help from others, you probably can uncover the reasons. What's important right now, however, is rousing yourself enough to take action.

The longer you let the blues rule your mood, the more damage they can do and the more likely it is that you'll sink into a downward spiral: You feel lousy, so you don't think or behave as well as usual, which makes you feel worse, which affects your relationships and job performance, which makes you feel worse yet...and so on. Because your body and mind are two aspects of one integrated system, all this takes a toll on your physical health. Just about every aspect of your life is colored by a blue mood.

Don't despair. In fact, get ready to shout hallelujah! You have in your hands a way to nip downward spirals in the bud. As its title proclaims, this book is about busting the blues and giving you the equipment to challenge them and win big. It offers a rich menu of activities to restore and strengthen your spirit. It won't ask more than you can give or exhort you to think positively when your life feels like a big minus sign. Instead, :60 Second Bluesbusters inspires you to do things to renew your energy and confidence so that you can work on whatever it is that's causing the blues in the first place, get through that blue mood quickly and get on with your life.

:60 Second Bluesbusters won't, however, cure clinical depression. There's a big difference between the blues and depression. It's a little like comparing a cold with the flu. Both can make you pretty miserable while the symptoms are raging, but one is more serious, more likely to linger and may even be life threatening. Depression is an illness that should be diagnosed and treated by a doctor. Sometimes that treatment will include medication, sometimes talk therapy, sometimes both. You'll find a list of symptoms in an appendix at the back of the book that will help you decide whether you need professional help.

Rest assured that as human beings first, therapists second, we too have had our share of ups and downs, minor and major. We've had personal as well as clinical experience with depression and antidepressants. There have been times in our lives when we were so far down in the dumps, we began to mistake the rim of the abyss for the horizon. Some days, we wondered if we'd ever find the handholds we needed to climb up and out. That has put us in a unique position to know what really works, not only for our clients, but also for ourselves. This book is a way to share that knowledge with you.

By the way, although we are two individuals, when we refer to ourselves or our experiences in the text, we use the first person, singular. In other words, we're writing in a single voice and we're doing this for several reasons. We think it's easier for you, we know it's easier for us, and, because we've been friends for so many years, we practically finish each other's sentences anyway.

One more thing. You don't have to read this book front to back, cover to cover. In fact, you don't have to read it at all, if you don't feel like it. Don't worry if many or even most of the activities don't appeal to you. Don't worry if some of them seem impossible in your current emotional state. Don't worry about anything. The important thing is not where you start, but that you start. Choose one idea that appeals to you, even if the appeal is slight. Then, as the slogan goes, just do it. Pick more than one thing to do if the spirit moves you, but don't risk feeling inundated. Whatever activity you choose, stick with the process long enough to begin to see some results. If you don't feel like it (*of course* you don't feel like it, you have the blues!), try not to use that as a reason to quit. Hang in there. You'll probably start to feel more like doing it after you get started, not before.

The activities in *:60 Second Bluesbusters* work most of the time for most people, so there's a good chance they'll work for you, too. You've already taken the first step toward losing the blues by reading this book.

Now, all you need to do is keep moving. Take the next small step and then the next. One step at a time is how you head toward better things; one today at a time is how you create your future. Using the tips and techniques in *:60 Second Bluesbusters*, we hope the road will be smoother and a lot more fun.

We're rooting for you. Please write to us care of the publisher if you have a *:60 Second* Blues-Busting idea to share or a story about how you used these suggestions.

PART ONE

Sweet Indulgence

It's practically impossible to feel pitiful and pampered at the same time. If you're feeling down, stop catering to others for a while and start caring for yourself. Inevitably, your spirits will lift when you relax, let go of everyday restrictions and indulge yourself in some simply delicious diversions. The thirteen chapters in this section suggest tried-and-true or fresh-and-new ways to pamper yourself. Any one of them can work wonders. But why stop at one?

Chapter 1

Ditch Your Diet

Never underestimate the value of a quick fix, especially when it tastes good! Comfort food doesn't just ease your hunger, it warms your heart and helps you feel cared for. So, if you don't already have some on hand, grab your coat, take yourself to the store and buy a few things just for the yum-yum factor.

When I was a kid, my mom made grilled cheese sandwiches and Campbell's cream of tomato soup when I came in half-frozen on wet winter days. These simple foods still warm my heart in frosty (or funky) weather. My daughter feels the same about oatmeal with brown sugar and raisins. For my buddy, David, raised in the Midwest, biscuits and gravy are comfort food, and Jenny, who grew up in Georgia, says it's gotta be grits. What does it for you?

Culinary Care Package

Put together a Blue Mood Food Kit. Possible contents: fixings for hot fudge sundaes, raspberry chocolate truffles, milk and cookies, imported brie and crusty rye bread, smoked oysters or caviar on melba toast, strawberries and really good champagne...make it a sampler of your favorite, most outrageously indulgent, soul-satisfying treats! Share with a sympathetic friend or feast on them all by yourself.

For me and many others, chocolate has special comfort status. Is it the incredibly smooth texture, the mood-altering chemicals or both? Who cares? I love it in all forms, but warm chocolate pudding always

3

makes me feel sooo good! When I was trying to lose weight, I kept a box of chocolate-covered cherries in the fridge. When in need of a treat, I took one, sat down (the better to focus and savor), slowly nibbled away the bottom of the chocolate shell, licked out the gooey center, then ate the cherry in tiny bites. My daughter prefers a chunky piece of dark chocolate fudge. When counting calories, she sucks on a low-calorie fudge Popsicle. Sometimes two or three.

If you're worried about your health, think you may have an eating disorder or are struggling with weight control, food smells can sometimes do the trick. A big part of the comfort we gain from food comes from aroma. You can buy candles that smell like chocolate chip or sugar cookies, warm apple pie, cinnamon, blueberry, strawberry, butterscotch, chocolate, vanilla, latte and other taste delights.

Next time you shop for groceries, splurge a little and buy a few items strictly for comfort value. Keep them around so you can treat yourself to something yummy on a yucky day. In addition, we now know that certain foods help us feel calm, alert or energized. Here are a few things to keep in mind when you make your shopping list:

- A few slices of whole grain bread raise levels of serotonin, the soothing, mood-elevating brain chemical.
- Chocolate boosts the brain chemical that stimulates euphoric feelings. It also adds a little caffeine kick.
- Bananas are rich in magnesium. Magnesium deficiency is linked so closely to stress that it's a good idea to add a banana to your daily diet. Nuts, beans, leafy greens and wheat germ are also good sources, or take a magnesium supplement.
- Lack of vitamin C can make you cranky. Tomatoes and citrus fruits are rich in C, so pour yourself a big glass of orange, grapefruit or tomato juice with breakfast or any time of the day.
- Iron fights fatigue. Foods rich in iron include beef, prune juice, soy products, garbanzo, navy, pinto and black beans, lentils, chard and spinach.
- Brazil nuts contain selenium, a trace mineral linked to upbeat moods. Selenium supplements are found in the vitamin section of your grocery or drug store.

Finally, don't forget water. Even mild dehydration can cause fatigue. Six to eight glasses a day are optimal. (By the way, coffee, black tea and most soft drinks don't count. They are diuretics and actually increase dehydration.) If you'd like to know more about the chemical effects of what you eat, take a look at the book *Food and Mood* by Elizabeth Somer, R.D.

Chapter 2

Splish-Splash, Take a Hollywood Bath

On my bathroom vanity is a greeting card sent by a friend. The illustration shows a woman in a bubble-filled tub and the caption: "When life gets me down, I take a nice, hot bath." Inside it says, "I've been in here since last Thursday!" It makes me smile, as she knew it would, because Hollywood baths are a favorite bluesbusting tool for both of us. With you as star of this "soap opera," here's how I'd direct the scene:

Decorate the set and choose a soundtrack. This is a key scene, so give yourself at least half an hour. A full hour is better. Post a Closed Set/No Admittance sign on the door and turn off the phone. Have your biggest, fluffiest towels nearby and make sure the room is nice and warm. Fill the tub as deeply as possible with water as hot as you can comfortably stand.

While the tub is filling, add bath salts, bath oil, water softener or a mountain of bubbles. If your skin is dry or itchy, try a handful of colloidal oatmeal, available at most drug stores. It makes the water feel like satin and gives you baby-soft skin. If your muscles ache, use a scoop of Epsom salts instead. To unwind, energize or stimulate your sexuality/spirituality, experiment with aromatherapy products. Lavender, traditionally used by herbalists to promote relaxation, is a good bet. Bring in a radio, CD or tape player and choose some relaxing music. Your soundtrack can be anything you like, as long as it fits with the way you want to feel. (When I'm the star, I choose dreamy instrumentals. Lyrics tend to engage my mind; disengagement is what I'm after.)

Lights! Camera! Action! Place candles around the room and switch off the electric lights. As you light the candles, a warm, flickering glow will transform the space and begin to calm and relax you. Scented candles take this lovely transformation a step further. Instead of candles, you could try a night-light and plug-in room fresheners or sprays.

Slip slowly down into the water. Notice the way the wet heat feels on your skin. Now, take a full breath in and let it out. If the water is deep enough, immerse your whole body. If not, submerge as much as you can. Slide forward, rest your feet on the rim of the tub or the wall and put your chest, shoulders, even your neck and head under. This feels terrific. It's also wonderful for your circulation.

If you can't immerse your upper torso, lay a wet hand towel over your chest and midriff. Dip it in hot water now and then to keep the temperature up. Close your eyes and cover your face with a hot washcloth. It's like being in your own, personal spa! If your eyes are puffy, try wet tea bags or refrigerated cucumber slices on your eyelids. Lie back on a bath pillow. Even if your tub has a sloping back (lucky you!), these inflatable cushions make a delectable difference in how relaxed you'll feel. Now, all you need to do is nothing. Maybe, from time to time, as it cools drain part of the water and add fresh hot water. Then, drift away again. Let your mind go blank. Focus on your breathing.

Post Production: An after-bath shower is a wonderful refresher. Cool water closes your pores, tightens your skin and stimulates blood flow. Keep the water warm, though, if you're planning to sleep soon or want to prolong the tranquility. Now, reach for those fluffy towels and dry off, then rub some rich body lotion and facial moisturizer into your skin. Follow with a dusting of powder or a spritz of cologne. When you are sure the scene is a wrap, find a mirror, admire your pink cheeks and take a bow. As you leave the set, try to take the serene spirit of your Hollywood bath with you.

Director's note: If the set decorator has provided only a shower, ask a friend if you can "borrow" a tub. Leave a spotless room and a small gift (scented soap?) behind. Or visit a spa and pay for a hot-tub/Jacuzzi. If that's not possible, produce a Hollywood Shower, followed by some mellow meditation, a massage or a nap.

Set the Scene

Transform your bathroom into a spa. Here are three ideas:

Tropical Rainforest: lots of hanging plants, jungle-print shower curtain, collection of pretty rocks, accessories in several shades of green, plug-in fountain

Roman Bath: fluted columns, cushy chaise, royal purple towels, gold accents, statue of Venus or Caesar, Pavarotti on the stereo

Desert Oasis: an assortment of cacti and succulents in terra cotta pots, sunny colors, heat lamp, Georgia O'Keeffe posters on the stucco walls.

Chapter 3

Make it a Bluesbuster Night

When you're blue, sometimes you need to think, problem-solve, rest, reflect, regroup. Other times, all you need is a little distraction. Remember, no problem is so big that you can't run away from it for a while, so *vive* VCRs! Let's hear it for DVDs and TiVo! When you're down in the dumps and doing your best imitation of a couch potato, haul yourself up and out long enough to visit the nearest movie-stocked store.

Choose an old favorite, one with parts you like so much you rewind and watch them several times (I could watch some scenes of *Bull Durham* until the cows come home and there are sections of *Best in Show* that crack me up over and over). Double-feature it with another film you wanted to see but missed. Academy Award or film festival winners are usually safe bets or take a risk and pick one you'd normally pass over. If you like sports, try one of the sports blooper tapes. They're great fun, as are most of the outtake or other blooper videos. Check out the live concert and comedy section while you're at it. Chris Rock, Tracy Ulman, Paula Poundstone, Sarah Bernhardt, Margaret Chu, Spalding Gray—all offer wonderfully funny video performances. Opt for something steamy, even X-rated. Watch Debbie, once again, do Dallas. What the heck, rent three or four, in several categories. Make a night of it.

Pictures Worth a Thousand Words

If you haven't seen any or many, rent a couple of classic silent films. Get one of the truly great (*Birth of a Nation, Intolerance*), one of the timelessly funny (Charlie Chaplin, Buster Keaton), one of the absolutely unbelievable (*Perils of Pauline, The Cabinet of Dr. Caligari*) and/or a terrific, modern black-and-white silent (*Sidewalk Stories*). Expect piano music and subtitles. Expect scenery-chewing acting. Expect to be enthralled.

Who can watch movies without something to eat? Popcorn is, of course, traditional. Ditch your diet (see chapter 1) and drench the kernels in melted butter. I love it tossed with grated Parmesan and a little cayenne pepper. Sometimes the salty-sweet flavor of old-fashioned Kettle Korn is what I crave; try it and see if it does something for you.

If you're not in the mood for popcorn, stop at the supermarket on your way home from the video store and pick up a few bags of your favorite snacks, or go all out and get fixings for whatever really delights you. My favorite is a big, fat, juicy sandwich—roast beef with horseradish on toasted rye, a dill pickle on the side and a pint of Cherry Garcia ice cream for the second feature. Movie night is the only time I eat roast beef, which makes it taste even better. Sometimes, believe it or not, it's tofu that turns me on. It now comes in flavors (lemon-ginger, southwest chili, honey-mustard) with dipping sauce—just the thing for a night of healthy big-screen feasting.

Tell your family, roommates or significant other that you're hanging up an invisible Do Not Disturb sign for a few hours and taking over the TV. Get comfortable (my movie-watching nights require sweats or pajamas, feet cozy in socks or slippers, propped up on an ottoman) and settle in for the evening. Give yourself over to the experience and give the experience to yourself. Laugh out loud, cry without trying to stifle your sniffles, make rude comments, boo and hiss, cheer and applaud, wax philosophical, let it all out.

Like taking a drive without a destination (see chapter 14), movie-night starts out solo, but at some point you may want to invite others to join you. If you want to change your private screening room to semiprivate, because you're feeling more willing to socialize and share, great! It may mean your blue mood is lifting. If, like Garbo, you'd rather be alone, that's fine, too. Have it your way, from opening titles to closing credits. And don't be surprised if you find yourself having an Oscar-winning good time while you're at it. After all, that's entertainment!

BLUES
FLASH!

When you're in the grip of a blue mood, curb the urge to ditch your razor. Letting yourself grow will only make you gloomier.

Instead, get the bare-to-there look you'd see if you were on the beach in Rio.

Don't, for heaven's sake, even think about doing this yourself! Make an appointment with a good salon, and pop a few Tylenol before you go, so you won't wince when they let 'er rip.

Then, buy a few pair of sexy, skimpy undies, and smile when you think about showing them off.

And men, either grow a beard, trim the one you have in a new, artful way, or shave off all that facial hair and treat yourself to a facial. Then show off your smooth, glowing complexion.

Chapter 4

Comic Relief

A tried-and-true way to banish the blues is with laughter. This is not news. Philosophers emphasize the importance of joy and religious teachers see it as healing. The symbol of the laughing Buddha, for example, represents the core of Buddhist teachings. Even if you're not into philosophy or religion, I'll bet you warm up more quickly to people who make you laugh. What's more, there's a lot going on when you chuckle besides having a good time.

After Norman Cousins, former editor of the *Saturday Review*, was stricken with a usually fatal neuromuscular disease, he did something unconventional. He checked himself out of the hospital, where he was becoming increasingly depressed and into a hotel, where he watched funny movies and videos for hours every day. Although he also used some standard medical treatments, Cousins swears that laughter had a great deal to do with his recovery. He told his story in *Anatomy of an Illness as Perceived by the Patient*, a book that helped launch a scientific inquiry into the relationship between emotions and the immune system response.

Maybe you're thinking you're too blue to laugh. And maybe that's true, right this minute. But black humor can bubble up in the midst of suffering and pain, making us laugh in spite of ourselves. Hawkeye Pierce had it in the TV show *M*A*S*H*. Shakespeare leavened his tragedies with it. Adolescents love it. After we laugh, even at something that isn't really all that funny, we feel better.

It's well known that humor helps us cope with stress. Finding a way to back off from your pain and problems for a minute or two and laugh can make all the difference. A few years ago, I was scheduled to speak at a conference of health care providers. My topic was the effects of workplace stress. Because of several unforeseen events and my own stubborn tendency to put things off until the last minute, I was running late that morning. At the last second, I snagged my pantyhose and had to change them; I couldn't find my keys anywhere; and I spilled a mug of tea on my notes. I barely made my train.

Once I was on the train, I began to settle down. It was then that I noticed the tea spots on my white blouse. That was right before I noticed my shoes: one was black, the other blue. I couldn't go home to change and still arrive on time at the conference. "Well, there goes my credibility," I thought. "They'll take one look at me and decide I'm one of the casualties of stress—and I am!" For some reason, this struck me funny and I started to giggle. I began my presentation with the story of my morning's mishaps, got a generous laugh, established myself as an imperfect person (like everyone else) and didn't hurt my credibility a bit. In fact, my willingness to laugh at myself and invite the audience to laugh with me was a great help.

Laughter instantly improves your quality of life. For starters, it empowers you to face difficulties and it relaxes you so you can communicate more effectively. Laughing might not solve your problems, but it will ease your pain, improve your disposition and lighten your load. After all, a problem that can be laughed at isn't the end of the world and a predicament that makes you giggle isn't one that will defeat you.

Crack Yourself Up

You may have heard that hearty laughter produces natural mood lifters in your body. But did you know that *pretending* to laugh also produces mood-boosting chemicals? If you're having a day so dark that nothing seems funny, try laughing anyway. Pretend you're an actor and the part calls for a big belly laugh. Fake it. Do "Take Two" in front of a mirror and see if it generates real giggles. Or start your own comedy club. It's free, it's fun and there's no cover. Ask friends to bring something good to eat and something funny to share. Before everyone leaves, have them stand in a circle and pretend to laugh as hard as they can for two minutes. Within seconds, you'll break up for real!

So take your problems seriously if you want to, but take yourself a little more lightly. Exercise your funny bone by sharing jokes and cartoons, reading humorous books (author Dave Barry is my daughter's favorite), visiting comedy clubs, watching comedy videos, or tuning in your favorite, funny television programs (I love *America's Funniest Home Videos*) or radio shows (*Prairie Home Companion's* annual Joke Show is a madcap marathon, available from the program's Web site at www.prairiehomecompanion.org).

Chapter 5

Sing the Blues (Away)

We probably remember Judy Garland best as Dorothy in *The Wizard of Oz*, but an equally vivid picture is this: Judy in a rakishly tilted fedora, man's suit jacket, dark hose and stiletto heels, belting out "Forget your troubles, come on, get happy...." Who could sit still? Who could resist the hand-clapping tempo of that old Gospel song?

Music changes how we feel. We've all experienced the mood-altering effect of a particular piece or type of music. Now there's plenty of research that confirms what we've felt: Music can pick you up or settle you down. It can focus your mind, set the stage for introspection or take you out of yourself. It helps you express and release strong feelings and makes pain-in-the-butt tasks easier (*Whistle While You Work*). It can also help you ditch a lousy mood.

Think back for a minute. What tunes have given your mood a boost in the past? Dig out those old LPs or tapes and listen once again to an upbeat, energetic melody you've long been fond of. For me, this works magic. I'm partial to vintage soul and rock and roll, so no matter how downhearted I feel, Chuck Berry or Elvis or Aretha can get me up and moving. I can't maintain a long face when Benny Goodman wails, either. Some more classic selections that do it for me are Beethoven's *Turkish March*, Brahms's *Horn Trio* and Rossini's *William Tell Overture*. I also love the soundtracks from *Chicago, Cold Mountain, Lawrence of Arabia and Raiders of the Lost Ark*. Go through your music collection, pick a few that appeal to you and play them.

Burn a Bluesbusting CD

With a two-CD-drive computer, even technophobes like me can burn a disk of their favorite bluesbusting songs. Shell out ten or fifteen bucks and any one of several Web sites will make it even easier. Just scroll through their song lists (Thousands! Tens of thousands!), point to the ones you want and click. Pay with plastic and you'll have your CD in a couple of days. Stash it away somewhere—or at least don't play it to death. You want it to sound fresh when you hear it again, next time you're in a funk.

Moving, dancing and/or singing along give the music much more mood-changing power than just sitting and listening. So does listening with earphones and really surrounding yourself with sound. Close your eyes and pretend you're the guest conductor or bandleader. Imagine that you're in total control of the music and that your gestures and expressions tell the musicians how to play. This may sound strange, but it's actually quite an empowering feeling. It's also fiendishly clever. Conducting means you have to let go of your mood for a while and give yourself entirely to the music. By the time you lay down your baton, the mood may have loosened its grip.

You may also want to try remembering and replaying music from your childhood. For Gillian, this means Scottish reels and folksongs. For Maria, it's anything played on an accordion. For me, it's a music box that plays Brahms's *Lullaby.* When my children were small, I sang them to sleep with *Morningtown Train* and *Good Morning Starshine.* My son used to call these his "love-a-bys." After they went away to college, both my kids used these songs as musical first aid when they felt lonely or afraid.

My clients use music in inventive, mood-altering ways, too. When one young man was feeling low and having trouble studying, he decided to see if music could help. He chose Gershwin's *Rhapsody in Blue* to play when studying and it worked. It served both as clear starting point (the opening notes signaled "it's time to focus") and motivator (upbeat, familiar but not distracting). It helped him stay on task despite his mood. A woman whose boyfriend had suddenly dumped her put Joan Jett's *I Hate Myself for Loving You* to good use. She cranked the volume up and stomped around the room, loudly singing into an imaginary mike. It made her feel strong, independent, in charge. I once did the same thing for the same reason to Boz Scaggs and *I'll Be Long Gone.*

One of the beauties of using music is that it's as easy as pressing *play,* plus it often works. Trust modern research and traditional wisdom: Whether you're feeling savage or sad, whether it's relaxation or stimulation you crave, the right music can orchestrate your mood.

Chapter 6

Throw a Tantrum

There's something to be said for losing it—feeling sorry for yourself with all the gusto you can muster. Entertaining fantasies of revenge and retribution. Ranting, raving and name-calling. In other words, having a four-star, freestyle freakout.

Think of it as a kind of surrender, because you're giving in to your feelings, but having a tantrum can actually help you defeat the blues. It's not only effective, it's easy. All you have to do is let yourself come unglued. Of course, this should happen in a setting where hysterics and histrionics are okay; your bedroom is probably best. It's usually wise to freak out in private, too. If you want a spectator, choose a close friend.

Freaking out works for two reasons. First, a good psychological rule of thumb is: *what you resist persists*. The harder you try to duck an unpleasant or painful truth, the more power it has over you. As long as you keep it out of your awareness, you feel pain-free. But the pain hasn't gone away; it's gone underground. To your body, emotions are ultimately chemicals. Positive emotions make good chemicals. Painful emotions make bad chemicals. Suppressed painful emotions make the worst kind of all. Next thing you know, they start reappearing in the form of rashes, ulcers, headaches, backaches, fatigue, anxiety attacks, you name it. When you're in the habit of sweeping your feelings under the carpet, you can't help but trip over the lumps. Freaking out is like pulling up the carpet and running the vacuum.

The other reason tantrums work is that such a high emotional intensity is tough to sustain. Think about it: How long can you engage in back-and-forth bickering when you're feeling irritable? Quite a while, right? And how long can that irritable mood last? Hours, days, maybe even weeks? Now, how long can you carry on a fierce argument when you're completely enraged and yelling at the top of your lungs? A few minutes at that intensity level is all most of us can take. We're just not wired for it. So, when you deliberately rev up the intensity of your bad mood, when you exaggerate it and take it to emotional extremes, it tends to burn out faster.

Drama Queens

If having a pity party means moping around feeling sorry for yourself, avoid it like the plague. If it means having an offbeat good time, do it in spades. Invite all your friends to a *Can You Top This?* pity party. Ask them to come prepared for sharing a personal tale of woe, past or present. Then try to top each other's stories. Announce that prizes will be awarded for the biggest tempest in a teapot and best actor/actress: "You think that's bad? That's bush league, baby! Listen to what happened to me." Fume, vent, rage, dis, carry on, crack up, cry. Do it all. Do it like soap opera stars. End the evening with comfort food—macaroni with cheese and a hot fudge sundae for everyone—maybe even a big group hug.

What does freaking out look like? Depends on who's doing it. Weeping, wailing, moaning. Punching a pillow. Breaking old dishes or anything else you don't care about that will make a racket. Beating your chest and jumping up and down like an ape. Pacing furiously. Swearing like a sailor. Yelling and screaming. Taking negative self-talk ("I'm such a screw-up!") to its nadir ("I'm the worst screw-up in the entire universe!"). If you are by nature a silent sufferer, this may seem impossible; believe me, you can do it. In fact, once they learn how, silent sufferers are amazingly good at throwing tantrums.

Here's what freaking out should *never* look like: Hurting yourself or anyone else. Breaking things you care about Losing it in front of kids. Add anything else that's outside your own definition of acceptable. The idea is to feel better when the eruption is over, not worse.

As you wind all that energy down and move into the chill-out phase, you may feel energized. More likely, you'll be sleepy. Go ahead and crawl under the covers. Before you give way to sleep, though, try this: breathe slowly and deeply. Tell yourself that when you wake up, you'll feel calm, clear and centered. Relax your muscles, especially the tiny ones in your scalp and around your eyes and mouth. Rotate your ankles, arch your feet and wiggle your toes. Remind yourself that you're the star of your own life, even if it seems like a soap opera sometimes. Of course, you're also the writer, producer and director. So, before you drift off to dream, take an extra minute or two to imagine what you'd like tomorrow's much-more-pleasant episode to look and feel like.

BLUES
FLASH!

Proactive Snacking

Believe it or not, you may be able to snack your way out of a slump. The key is high carbohydrates, which promote formation of the feel-good brain chemical, serotonin.

Be careful what kind of carbs you consume. Bagels and pastries please your mouth and are a quick fix for low energy. They metabolize rapidly, though, so your "up" may fast be followed by a "down."

Instead, reach for complex carbs (like whole grains). They give you the mood boost you want without the swings in blood sugar, so you'll have fewer cravings later.

Chapter 7

Baby Yourself

Feeling tuckered out by your To-Do list? Tired of taking care of others? Don't know which way to turn to fill your own cup? Ask for help.

It sounds simple enough. For many of us, however, it is not. When you feel unimportant, incompetent, lonely or unloved, you tend to keep others at a distance. You may even withdraw from the very people who are most likely to help. You're only trying to protect yourself from being hurt by rejection, apathy or the negative judgments you anticipate, but you end up alienating others, isolating yourself and feeling lonelier, less worthy and more lost than you did in the first place.

At times like these, you may need to open yourself to be taken care of. A young mother I know who has three little kids and a husband who expects a lot of emotional support summed up her own situation perfectly: "I need someone to take care of me." How about you? What do you need?

Maybe, like so many staunchly independent Americans, you think that you should be able to handle everything yourself. But maybe that's not such good thinking. You don't have to tough it out alone. Asking for support and assistance is not wimping out, it's mustering the initiative to spring yourself from your self-imposed solitary confinement. It's being brave enough to admit you're vulnerable (like the rest of us). It's taking a risk (What if they refuse to help? What if they can't? What if they don't care?).

Remember, this is not about how much your friends and family care. It's about how much *you* care. Besides, not risking is the biggest risk of all. When struggling with a dark mood, my first impulse is to pull back into a kind of cocoon. Experience has taught me that I need to fight this impulse by pushing myself to seek out others. Unless you do it all the time, asking friends for help doesn't make you disgustingly needy in their eyes. On the contrary, your willingness to be open and vulnerable lets them know you value and trust them. It also gives them tacit permission to be just as open with you and to ask for help when their blue times come. Assuming you're feeling like yourself again when that happens, it may feel satisfying to take care of someone else. While you're asking for support from friends and family, it's good to know that what they give you makes them feel good, too.

With a Little Help from My Friends

As long as you're asking for help, why not ask big? Get a group of family or friends together (like an old-fashioned barn raising) and paint your apartment or house, inside or out. Clean the basement, garage, or storage area. Build a deck, patio, or sauna. Do a yard or garden cleanup. Wash windows. Organize the spare room that looks more like a junk shop. Make it a work party, with plenty of both. You provide supplies and an abundance of good things to eat and drink. Don't scrimp. Videotape highlights of the process or take Polaroids. Make sure everybody gets to be a star. When the job is done, chuckle together over the "instant replay" or give everyone a snapshot of themselves to take away, along with bear hugs and effusive thanks. In a week or so, send thank-you cards, or bake and deliver something yummy to each helper.

There are lots of ways to baby yourself. Is your house a mess? Ask a good friend or family member to come over and help you clean. Send out for pizza or Chinese. When it's spic and span again, give your helper a hug, kiss, your most heartfelt thanks and a promise to reciprocate. Then go take a nap. Longing for a sympathetic ear, a smiling face, a bear hug, someone to sit with over coffee and Danish or someone to take your car in for a brake job? Arrange it. Ask for whatever you need right now—solitude, help with the kids, creature comforts, a foot rub, homemade rice pudding or chicken soup, a fire in the fireplace, someone to read to you. What would help you most?

If lounging around in silk pajamas and marabou feathered mules would make you feel better, do it. If taking a day off work and going to a ballgame—complete with hotdogs and beer—would make you happy, do it. If an ultimate spa day with everything from mud baths and herbal wraps to scalp massage and a pedicure lights up your eyes, do that. Don't rule out hired help, either. Dream of spending the day in bed, eating bon-bons and reading magazines while a paid professional does your shopping, cooking, cleaning, child care, you name it? Go for it! As they say in shampoo ads and royal families: you, my dear, are worth it!

Chapter 8

Give Yourself
a Mmmassage

A blue mood happens to your body as well as your heart and mind. Anxiety, sadness and anger cause your muscles to contract and stiffen. You may not realize how tense you are until you find yourself reaching for the aspirin, but painkillers are Band-Aids that do nothing for the underlying stress. They allow you to keep going when what you really need is to slow down or stop for a while and relax.

Some people relax through aerobic activity. Others prefer meditation, music, a Hollywood bath or a catnap. For many, there's nothing like a rubdown. We've known for a long time that, in addition to making us feel good, massages are good for us. Now there's proof. Recent studies say that regular massage leads not only to less stress, but also to better-functioning "natural killer" cells, the ones that attack disease.

How wonderful to do nothing for an hour, but lie still and surrender to the strong, gentle hands of a massage therapist! Mine, whose name is Annie, works in a dimly lit room. The colors are soft aqua, gold and rose. The sounds are water trickling over pebbles, bamboo flutes and chimes. The massage table is covered with warm flannel sheets in winter and cool Egyptian cotton in summer. Bliss and double bliss!

If you're new to therapeutic massage, it's easy to get started. Licensed massage therapists are almost everywhere. Ask friends for referrals or check the yellow pages. Massage schools offer great discounts. Ask a few questions before making an appointment, as there are several types of massage and many therapists specialize. A brief conversation will tell you what you want to know about length and cost of sessions and the kind of massage you'll be getting. Ask about training and experience, too. Consider whether you'd be more comfortable with a man or woman and if this will be your first professional massage, be sure to say so. It's important that you feel at ease with the person who'll be working on your body, so keep searching until you're satisfied.

Scheduling time with a professional is the most common way to give yourself a relaxing massage, but did you know that you can also do it yourself? As Annie points out, we're naturally drawn to self-massage. When muscles are tense for too long, we instinctively knead the ache between our shoulder blades or press fingers on painful eye-sockets, but it usually doesn't last long enough to do real good. Annie is convinced that we would all feel better if we massaged ourselves more often.

Here's how to give yourself a mini massage. Sit comfortably, close your eyes and take five or six slow, deep breaths. Try to breathe all the way down into your belly instead of high up in your chest. Next, slowly rotate your head, first in circles to the left, then to the right. Do this three or four times on each side. Shrug your shoulders as high up as you can, then let them fall. Do this several times, too.

Cross your arms in front of your chest and knead your shoulders and upper arms for a minute or two. Then, with arms relaxed, use your thumbs to massage each hand in turn, making small circles around the bones and joints. Rotate your ankles, first clockwise, then counterclockwise. Wiggle your toes, point them hard for ten seconds, then flex your heels for another ten seconds. Use your intuition as you massage insteps, ankles, calves, thighs and hips. Move your fingers in tiny circles or try long, deep strokes. Experiment with slapping. Press hard, if that's what you like, or gently if that feels better. Do whatever feels good. Imagine your body releasing all tension, tightness, pain and stress. Picture a warm, golden light entering your body through your fingertips, penetrating, soothing and healing. When you're ready, end your massage as you began it, with a half dozen slow, deep breaths.

You've Got that Magic Touch

If you have tense or knotted muscles, but can't do a self-massage because you're driving, in a restaurant, at a meeting, etc., try this: Gently lay the palm of your hand on the tight area of your body. Rest it there for about thirty seconds. Don't try to rub or knead or press. Shift your attention to the sore place, breathe deeply (at least once; two or three times is better) and imagine the tension dissolving. Imagine it simply melting away. This technique is so simple and effective that Annie (masseuse extraordinaire) calls it The Magic Touch!

Chapter 9

Slob Appeal

In Part Three, you'll find a chapter entitled "Dustbusting" and another called "Make Your Bed Like Mama Said." They're about bringing a sense of order to some of the more chaotic parts of your life so you'll feel—and be—more in control. That's good advice, assuming you've been letting things slide, dropping the ball a little too often. But if you're someone who feels that you can *never* drop the ball, it may be high time you did.

Lauren is a perfect example of a highly scheduled, in-charge individual. She has a high-pressure job, two kids in their teens and a parent in the early stages of Alzheimer's disease. She teaches Sunday school, cleans and cooks and is active in the PTA. She also has several friends who are important to her, not to mention her commitment to an exercise program that includes aerobics and weight training. Lauren has so many balls in the air she could be a juggler, if she could fit it into her schedule. She's also very smart. She knows that if she's going to do all this (and, for the time being, that's what she chooses), she has to have time for herself. She has to be able to drop some of those balls and let go of her responsibilities for a while. She needs to do it on a fairly regular basis, too or else she'll go nuts. Or get sick. Or her mood will turn dark.

Many of the activities in this book describe specific ways to create stress-free time for yourself—time when you can drop some or all of your "have-to's" in favor of a "want-to" for a while. Here are some additional ideas: Don't pick up after yourself or anyone else. Things may become cluttered, but you can always take care of it later when you're feeling better. Believe it or not, you may not even have to. What often happens when you drop the ball is that someone else picks it up. Don't wash your hair, shower or shave, if you don't want to. Don't put on makeup. Stay in your pajamas or your sweatshirt all day if you feel like it. Get in touch with your inner slob.

Call for takeout food, eat frozen dinners or directly out of boxes and cans. Never mind what your mother would say if she knew and if she finds out, who cares? Don't open your mail, return your calls or read the newspaper, if these feel like things you're supposed to but don't really want to do. I promise, the world will not end or even pause. And you will not fall so far behind that you can't catch up when your energy comes back.

The Glory of Grunge

The secret of slob appeal isn't entirely in how good it feels to let yourself go. It's also about how enlivening it feels to spruce up afterward. When you've been slumping around with briar-patch legs, dirty hair, a bristly growth of beard, greasy skin, chipped nails—feeling and looking like an unmade bed—you don't have to put on a ball gown or tuxedo to be transformed. Just making the shift back to normal is all it takes. So go ahead, let yourself go to pot for a while. A few days, maybe even a week. Then rein yourself in and spruce up again. By comparison, you'll look and feel great!

Of course, if those who are helpless (small children, pets, the frail elderly) depend on you for care, those balls can't be dropped without making arrangements for others to step in. But don't confuse pseudo-helplessness with the real thing. Your spouse *can* do laundry, cook, pay the bills and make sure clothes get to and from the dry cleaner, even if you're the one who usually does it and you do it much more efficiently. Ideally, you'll talk it over first and negotiate a trade so that each of you gets a "drop the ball" day every couple of weeks. If you're blue, though, don't be reluctant to explain that you need it right now. Pay it back when you're feeling more like yourself again.

Ask other people for help, too (see chapter 7, "Baby Yourself"). Neighbors, kids, professional helpers, church members, relatives, friends—all can be called on when you need a rest or getaway. You don't have to manufacture a conventionally "good" reason for asking, either. You don't have to give a reason at all, if you'd rather not. Just say "I could really use help on such-and-such a day," and describe what you want. Pay for their time, if that seems appropriate or offer to trade. The important thing is that you feel comfortable asking for help when help would make your life easier.

Remember, by dropping the ball and taking a time-out you aren't quitting. You're just putting yourself on the sidelines for a while. When you've played so long or hard that your spirits and energy are flagging, that's exactly where you want to be.

BLUES
FLASH!

Sweet News

There's always been something about chocolate that makes us feel good. Turns out it's not just texture and taste.

In cold weather, cocoa warms your tummy, tastes yummy and is loaded with antioxidants.

It does more for your immune system than green tea or red wine and—get this—a cup of cocoa is lower in saturated fat (3 grams per cup) than a chocolate bar (8 grams per bar).

What's more, new research indicates that dark chocolate contains flavonoids, compounds that make your platelets less sticky and are, therefore, good for your heart!

Chapter 10

Take a Break

Ugh! Another rush-rush, too-busy day. If you feel overwhelmed or exhausted and think your brain has given up the ghost, maybe it's time step on the brakes and take a break from your daily maddening rush. Don't just slow down—STOP! Push back from your desk, walk away from the dirty dishes or unpaid bills, turn off the phone and quit what you're doing.

Taking a break gives your mind a chance to rest and gives you a chance to shift out of overwhelm and stop circling around the "this is impossible" loop. A break allows you to deliberately interrupt negative thoughts, breathe deeply and set yourself free for a while. I won't write even one of these short chapters without a little break. When I'm working on something longer and/or less fun, my breaks tend to become less frequent, but they last longer; I need those rewards and build them into almost every kind of work I do.

Breaks can last from two minutes to two days, depending on what you need and what's practical. A break that's too short won't give you the lift you're looking for. One that's too long can generate anxiety and guilt. Here are a few ideas for two- or three-minute breaks: Look out a window and let your mind drift. Focus on a favorite piece of art or photo and try to see it in a new way. Or simply turn your attention to your breathing and feel the path the air takes as it moves in and out of your body.

I keep a kaleidoscope on my desk. When I feel over-the-top or down-and-out, I find a pattern I love and focus on it for a couple of minutes. If you'd prefer something more active, keep a stress ball handy. If you haven't seen them, they are pliable plastic balls about the size of a child's fist (some even look like a face), found in many drug, notion and grocery stores. You can punch, scrunch, step on, squeeze, twist and otherwise abuse them. Then they return to their original shape.

If you have more time, try meditating, taking a short walk (outside is best), or a set of looong stretches. Reach for the ceiling, hold for twenty seconds, then roll down and touch the floor, holding again for twenty seconds. Never stretch so hard you make yourself hurt. Be gentle. Roll your shoulders and your neck, then rotate your waist. Loosening the muscles usually loosens the mind. Remember that music has charms to soothe the savage (or stressed out) beast, so try listening to something relaxing. Or just sit for a few minutes, drink a glass of herbal tea, juice or water (no more caffeine!), nibble on a piece of fruit and daydream a little.

Have an hour or two? What a boon! *:60 Second Bluesbusters* is full of fun, easy activities that will have you feeling better in a snap. If you need to get your nose back to the grindstone soon afterward, the following chapters may have special appeal: chapter 2, "Splish-Splash, Take a Hollywood Bath"; chapter 16, "Dance with Your Demons"; chapter 28, "Breathing Lessons"; chapter 41, "Paint Your Mood"; chapter 58, "Get Lost in Cyberspace"; chapter 60, "Write from the Heart"; chapter 85, "No Place Like Om"; chapter 86, "Stage a Great Escape."

Indulge yourself with a total sensory shutdown: grab a blankie and take a nap—one of my all-time favorite tension-tamers. During the time when I worked away from home, I kept a Therm-a-Rest inflatable camping pad, eye mask and earplugs in my office, as well as a Do-Not-Disturb sign to hang on the door. When I didn't have an office with a door I could close, I went to my car and "pitched my tent" there for a half hour or so around noon. It made a world of difference in my energy level and mood.

Get Away for Real

Take off for a day or two. Leave the pressure, the problems, your issues and your cell phone behind. (I'm serious about the cell phone. Pretend it's ten years ago). Go solo and check into a hotel, bed and breakfast or spa. Let yourself be pampered, fed and entertained. Or take off with an old friend or new lover. Enjoy a scenic weekend cruise, find a retreat that speaks to your soul, go camping or just sequester yourself in your den or bedroom. How about a bookstore with overstuffed easy chairs and a snack bar? Curl up with a good book, something yummy for your tummy and nobody to interrupt. If you're an outdoor person, go horseback riding, kayaking, skiing, hiking, stargazing or mountain climbing. Drop me a postcard.

Chapter 11

Free Your Inner Bookworm

Over the years, I've tried many things to get through the blues. Most are described in this book. None works for me *every* time, which is why *:60 Second Bluesbusters* has such an array of strategies to choose from. None, that is, except this one. Because I am such a lifelong, dedicated, died-in-the-wool, voracious reader, this method has never failed me.

Books have changed my life for the better, over and over again. When I was very young, my mom read to me every day. Later, as the only child of a single-parent, working woman, I spent plenty of time alone. An introvert by nature and nurture, books became my best friends. I was enthralled by the people I met in their pages, the places they could take me, the ideas they stirred up and the emotions I felt when they touched my heart. Though I now have a wonderful, widely scattered group of real-life friends and extrovert leanings, I still treasure the experiences and people in books.

I find good ones by reading all sorts of book reviews, including those in the venerable *New York Times,* going to book readings and book fairs, asking for recommendations from friends and booksellers and generally keeping my ear to the ground. I've made a short list of books I think will lift your spirits. It has been gleaned from my current personal best-of-the-best and a terrific book by Nancy Pearl called *Book Lust: Recommended Reading for Every Mood, Moment and Reason.* Some are deeply moving, some escapist fiction, some fascinating true-life tales, some laugh-out-loud funny and some defy genre or easy description.

They are listed in no particular order. Because I'm a big library fan, I seldom buy a book until I've borrowed, read and know that I love it. If there's no library near you, see what you can find in a used bookstore, a great place to while away blue hours. If you're in a hurry, try a new bookstore or visit

Amazon.com, justly famous for having almost everything (new and used) in stock and getting it to you in a hurry. Then, settle down with cookies and milk or chamomile tea and let these wonderful writers take you to another place.

- **Anything written by Elinor Lipman.** She creates comfort food for the mind. All her books are about relationships (not just between men and women) and all are smart, funny and totally believable. You might start with *The Way Men Act,* but they're all delightful.
- *The Vintner's Luck* by Elizabeth Knox. Reading this strangely convincing story about the relationship between a male angel and a nineteenth century French vintner is like drinking a little too much fine red wine: it goes straight to your head.
- **Anything written by Richard Russo:** My favorites are *Straight Man,* a scathingly funny serious novel and *Empire Falls,* for which he won a Pulitzer Prize.
- *The River Why,* an offbeat, funny, sweet voyage of self-discovery; and *The Brothers K,* the story of a quirky American family with whom you'll fall in love. You won't want either book to end. Both are by David James Duncan.
- *What She Saw In...* (the entire title is too long to list, as it names all fifteen guys) by Lucinda Rosenfeld. It's the story of Phoebe Fine's relationship with 15 men, from the first boy she kissed to her married lover. A fine, fun read.
- *The True and Outstanding Adventures of the Hunt Sisters* by Elisabeth Robinson is a novel written entirely in the form of letters that is as touching as it is hilarious.
- **Anything written by Dave Barry.** He's rude, crude and side-splittingly funny. I laughed so hard reading *Dave Barry Does Japan,* I almost wet my pants.
- *Three Junes* by Julia Glass, a first novel about one family and three summers that is so full of compassionate wisdom and wonderful writing it takes my breath away. It richly deserves the awards it's garnered.

Three-Hanky Reads

As Nancy Pearl says, "There's something cathartic about crying over a book—it feels less self-centered than tearing up for oneself." Open a fresh box of Kleenex, settle in and try one of these:

A Lesson Before Dying by Ernest J. Gaines, one of the most profoundly moving books you'll ever read and one of the most beautifully written.

Talk Before Sleep by Elizabeth Berg and *The Saving Graces* by Patricia Gaffney, both about women's friendships and serious illness, deeply sentimental but never sappy.

The Good Mother by Sue Miller. No death, but plenty of big-time emotion.

Paula by Isabel Allende. A soul-baring, lyrical memoir written for her twenty-eight-year-old daughter while she lay gravely ill and in a coma for months.

Disturbances in the Field by Lynne Sharon Schwartz. I can't describe why this book makes me weep every time I read it. Just trust me on this one.

There's nothing like a fast-paced thriller, chilling true crime or clever mystery to transport the reader away from everyday cares. Try the best-selling authors, of course, but do some research and ferret out the little-known or up-and-coming masters of these genres.

Chapter 12

Easy Listening

Really bummed? Don't even have the energy to read? Try an audio book. All you have to do is pop in the tape or CD, press play and a world of literature is at your fingertips or, more accurately, your ears. We're not necessarily talking about lit-er-ah-toor in the classic sense, either. There's something magic about listening to a terrific story told by an accomplished storyteller. It engages your mind and imagination while you get caught up in the problems, pleasures, and lives of others. Choose a mystery, romance or historical novel, a biography of someone you admire or are curious about, a best seller or anything else that tickles your fancy.

Find a story about somebody in much worse shape than you (*Angela's Ashes* by Frank McCourt, maybe, or Dickens' *Oliver Twist*), someone with a fascinating life (Patrick Dennis's *Auntie Mame* is fun), a hot (or not) romance (dip into Anita Shreve's collection), or someone caught up in a compelling mystery (every one in Sue Grafton's alphabet series is marvelous, and they're all on audio; start with *A is for Alibi*; for something a little more *noir*, try Dennis Lehane or Ian Rankin's Inspector Rebus novels or the always satirically witty Elmore Leonard). Audio books are easy to find at the bookstore, library or online. Picture yourself lying in bed, letting go of your bad feelings with little or no effort. Sound good? It gets even better.

If you find long car trips or everyday commutes boring, aggravating or even occasionally enraging, pop in a CD or tape and listen to a good book. Instead of depressing news programs that bring you down, let an interesting book lift you up. Did you know that listening to educational tapes twice daily during a one-hour commute can give you the knowledge equivalent to taking classes and earning six college credits in less than three months?

Prone to fits of road rage? Comedies on tape can help you avoid that trap. When you take your mind off your frustration and put it on Ellen DeGeneris, Jerry Seinfeld, Margaret Cho or the master himself, Bill Cosby, you're much less likely to get angry at other drivers, no matter how stupid or inconsiderate they are. On long trips, especially alone or at night, an engrossing book can keep you from falling asleep at the wheel and entertain you at the same time. Not only that, a well-written mystery can even increase your brainpower. When you listen carefully, follow the clues, and try to solve the case before they let you in on who-dunit, you exercise your brain and may even improve your memory.

Many people find it easier to listen to instructional material than to read it. Studying psychology, finding out how the ancient Egyptians built the pyramids or how you can build a deck or create your own Japanese garden can all be done as you commute to and from your job. Pick something you're interested in, but haven't gotten around to studying. Try listening, instead of reading about it, and see what happens.

Audio books can be a wonderful source of spiritual growth and motivation, as well. Jeff felt frustrated and bored with his life until he started listening to Brian Tracy's motivational tapes as he drove to work. Tracy's positive, upbeat message and style helped him replace his cynical, passive outlook with a more hopeful, proactive point of view. He followed Tracy with Wayne Dyer and Pema Chodron, and you ought to see him now!

Fave Rave

As a devoted audio book fan, I've been disappointed as often as thrilled. A poor or mediocre reading can spoil a terrific book. And always look for the unabridged version—you want the full experience and all the pleasure. Here, to save you some shrugs, are a few of my all-time favorite audio stories, all masterfully told.

Killer Diller by Clyde Edgerton. This tale of a talented teenager in trouble is laugh-out-loud funny, and, like all of Edgerton's books, wise without trying. If you like this one, get *The Floatplane Notebooks* or *In Memory of Junior* next. Norman Dietz as reader is just right.

Plainsong by Kent Haruf. A finalist for the National Book Award, this is a marvelous story of how members of a tiny prairie community come together in the face of trouble to form one of the most appealing extended families ever. It's profound, witty, warm hearted, and tough minded. Tom Stechschulte's reading is a tour de force.

Oldest Living Confederate Widow Tells All by Allan Gurganus. An oldie but goodie, hearing this was a much different experience than reading it or watching the television version. It's a stirring tale, beautifully read by Donada Peters. Make sure you get the unabridged version and settle in.

You too can have all this "reading" pleasure and barely lift a finger. "Read" while you clean house, fold laundry, jog, paint the house, wash dishes and scrub the tub or just curl up on the couch or in your favorite chair, slip on the earphones and listen while the minutes and your blue mood melt away.

Chapter 13

Flying Solo

How's your number 1 one-on-one doing? I'm talking about that all-important relationship with the only person who means everything to you. That person, of course, is you.

Though the question seems casual, the answer can make a big difference when you're feeling low. During courtship, sweethearts spend time alone as a couple to get to know each other and build a sense of closeness. Long-term partners do the same thing for the same reason, especially if they suspect that their relationship is in trouble. It's common for couples to set aside time to be alone, talk and listen, have fun and pay special attention to each other. It can be a great restorative. But here's a no brainer for you: It works that way for individuals, too. So, if you're feeling downhearted, it may be because your relationship with *yourself* needs some extra attention. Welcome to the club.

Here's what I recommend: Ask yourself out. No kidding. Set aside a couple of hours to spend alone, having fun if you can, but even if not, paying special attention to yourself. Use the time any way you like, but schedule it in advance and decide how you're going to use it beforehand. That makes it much more likely to actually happen.

Maybe you feel like staying at home, pampering and soothing yourself. In that case, you might enjoy baking some bread (chapter 31) or producing a Hollywood bath (chapter 2), casting yourself as the star. Maybe you love to get out and explore new things, but haven't done much of it lately. If that sounds like you, go someplace you've never been before (chapter 23, "Unlikely Places, New Faces"). If you'd rather do something familiar and reliably pleasant, how about a trip to a second-hand or antique store, a museum, art gallery, aquarium or zoo? Long walks in the woods or on the beach are also tried and true ways to clear mental clutter and restore perspective.

If spending time alone is rare for you, expect it to feel strange at first, especially if your inner landscape is gloomy. Hang in there. Feeling comfortable by yourself may take some getting used to, so ask yourself out (and say, "Thanks, I'd love to") more than once. Why not do it regularly, even once a week? If you invest time and energy in this valuable relationship— in any relationship that matters—you're guaranteed a big payoff.

To get to the prize, however, you have to honor your commitment to yourself. Take your solo time seriously. Don't give it away to others (unless, of course, something truly wonderful comes up) and don't even think about standing yourself up. The negative message that sends is clear: You don't matter. But that's not true. This is time you've set aside to give yourself what you need—to pay attention to what you're feeling and thinking. Treat it as important and it will be.

Not Such Risky Business

Go someplace you don't normally go alone, a place that feels a teeny bit scary. No safety risk, mind you; just a stretch for your comfort zone:

Eat Out. If you never do this alone, start small. Get an ice cream sundae or a sandwich at a deli and sit down to eat. Move on to bigger restaurants. Hold your head high when you say, "Table for one, please." Tip big.

See a Movie or Play. Make it something hot that your friends have either seen or are dying to see so you can talk it up later. If you attend live theater, consider trying to get autographs from the actors.

Walk on the Wild Side. Spend an evening someplace you'd normally not be caught dead: video arcade, dance hall, karaoke bar, bowling alley, waterfront dive. Let your hair down (while staying safe). Take a cab home.

If you allow yourself to be yourself, whoever and however that may be, you never know which part is going to show up to keep you company. You may find yourself wanting to comfort the aspect of you that feels weak, insignificant, helpless, frightened or dependent. Good. Maybe you'll trade caustic comments with your inner bitch for a while (I do this every bit as well as Roseanne Barr!). Or maybe you'll have an opportunity to touch base with your higher self, who can open your eyes to a perspective larger and more loving than the way you feel right now.

So try this. For a few hours, let yourself be whoever you feel like being, without censorship or judgment. Be like Popeye: "I yam who I yam." It could be the start of a beautiful friendship.

BLUES
FLASH!

Real women have curves (didn't you *love* that movie?), and some of those curves have health benefits!

A recent study in the journal Circulation has good news for gals who don't always appreciate their rounded contours.

Researchers looked at the arteries of women ages sixty to eighty-five and found that "peripheral" fat (located on arms and legs) seems to protect against heart disease.

"Central" fat (in the midsection) increases risk. So does obesity. But those hefty thighs? They do your body good!

PART TWO

Wacky, Wild and Wonderful

When you're feeling blue, your mood and the days can seem endless. Who needs that? Break free! Shake things up a little. Leave your list of troubles behind and do something different—something a little zany, something you've never tried, maybe something you never thought you would. Go somewhere you've never been before. Who cares what your mother would say!

Chapter 14

Hit the Road
without a Map

Sometimes home sweet home can feel stifling—too crowded, lonely or full of things you "should" be doing. You don't want to abandon responsibilities or relationships, but a change of scene would do you good. If you can't swing for a real vacation, try going for a drive with no destination.

Driving with no place to go is much different from driving to go someplace. It can feel wonderfully freeing. Give yourself at least an hour or two and a full tank of gas. Let instinct, whim or a coin toss decide which way you'll turn. You may end up on strange highways or small back roads, in a new neighborhood, a different part of the city, in a forest or farmland. During your meanderings, you'll notice things you'd never see if you were driving with a destination in mind.

I tend to notice trees and flowers, but I also love to spot unusual buildings and interesting front doors. Once, I saw a dilapidated Gothic mansion that looked like the Addams family should live there. I like to look for road signs with double meanings, too: Congested Area (Will I need tissues? Nasal spray?) Slow: Children at Play (Wonder where the fast kids hang out?) Not highbrow humor, but it suits me fine and makes me smile.

My pal Ivy takes drives in her car to chase sunsets and look for rainbows. She has seen too many beautiful sunsets to keep track of and four spectacular rainbows, including a double one. Sam takes a camera on his getaways and stops now and then to snap photos. He showed me his favorite: the shell of a tall building under construction. Standing on the steel beams are a half-dozen mountain goats! That drive definitely gave his mood a boost and the photo did the same for mine.

On my mini runaways, I often stop at general stores, coffee shops or unusual roadside stands and attractions. Last year, a billboard that read

Dream Place Ahead instantly grabbed my attention. Unfortunately, it turned out to be a strip mall! I was so disappointed, I decided to look for a real dream place. I found it ten miles later at a little overlook with a spectacular view of a river rushing through a gorge and a waterfall tumbling down a cliff. On another drive, I came across a silo with a sign proclaiming "World's Biggest Kaleidoscope!" I collect kaleidoscopes, so stopped to take a look. I found myself *inside* a giant kaleidoscope, so big that visitors had to lie on the floor and look up at the display on a domed ceiling. I stayed for nearly an hour, entranced by the intricate dance of jewel-like colors and shapes.

Whimsical Wandering

Go for a penny walk. Carry a pocketful of coins. At each crossroad, inter- section, T, or fork in the road, toss a penny: heads, go straight; tails, turn. Toss twice for turns: heads, right; tails, left. Leave the pennies as a kind of bread- crumb path or good luck tokens for a child to find.

Close your eyes and throw a dart (or jab your finger) at a map. Drive or take public transportation to get there. Eat at the café, if there is one. Wander around; pretend you're a reporter or foreign tourist. What makes this place interesting? Would you like to live here? Why? Why not? Snap a few pic- tures. Chat with some locals. Tell them you're thinking of buying a house. Ask how long they've lived there. What do they like and dislike about the place?

When you're blue, your ability to concentrate may be off, so it can help to do things you can't mess up. Many of the suggestions in this book fall into that category: no pressure, no schedule, no rules. This is one of them. Just let yourself wander wherever you choose. You may find yourself miss- ing the very things or people from which you're escaping. Perhaps you'll have an urge to share your discoveries or find something to take back as a gift. Or maybe you won't give anyone else a thought. Either way is fine.

Shortly after we got driver's licenses, my friends and I used to go for rides just to see how long it would take to get lost. These days, if I have no destination, I can't lose my way. I'm always *someplace,* which is where I was headed. Besides, I can read a map and don't mind asking for directions.

Next time you feel like chucking it all and running away, get behind the wheel instead. If you can't or don't like to drive, take a bus, bike or simply walk for an hour or so in an unfamiliar neighborhood. Be an explorer. Take yourself to a place you've never been and notice what's there and how you feel. Get yourself lost and then found again. It's a consciousness-expander, confidence-builder and quick relief from a stifling mood.

Chapter 15

Dye Your Hair
to Match Your Mood

Maybe blue hair is a bit far out for your lifestyle, maybe not. Either way, blue days are a fine time to play dress-up. Since it's no fun being you right now, be someone else—you can be anyone or anything you want: movie star, medieval queen, cowboy, Playboy bunny, astronaut, flapper, Southern belle, even a flower or inanimate object. Adopt a new identity or adapt your old one. All it takes is a well-stocked closet and makeup kit and whatever you can improvise to create your illusion.

Who or what would you like to be today? Gauguin in Tahiti or one of the islanders he painted? The glamorous star of film noir? A safety-pinned punk rocker? A call girl, a la *Pretty Woman?* (I tried that one Halloween. My six-year-old son said, "Oh Mommy, you look sooo beautiful! You should dress like that every day!") Clowns are easy to create. So are ballerinas, belly dancers, bikers, or flower children.

Don't stop now. Spike your hair, curl it, sweep it into a topknot or buy a cheap wig. Paint your lips black or burgundy. Take off your underwear or let it show. Consider glitter, fur, skin-tight spandex, black lace, fishnet stockings, a silk robe or feather boa, biker boots, picture hats, over-the-elbow gloves, ten gallon hats, temporary tattoos, thigh-high boots, a studded leather jacket—anything goes. Take your time and make it look right. Sometimes it's more fun if you invite a friend. Cheer each other on, take pictures and laugh at your own outrageousness. You might even decide to make it a party (see chapter 43).

Last February, with no place to go and nothing exciting to do, I gave a *Come as You Wish You Were* party. I dressed as a cat, because all I wanted to do was curl up and nap. Carole had tropical island fantasies, so she came in a sundress, with beach bag, sun hat and sunglasses. Her husband, Dave, who can't wait for spring, smeared dirt on his face, wore gardening grubbies and handed out daffodil bulbs to everyone.

Dress to Kill (or Fill)

Don't wait for Halloween. Decorate the place and get creative with invitations (paper skulls, etc.). Then, summon your friends to a *Dress to Kill* bash. Ask everyone to outfit themselves as their favorite villain. Award prizes for most clever or worst dressed. Play Clue or charades with words that pick up the theme: Hannibal Lector, Bonnie and Clyde, the vampire LeStat, Dr. Jekyll or make it a potluck and throw a "come as your favorite food" shindig. Imagine dressing as a Caesar salad: toga with romaine lettuce stapled to it, laurel and garlic wreath and stick-on croutons!

The idea is to become a kind of escape artist, freeing yourself from the confines of your usual style and breaking out of your mood. If you're one of those folks who doesn't hang on to old clothes (more power to you!), visit a local thrift shop or second-hand clothing store. You can have a fine time poking fun at other people's cast-offs and trying on the most outrageous things you can find.

How about pretending that you're going someplace really special—a black-tie wedding, a formal New Year's Eve wingding or dinner at an elegant restaurant? Take time with your hair and makeup. Trim that beard, shine those shoes. Aim for fabulous. Try false eyelashes if you're sure-handed (I always make a mess). Pin a flower, real or not, or jewelry in your hair. Try a new aftershave or cologne. And, remember, looking good helps you feel good, so shimmy into your most outrageous underwear (that goes for men, as well—if you don't have anything *outré*, get some!), paint your nails and go for the gold, or at least the glitter. When you're finished, take a long, lingering look at yourself. Better yet, snap a picture, if you have a self-timer or ask someone else to do it. Take several.

Consider going public while you're dressed to the nines. Maybe you'd like to be noticed while you pretend not to notice. Maybe you'd like to flirt with strangers. Stay safe, but not so safe you don't have any fun. If you go solo, be your best self—poised, relaxed, confident, gracious. Or pretend to be someone else—glamorous, mysterious and incognito—and act as you think that person would. Don't worry, though, if you lack the chutzpah to wear your dress-up clothes outside the house. That can be interesting and fun, but it's entirely optional. Instead, put one of the photos you took on the refrigerator as a reminder: Like me, like all of us, you have many possible, potential selves. Some are fun, some are silly. Some are exotic and glamorous. Some are strong and self-reliant. Feeling low is temporary. Just like fishnet stockings, blue hair and wash-off tattoos.

Chapter 16

Dance with Your Demons

If the blues have you feeling like you're running on empty, here's a great way to put a tiger in your tank: Dance! Get your mojo working and shake your booty. Dancing raises your pulse and stirs your blood. It's expressive and creative, the kind of good-for-the-soul activity—like singing, painting or digging in the dirt—that you did as a kid, but may have fallen away as you grew older.

If you'd rather collapse and devote yourself to some serious self-pity, that's okay for a while. Too much couch time feeds a blue mood and encourages it to linger. Besides, dancing is one of those things that you won't feel like doing until after you're doing it. Then the effects are almost miraculous.

Maureen dances to help cope with a condition that causes total, permanent hair loss. She is a perfect size six, with a lovely face and several beautiful wigs, yet hairlessness sometimes makes her feel deficient and unattractive. As part of a strategy to combat those feelings, she created a weekly Saturday Night Dance. She has a glass of wine, closes the blinds, dons a sleeveless leotard and plays music with a strong beat. Using colorful body paints, she decorates her face, neck, hands and arms with fanciful designs. Then, she dances for an hour or so, celebrating herself as a woman who, hair or no hair, is committed to being fully alive.

If you took dance lessons as a kid, you probably remember a few moves. Who cares if you're any good? Play some music and pirouette, time step or lunge around the room. Create a little recital for yourself. What kind of dancing did you like in your teens? Dust off some old tapes or CDs and take yourself back to disco, twist, funky chicken, swing, slide, stroll, cha-cha or Charleston. Maybe you'd rather try some amateur belly dancing or create your own unique moves. Do whatever feels like fun. Turn up the music and get down!

Sometimes watching others dance can get you in the mood. Turn on MTV and see what's happening or check out the Nashville Network for some tricky two-steps and line dancing. You can even find shows that give lessons and demonstrations. Take it a step further, if the spirit so moves. Go out to a club, lounge or tavern and dance to live music. Go alone or rustle up a friend. For a really good time, get up a group. Dancing comes in as many varieties as ice cream—everything from Argentine tango to zydeco and, remember, there's nothing square about square or contra dancing.

All God's Children Need Dancin' Shoes

You should have at least one pair of shoes in your closet that make you feel like dancing: lightweight, well-made, securely fitted and fastened (no sliding around on your foot makes for expert moves on the floor), a mid-height heel and very sexy, if possible. There's a large, active recreational dance community in my city, so there are also a couple of shops that specialize in dance clothing and shoes. Your city may have some, too. If not, any good shoe store can fit you with what you're looking for: black patent leather loafers, Cuban-heeled tango shoes, strappy high-heels—shoes that make you want to strike up the band and go out dancing!

If you're too self-conscious to dance in public without any expertise or experience, classes are everywhere—continuing education departments at local community colleges are a good bet or just check the yellow pages. Professionals will show you how, provide music, support, partners and an opportunity to make new friends. If you can't find a class, try a video. Maybe even one aimed at kids. I play one for my grandsons called *Big Bird's Get Up and Dance!* Even with two left feet, I look graceful compared to Big Bird, who teaches us all something about feeling comfortable as novices. If you can't find/don't want a partner, use a pillow, a blow-up doll (à la Ally McBeal), a broom (remember Fred Astaire?), or even, as Jailhouse Elvis recommended, a wooden chair.

A greeting card I saw recently suggests, "Dance like no one is looking!" An excellent idea and a wonderful way to waltz (or watusi) your blues out the door.

Chapter 17

Make a Friend
(Literally)

Some blues are born out of loneliness. You'd love to share your thoughts, feelings, hopes and fears with someone, but you can't right now. For the time being, you're alone, with no one to talk to. You could use a friend and you probably are able to describe in detail the kind of friend you'd like.

When the real thing isn't available, that description can help create a friend. A bona fide, for-real, *imaginary* friend. Hold on before dismissing the idea out of hand. Little kids hang out with imaginary pals all the time, until they learn they're not supposed to because it makes grown-ups uncomfortable. But what if kids with invisible friends are just being natural self-therapists? After all, it's creative. It's inventive and resourceful. And it really is comforting when someone listens whenever you want to talk.

If you're up for this game, I applaud you. I also suggest that when you're ready to create an imaginary friend, you make one with traits you admire—a person you'd honestly consider a role model and inspiration. Make him/her a warm, loving, wise person to whom you can turn for advice and counsel. Base this character on a real person or make up a composite of several people—historical figures, fictional heroes, real-life people from your past or present—whatever feels good. As long as the friend you create has traits you admire and to which you aspire, you can't go wrong.

What's Your Sign?

Choose or invent a tangible symbol that represents the essence of your fantasy friend: hearts always equal love, roses speak of passion, teddy bears mean innocence and warmth, books stand for wisdom, stars for brilliance. You could create a doll or collage or sketch an image. Make it tiny or sizeable, primitive or polished—suit yourself. Just make it speak to you. Display it where you'll see it every day or carry it with you. It'll heighten your awareness of this important part of yourself and remind you to call upon it often.

Dorothy, who lives alone, created a "pocket shrink," a new, improved version of a former therapist, whom she decided to imagine as a mentor and friend. She told him about her relationship dilemmas, job and family problems, anything that was troubling her. She asked for advice—and got it. In fact, Dorothy says it worked amazingly well. Unlike a real therapist, he was always available. Imagining what his advice might be led her toward a more balanced perspective and inspired new ways to behave. She used her imaginary pal to access the part of herself that was loving, thoughtful and wise.

After hearing about Dorothy, I suggested the idea to a workshop group. Participants decided to begin by listing traits they would find admirable in a mentor or close friend. Next, they visualized someone (or several someones) who had these characteristics. The final step was to "create" their imaginary friends by making them as real to themselves and each other as possible. They described their friends' appearances, values, habits, quirks and traits. Some named their friends: Eleanor, after Mrs. Roosevelt; Albert, for Einstein; Arnold Schwarzenegger; Athena. A man who had been especially close to his grandfather "reincarnated" him. One woman invented a character like the imaginary teddy-bear friend she had as a child and named her Theodora (Teddy for short).

After six months, the group had a follow-up session. Not all of the participants had maintained their imaginary friendships, but those who did were pleased with the results. One group member said her friend had a wacky sense of humor, which helped her laugh at herself and her problems. Another reported that her imaginary friend/counselor, while always loving, was also confrontive and focused on continuous improvement. One said hers gave out invisible gold stars.

Why not give it a try? Compose a list of desirable characteristics, then go ahead and create a friend. You don't have to tell anyone what you're doing. On the other hand, why not? Friends have a wonderful way of encouraging each other's well-being, especially when times are tough. If you tell a real-life friend and it gives you a giggle, that's great. Of course, when you create an imaginary friend, you're really learning how to be better friends with yourself. What a terrific idea! Pass it on....

BLUES
FLASH!

**Make your day a little more strange
and your life a little less blue**

Twin-cities based artist and curator Jo del Pesco suggests a few amusing/absurd actions:

Write messages on Post-It notes and stick them up around town.

Write one line of a multi-line poem in chalk on each street corner in a four- or five-block radius.

Plant veggies or flowers on a traffic island.

Learn to play a song using the numbers on your phone. When a telemarketer calls, play it for them.

Sew a fabric covering for a park bench. Consider padding it like an old-fashioned tea-cozy.

Chapter 18

What the Hell, Cast a Spell

A little magic can charm you right out of a low mood. Literally. Go ahead, clap your hands and say, "I believe!" Then consider this: In many parts of the world, even today, amulets, charms, talismans and special rituals or ceremonies are routinely used to help heal illness, bring good fortune and ward off harm. Whether they "work" or are scientifically sound is beside the point. Belief is powerful; all that really matters is how those beliefs make you feel.

Even if you think yourself too rational to dabble in magic, I'll bet you occasionally bless a sneezer, sneak a peek at your horoscope or wear something you consider lucky on important occasions. Who doesn't? Deep down, most of us are in awe of the incomprehensible universe. We'd love to be able to believe in magic, like kids clapping to save Tinker Bell. If childlike belief is too big a stretch for you right now, try simply suspending your disbelief for a while…long enough to have some magical fun.

You could start by making an amulet or talisman small enough to be worn on your body, carried in your pocket or purse or put in a special place. Make it from objects (or symbols of objects) that feel sacred, close to your heart. Sacred doesn't necessarily mean holy. You transform the things you care about into sacred objects by repeated attention and devotion. Have you always loved orchids, Siamese cats or sailboats? Do you long for a true love, an exciting career or exotic travel? Do you collect rocks, shells, fossils, ceramic angels or miniature frogs? How might you symbolize your passions or deepest desires in a talisman?

Once you've chosen your object(s), think about how to invest them with power. My niece, Sarah, took a beautiful silk scarf, a gift from an ex-lover, and cut it up to make a tiny pouch. Cutting it symbolized the end of her attachment to the past and her commitment to moving on. Because Sarah loves and grows roses—their scents both soothe and stimulate her—she tucked a few dried rosebuds into the pouch. "Roses are for romance," she said. She added a sprig of rosemary, "So I never forget the lessons I've learned." Sarah hung the amulet from a fine gold chain, a gift from her grandmother on her sixth birthday. At that time, the chain nearly reached her heart, and her favorite pendant was a miniature Tinkerbell. Now the chain is collarbone length. She wears her amulet when she feels sad or lonely and says it reminds her of her own strength and lovability.

Some objects naturally create a powerful emotional response. Some gain power when combined with others. Some remind us of what we value. A select few do all three. When her mother died, Lisa found a perfect remembrance talisman. An archaeologist, she knows a lot about burial customs and ancestor worship. In one culture, she says, people preserve the bones of their mothers to lend strength to future generations. Among her mom's possessions was an old bone-china teacup, hand-painted with wild roses, full of unbroken wishbones from long-ago dinners of roast chicken and turkey. Lisa decided to call these her "mother's bones." She keeps the cup on her dresser as a talisman—a potent, love-filled reminder of her mother.

You may want to give your charm or amulet special meaning by chanting a prayer, incantation or affirmation over it. The exact words don't matter; say anything that feels right and put your heart into it. For example, "When I see this, I renew my choice to live a happy life." Or, "This is a symbol of strength, abundance and appreciation. I am grateful for all I have and I have all I need." Or even, "Hear my wish, powers that be. May joy and love come home to me." Then clap your hands and affirm your belief in yourself and all the other powers that be!

Spirit-Lifting Séance

Ouija boards were all the rage back in the 1930s. Buy one at a second-hand store or where games are sold or make your own. Write each letter of the alphabet on a small square of paper. Add two more for "yes" and "no." Arrange them in a circle (about two feet in diameter) written side up on a table or other smooth, flat surface. Turn a drinking glass upside-down, place it in the center and use it as a "pointer." Now, you and a couple of friends (the glass won't accommodate more) place two or three fingertips of each hand lightly on the edge of the glass bottom. Don't rest your arms on the table; they need to be free. Sit quietly and wait until the glass begins to move, on its own, without anyone pushing it. It almost always does. Eerie. Then, ask it questions. The glass will move to various letters, spelling out answers. See if you can "raise some spirits" and lift your own at the same time.

Chapter 19

An Astronomical Idea

Some people find that looking at the stars and planets in the night sky makes them feel small and unimportant in the cosmic scheme of things. This kind of outlook can make your problems and concerns seem smaller and less important. Like most things, what you think and feel when experiencing something depends on your conditioning, your expectations and your intentions. My friend, Pat, an enthusiastic amateur astronomer, feels that stargazing deepens his spirituality. It can also lift your spirits as well as your chin and put your blue mood into a new perspective.

H. A. Rey (author of all those wonderful *Curious George* books and one-time teacher of astronomy in Cambridge, Massachusetts) compares gazing at a sky full of stars to looking at a giant picture book. The clusters of stars (constellations) form outlines of mythical beasts, birds, fish, warriors, kings, princesses, even a few inanimate objects (the Big and Little Dippers, for instance). Many have fantastic and fascinating legends associated with them; learn what they are at the library or on the Internet.

To find and enjoy the constellations, you have to know how and where to look. A star map, found in any basic astronomy book, will help. You may need several, because the sky changes day to day throughout the year. It even changes as the night progresses. You won't need a telescope or binoculars, although once you've found a particular constellation, it's wonderful to see it magnified. You don't have to get away from city lights, either, although the darker the viewing place, the more you'll see. Choose a spot where trees, buildings or streetlights aren't in the way. In the city, the roof of an apartment house or another tall building makes a good observatory. Beaches, baseball fields or even your own back yard, if it has an unobstructed view, are also great places to stargaze. Bring a blanket or beach chair, pick a clear night without a moon, lie down lest you develop a crick in the neck and behold the beauty.

You could begin by finding the Big Dipper and Polaris, also called the North Star, to get your bearings. Polaris is the brightest star in its part of the sky. Because it's the only star that never noticeably changes its position, it has been used as a point of navigation for centuries. To find it, look for the Big Dipper and draw a line straight out from the two stars in its bowl, which are called the Pointers. Extend the line about five times the distance between the two stars and you'll hit it.

Star Date

There's nothing wrong with solo stargazing, but it can be even more fun with a friend. Pack snacks and something good to drink—hot cider or buttered rum in a thermos if you're looking at the winter sky; icy mineral water or sangria in summer. If you plan to be out for more than an hour, aim for comfort. Bring a camping pad, good-sized chunk of foam, lawn recliner or blanket to lie on, maybe even a pillow. If it's really cold, a sleeping bag is just the ticket. P.S. One of the loveliest sights in the sky is the Pleiades, a small group of stars in the Bull constellation that are so close together they look like a tiny silver cloud. See if you can find it, but don't stress about what you can or can't identify. If you have a hard time finding things, just hold hands (if he or she is that kind of friend), and let yourselves drift. There's literally no end to the pleasure heavenly bodies can give.

A wonderful place to find star maps is in two more books by H. A. Rey: *The Stars: A New Way to See Them* and *Find the Constellations* contain all the star maps (Rey calls them sky-views) you'll need to get started, as well as clear instructions on how to use them. He wrote the latter work for kids, but Dr. Hugh Rice, of New York's famed Hayden Planetarium, says, "Mr. Rey's outlines of the constellations are the best I have ever seen." Good enough for me. Two other helpful books are *Star-Hopping: Your Visa to Viewing the Universe,* by Robert A. Garfinkle and *Turn Left at Orion,* by Guy Consolmagno and Dan M. Davis.

Go make friends with the stars. See how many constellations you can find and call by name. Look for planets, too, and shooting stars (meteors). Make a million wishes on the Milky Way. Bring a flashlight so you can read the star maps (paint the glass with red nail polish to cut the glare). Then beam yourself up, Scotty.

Chapter 20

Lighten Up

Come out of the dark ages! Open the curtains, roll up the blinds and throw a little natural light on the subject. Now, turn on the electric lights, too. Yep. The brighter, the better. On a dark, gloomy day, forget conservation; turn them *all* on! Low light is romantic for a candlelit dinner or relaxing in a bath, but if your living spaces lack light, its absence can sap your energy and send your mood down the tube.

That's because humans are light-sensitive, light-seeking creatures. Did you know that more people die at night than during the day? It's true. Light and life go together. We sleep in the dark and awaken to the light. We fear the dark, dislike feeling "in the dark," and when confused, we want someone to "enlighten" us.

The solution? Simple. Try replacing your 45- or 60-watt bulbs with 75s, 100s, or even 150s. It may not be energy efficient, but it can certainly boost your personal energy supply. Try soft white or even pink bulbs. Their subtle glow makes a room feel warmer, cozier, more inviting. They make you look better, too. It's a little like looking through rose-colored glasses.

By the way, you as an individual may be more affected by lack of light than most folks, particularly in fall and winter. Seasonal Affective Disorder, commonly called SAD and triggered by lack of daylight and a natural tendency to spend more time indoors, causes fatigue, irritability and low moods. If that sounds like something you go through each winter, one of the best treatments is also the simplest: spend more time outdoors. Even if it's cold outside, bundle up and take a walk in the sun. Early morning light has the most uplifting effect, so try to get out before your day gets rolling. It's a powerful energizer to take early walks, but if you're not a morning person, don't despair. A thirty-minute outdoor break during the day will also brighten your outlook. But it doesn't have to be thirty minutes to matter. Make it a habit to get outside whenever you can. Garden, walk, wash your car or your dog, window shop or just find a pleasant place to sit. Remember, no matter where you live or what the season, it's a good idea to wear sunscreen, so keep a trial-size container in your pocket or purse.

To combat SAD, many people use a light box or special bulbs that emit full-spectrum daylight without harmful UV rays. Sit next to one of these devices for an hour or two a day and you'll feel a difference. In fact, if you think you might have SAD, ask your doctor for more information. Many insurance plans now cover full-spectrum lights, if prescribed by a physician. They're available, new and second hand, on the Internet.

If you work outside your home, as most of us do, don't forget the light in your office. You're probably spending most of your daylight hours there, so if you're lucky or important enough to have a window, open the blinds! If not, see if you can substitute full-spectrum tubes for plain florescent or at least up the wattage. If you spend lots of time in front of a computer monitor, take frequent one-minute breaks; just stand up, turn your face toward the brightest light you can see and let your mind wander. A simple thing like this, done often enough, can make a world of difference.

Light Dressing

Dark mood got you stuck in sartorial gloom? When your spirits are low, lighten up your clothing choices. Shove the black, brown, gray, khaki, maroon, and navy blue things to the back of the closet. Instead, pick light colors for a few days: gold, yellow, cream, white. Bright colors are also good. Think tropical: red, orange, turquoise, bright blue, lime green, hot pink. Look around the house, too. Would a fresh coat of bright white or creamy yellow paint do something for your surroundings?

Lighten up on the inside too, while you're at it, and give yourself a double dose of good energy. Most of the chapters in this book are designed to help you do exactly that. Dark moods encourage dark thoughts. Light-hearted thoughts do for your mind and spirit what basking in sunlight does for your body. Remember the laughing Buddha (they don't call it en*light*enment for nothing).

Chapter 21

Assemble an Alternate Family

Sometimes we feel down in the dumps after spending time with our families. Between happily-ever-after movies, Kodak moments, TV sitcoms and saccharine ads for instant coffee or long-distance service, we've been programmed to expect warm (or at least congenial), ever-loving, two-parent families. The kind where prodigals are welcomed back; attractive, supportive grandparents love to baby-sit and adore your spouse; and grown children get along with their siblings, laugh a lot and can imagine nothing better than spending holidays at home.

To save your sanity, it's time to get real. If being with your family makes you feel angry, sad, frustrated, disappointed or disgusted, stop hanging around them so much. In fact, why not create a new family? Creating a new family doesn't mean giving your current kin the boot. In fact, once your needs for warmth, companionship and support are met elsewhere, it'll be easier to accept your blood relatives as they are, warts and all. Even if you're one of the lucky few whose family is wonderful, but too far away to be there for you, a new family will come in handy.

Assembling another family will take focus, time and perhaps several tries. You'll need to seek out and get to know people who behave and feel the way you wish your real family would, whether that's warm and loving or fun and hip. Whatever you do, it's a good idea to make friends with folks who support and applaud your growth and give you a gentle push when you need it. You're likely to find some of your "adopted" family among your old friends, but you'll probably need to broaden your scope a bit, too. Open your heart and make room for new people. Join a club or take up a hobby that connects you with like-minded others. Go to a church, temple or mosque and find new friends there.

When someone seems special or interesting, reach out. Risk taking the first step, which may be as simple as saying "Hello. How are you today?" But don't try too hard. Good relationships take time to develop. If you feel like you're forcing it, back off a bit. As things progress, be open about who you are and what you're hoping for. Be supportive and accepting of others, too and interested in what they want and need. As the old saying goes, to have a friend, be a friend. It's not all about you.

As you imagine a new family, consider whether there are certain roles you especially want to fill. Are you looking for parent-types? Do you currently have any older friends who might fill the bill? What about the parents of a close friend? Might they be willing to accept you into their brood? How will your friend feel about this? Retirement homes are filled with people who would love to connect with an attentive surrogate daughter or son.

Maybe what you really want are some kid substitutes. Many young parents would be delighted to share their offspring with another adult, especially one whom they have grown to like and trust. Siblings are, of course, easiest. Look for people of your generation with whom you feel a good connection and just keep doing what you're doing.

Sometimes new families just happen over time—friends end up together on holidays and special occasions because they like each other, their own families leave a lot to be desired or distance keeps them from their blood relatives. Often nothing is ever said among close friends about being or acting like a family. On the other hand, if the others are willing and it doesn't feel like belaboring the obvious, it's fine to discuss mutual wants and needs, plan holiday get-togethers well in advance and express your appreciation and affection.

Begin a New Tradition

Even if you aren't interested in creating a new family, perhaps you still might like to find more satisfying ways to enjoy special days with like-minded people. Many religious organizations, schools, diversity coalitions and community outreach groups routinely organize and offer open holiday meals. If you can't locate a group that's already doing this, start one. Phone or visit a likely place and suggest creating a Thanksgiving, Christmas or Passover dinner. Or talk to your friends and see who'd like to share such an experience. A potluck or progressive dinner can be a wonderful way to spend a holiday, birthday or other special occasion.

BLUES
FLASH!

The Tee-Hee Technique

Seems terminally silly, but it works.

Developed by psychotherapist Annette Goodheart, simply add the words "tee-hee" to the end of a sentence describing your problem. Then say it out loud.

"I didn't get the promotion, tee-hee."

or

"My car won't start, tee-hee."

or

"I've burnt the roast and company will be here any minute, tee-hee."

It sounds so ridiculous, you just might laugh, even (*especially!*) when there's nothing funny about it.

Chapter 22

Try the
Rhythm Method

If you love the beat of the bongos, your solar plexus stirs to the boom of a big bass and you can't keep your feet still during a drum solo, why not play a little percussion yourself? Let's face it, rhythm is in our blood. The lub-dub, lub-dub of mamma's heartbeat was the first sound your little ears ever heard. Later, the rhythm and beat of nursery rhymes made words easy to remember. Games in which you clapped your hands and stamped your feet made you feel good and created a unified group out of twenty second-graders. In high school, you danced to music that would have left you bored and sitting still if not for the beat set down by the drums. As my teacher, Simone LaDrumma says, "Drumming is hot." Meaning exciting. Primal. Sexy.

Drumming is a universal language. It doesn't matter whether you're a novice or expert or whether you play a little pair of bongos, a big Cuban conga, a stately Japanese taiko, a beaded African djembe or rock and roll on a full drum set in your garage; when the spirit of the drum speaks, your body wants to listen and what it hears can make you feel happy and connected to something basic and deep.

Maybe that feeling of connection is why community drum circles have become so popular. A community drum circle is the use of a rhythm-based event as a tool for unity. It isn't a drum class and it doesn't use culturally specific rhythms. It's a fun, family-friendly event in which people empower each other in the act of celebrating community and life through rhythm and music. People of all levels of musical expertise come together to share their spirit with whatever drums and percussion instruments they bring to the event. It's a freeing and inspiring experience, one in which an entire group comes together in one beat.

Get your RDA

When discussing nutrients, RDA means Recommended Daily Allowance. If you're talking about drumming, RDA means Rhythmic Daily Allowance and, no, you're probably not getting enough. The beat in music is the driving force, the contagious element, the energy. Choose a song with a beat you love to begin your day. Drive to work moving to the beat. Tap your fingers and feet. When you're at home, play a drum to the tune or grab a couple of chopsticks or pencils and play whatever's handy: a wooden table, glasses on the dish drainer, a plastic milk bottle, the stainless steel sink. When the tune has finished—and this is the essential part—don't stop. Keep going; take that beat and make it your own. Improvise, play around with it, challenge it and let yourself feel free.

You don't have to be a drummer to take part. Sometimes people just use their own two hands. Everyone has something to offer the circle and everyone is welcome. Whether you're in Arizona or Arkansas, California or Colorado, chances are there's a drum circle scheduled soon. Go online and find out. Start with www.drum-circle.org.

Drumming can heal as well as make heat. Some of the psychological applications in which hand drums are being used include assisting military veterans to release the emotional pain of post-traumatic stress, releasing the pent-up anger and negative emotions of at-risk teens and promoting health in corporate executives through releasing their day-to-day tension. In the medical field, the hand drum is being used to help Alzheimer's patients improve short-term memory and increase social interaction, as well as help autistic children increase their attention spans. In some cases, it's not necessarily the hand drum that sparks positive change, but a rhythmic device such as a metronome. Tools like these are also being used to aid Parkinson's patients and stroke victims to regain control of movement.

In this century, we seem to be moving farther and farther away from ourselves and our deeper needs. The drum, through its simplicity, effortlessness and naturalism, offers us a link to a time before technology began to separate us from our souls. Through providing a channel back to our deeper nature, the drum gives those who use it a tie to others. Drumming seems to have the capacity to unite people who choose to experience it together. Despite race, religion, color, creed, background or ideology, all are joined together through this ancient instrument's calling.

Beg, borrow or buy a drum and make it come alive in a community circle, with a teacher, other students or friends who dig the sound. Do it with sticks, mallets or the palms of your hands. Accompany a favorite CD, another musician, a song on the radio or the sound of the rain. Beating a drum sure beats a blue mood.

Chapter 23

Unlikely Places,
New Faces

I've said it before and I'll say it again, just in case you missed it: it's nuts to do the same thing over and over and expect different results. That's why so many of the suggestions in these pages ask you to try something new, do something different, change your habits. Change that's forced upon you from the outside can feel threatening and stressful. Change that you initiate yourself often feels exhilarating, exciting and growth producing.

Here's an idea that definitely falls into the "something different" category. Most of us have life routines that take us, over and over again, to the same places. For example, in a typical month, I'll spend time in the library, my office, yoga class, my drum teacher's studio, the gym, several grocery stores, family members' houses, a few favorite restaurants and coffee houses, the route I walk between my house and the beach, several bookstores and Home Depot (I *love* Home Depot). That's pretty much it. Does it ever get boring? All the time. Your routine gets tiresome, too, I'm willing to wager. When that starts to happen, try doing what I do. Shake things up a little.

Last month I went to a poetry slam. (I can't describe how much fun I had!) Next week I'm scheduled to check out family night at a karaoke bar with some friends. It'll be my first live karaoke experience and, yes, I plan to sing. The "Monster Car and Truck Show: Chrome, Cabs and Carbs!" is coming to town soon and I think I'll go just for the fun of it. A weekend glass-blowing class offered at a local art institute sounds intriguing, too. Not one of these things is a bit like me. Not the usual, everyday me, anyway. That's a huge part of their appeal. Don't you hate it when someone stereotypes or typecasts you? So why do it yourself?

Don't get me wrong. Routines are fine. They're comforting and, to a certain extent, they define us. I *like* the library and my walks to the beach and hanging out in bookstores. Too much routine, however, is deadening. If I do the same things all the time, day in and day out, I grow stale. Bored and boring. Playing certain roles is fine, too. I'm a writer, therapist and corporate trainer; a friend, mother and grandmother. Those are good things to be. But if they are all I am for the rest of my days—if I never try anything new and different—there's a strong likelihood that I'll stagnate and start to feel blue.

You know better than anyone what breaking out of your routine means for you, but here are a few suggestions. If you've never been, go to a gay bar or to see a male or female stripper (best done and more fun with at least one or two friends). If you're the queen of Neiman Marcus or the king of Brooks Brothers, spend an afternoon thrift-shop hopping. Does the appeal of Home Depot escape you? Spend a couple of hours walking their aisles and really looking at the incredible array of stuff they sell; get some spare keys made while you're there. If you're not the religious type, attend services at a church, mosque, temple, synagogue or meeting hall. If you are a regular churchgoer, see if you can visit a witches' coven (see chapter 26). If the ballet is your cup of tea, go to a country line dance or vice versa. Are you a regular moviegoer? Take in a play. If you listen exclusively to classical music, go hear one of those alternative bands with the weird names.

Adjust Your Attitude

When you break out of your routine and leave what's commonly called your comfort zone, you can expect to feel a bit nervous at first. That's normal. On top of a blue mood, though, it may feel like too much. Here's one way to minimize the stress of new behavior and get back to feeling relaxed. First, monitor and control your thoughts. Nip in the bud anything that remotely resembles: *This isn't like me! What am I doing here? I'm out of my element!* Instead, tell yourself something like: *I enjoy trying new things and am an adventurous person!* Second, play Let's Pretend. How would you behave if doing things like this were second nature? Try behaving that way. Finally, remember to breathe and smile at people (yes, even punk rockers and male strippers). It's amazing how smiling at others makes you feel at home and on top of things.

If there's a place about which you've said, "I wouldn't be caught dead...," go there. Just once. Doesn't matter what or where, as long as it's different (and, of course, not actually dangerous). Sometimes different is all it takes to break free from a confining, low-down mood.

Chapter 24

Talk to
Your Toothbrush

Down in the dumps and down on yourself? Your internal critic can make you miserable and keep you that way as long as you listen. So don't listen! Instead, replace that critical voice with some unique and unusual ones. Talk to your pets, machines, furniture, clothes, even your toothbrush!

This isn't as weird as it sounds. I'm sure you know people who talk to their pets; you may even be one of them. You probably also know someone who talks to his or her car, computer or television set. Lots of people do. From time to time, I talk to my cat, computer and those annoying television pundits. I've even suggested this as a coping tool to my clients and some have found it quite useful.

With pets it's easy; you already tell them what to do and not do. Simply increase your communication. Tell them how you feel and ask about their wants and needs. What do you have to lose? Ask their advice; you may be surprised by the responses you get. Besides, communicating with pets is fun and can keep you from feeling alone.

At first, you may have a little trouble talking to inanimate objects, like a radio or computer. However, it'll get easier as you do it. If you make these conversations frivolous and fun, there's a good chance they'll improve your mood.

A good way to start is to let your objects make helpful suggestions. For example, your vacuum cleaner might propose, "Why not use me more often? I love making things look bright and clean and I know you feel better when they do." Isn't that better than thinking to yourself, *You slob! Get out the vacuum! I can't believe the way you let this place go.* Your toothbrush could say, "You know, I wish I could do more to keep your teeth and gums healthy, but there are areas I just can't reach. How about trying some floss?" Not only do these suggestions work better than dis-approving put-downs, you're also more likely to listen and respond positively.

Over the Top

If you think talking to your pets and your stuff sounds silly, great! Run with it. See if your things know any good (or bad) jokes. Tell them some of yours and see how they react. Imagine a house full of laughing objects. Share all the clever responses you think of too late to use with real people and get some appreciation for your wit. Learn all the latest gossip about who's doing what with whom. Tell dishes or silverware the story of "The Cat and the Fiddle," and see what they think. Ask your salad bowl what the lettuce said to the tomato ("Let us alone.") Not Saturday Night Live material, but worth a giggle. Be as goofy and irreverent as you can. If it's worth doing, it's worth overdoing!

Once you're able to fold your self-negating voices into friendly suggestions, you'll find it's comfortable and rewarding to have these conversations. You can also use them to encourage mechanical things. I kept telling my computer that it needed to get a move on and speed things up. To my surprise, it suggested I get something faster than a dial-up connection. I got cable and we're both happier now. I have a friend who has an old car she calls Lizzie. She talks to Lizzie all the time and swears that the car keeps on working, because she keeps telling it that it can.

Set yourself up to feel good. Be flirtatious with your clothes. Ask your nightgown to go to bed with you, or sweet-talk your blanket while you snuggle up to watch TV. When trying to lose weight, there's nothing better than having your jeans say, "Good job, girlfriend! We fit so much better now!" Who would know better?

These seemingly absurd conversations can flatter and encourage you, quiet your inner critic and make you aware of how the things you own serve you. You'll feel more connected to your day-to-day experience, less likely to be annoyed when things don't work and more inclined to be grateful when they do. Two small caveats: Talking to pets and inanimate objects may help you feel better, but it shouldn't replace reaching out to other humans. Your relationships with people are most important. Also, you should probably limit this behavior when around others, so they don't think you've flipped your cork.

Chapter 25

Constellations, Cards and Clairvoyants

You don't have to believe in astrology to have your chart made and you don't have to give credibility to anything even slightly occult to have your Tarot cards read. In fact, I think it's a more interesting experience if you're simply curious and reasonably skeptical. One of the best reasons to have your chart done or cards read is to see what it's like. One of the best times to do it is when you're feeling down in the dumps, because it's almost always an uplifting experience.

People who have made astrology or any of the "psychic sciences" their profession take it very seriously (which doesn't mean you have to). More importantly, most of them are genuinely committed to helping others learn and grow. They use planets, stars, cards, runes and other ancient symbols to help you look deeper into yourself, discover or appreciate your unique gifts and make choices that enhance your life and make you happier. They don't charge unreasonable fees and they certainly don't expect you to run your life based on what they tell you.

For years, I resisted having an astrology reading, even though several friends had reported positive experiences. One day, when I was in a just-for-the-hell-of-it mood, I made an appointment. I was pleasantly surprised by the results. It was like gazing into still, deep water and seeing my own reflection in a clear light—only more fun. It helped me see some of my behavior patterns, dilemmas, strengths and weaknesses with fresh eyes. I came away feeling lighter, hopeful and recharged.

I've had professional Tarot readings several times (the first was a birthday gift from a friend); each was fascinating and worthwhile. I've spent a lot of time learning about myself in more conventional ways and have little trouble trusting my intuition or whatever you call the uncanny internal guidance system we all have. But I'm also open to information from other sources, especially when my usual methods aren't working and confusion persists. If some of those sources are a bit unconventional, who cares? The best question to ask is the one we hear so often from Dr. Phil: How's it working for you?

Some of my colleagues scoff at using astrologers, card readers, psychics and others to gain personal insights. Not me. The way I see it, the message is always more important than the messenger. If what's said makes no sense, forget it. If it's useful and it helps, why discount it? Besides, when you're feeling really crummy, it's nice to just sit there without having to do a thing (except maybe hold out your palm) and listen to someone else. Therapists prefer that you participate, do some work; card readers don't.

Ask around until you find someone with a good reputation who's been in business for years. Take a tape recorder or take notes so you can review your session later. You'll be surprised by how much more you'll glean from a second go-through, especially if your mood is improved. If you're hesitant, remember that no one is going to tell you what to do, try to persuade you to ignore common sense or tell you to come back again for the really important information (if they do, it's a sure sign you're talking to a scam artist or fake).

Again, astrology, Tarot and palmistry are merely tools to gain insight; judge them on the basis of their usefulness and cost-effectiveness. Approach your experience with an open but discerning mind. Don't expect to come away with specific answers, but you may become clearer about some important questions. While you're at it, you may even get a quick fix for your blue mood.

Cozy Up to a Tree

A Native American healer in my city conducts workshops for people who'd like to develop their psychic powers. She says if you want to tap into some deep, strong, calm energy, there's nothing like a tree. In fact, she asks student psychics to find a particularly beautiful old specimen and sit next to it for an hour every day for a week. Her advice: close your eyes, breathe deeply and try to match the tree's energy. Feel its steadiness and strength. Try to sense your connection with it and everything else in nature. Imagine what it would be like to be a tree. Thank the spirit of the tree before you disengage. Leave a symbolic offering at its base.

Chapter 26

Which Witch
is Which?

Black mood making you feel like a witch? Fly with it! Modern witches don't have warts, ride broomsticks or poison sweet young things with apples. During the sixteenth century, witch-hunts were carried out here and throughout Europe. Healers, midwives, herbalists and women who were seductive, independent or freethinkers were considered dangerous to the powers that be, so they often were branded as witches, hunted down, tortured and killed. In fairy tales, bad equals ugly and frequently old, hence the old, ugly, mean-spirited stereotypical witch. Twenty-first century witches blow away the stereotypes.

Today, many women and some men practice witchcraft, attend coven meetings and celebrate The Goddess—the powerful mystical feminine. Witchcraft, sometimes referred to as Wicca, is an ancient religion with teachings drawn from nature. It takes inspiration from the movements of the sun, moon and stars; the changing of the seasons; and the elements of earth, wind, fire and water. It involves worship of the Mother Goddess, who brings life to all things. Coven meetings are formed to invoke her and preserve her knowledge. If the idea of worshiping goddesses and celebrating/invoking female power is a bit threatening, don't worry. I'm not suggesting you attend a coven, although you might find it educational, inspiring and fun. But you might like to experiment with finding the witch in you. It can be interesting, amusing, liberating and spiritually uplifting.

The witch symbolizes your own fierce, strong, competent, wise, growing self. She knows what she wants, goes after it and usually gets it. She refuses to tolerate abuse, even in jest, constantly makes her presence known and won't be dismissed. The witch keeps you blooming, bouncing back and forging ahead.

Backyard Magic

Real magic is created through thought and behavior, not smoke and mirrors, but sometimes we need a little help. If you have trouble feeling connected to your witch, take a moment to ask her what kind of charm or talisman will help. It may be as simple as lighting a candle or drinking a cup of herbal tea. Maybe you'll need to create or find a specific charm, light a fire or stand in the light of a full moon for a while. Here's an exercise that may help if you're having trouble accessing or understanding your witch's advice. Go outside and look around until you see a rock, stone or piece of wood that calls to you. Pick it up and handle it for a minute, exploring its contours and texture. Try to find some images or signs embedded in it. Use your creative imagination. See if you can find three images. Then ask each what you need to do to reach the witch in you.

Witches believe that women are natural nurturers, have the ability to create life and the strength to maintain it in themselves and others. They respect their own instincts, act confidently on their intuition and see the details while maintaining an overview of the big picture. You're familiar with damsel-in-distress legends, but if you listen to them with a witch's consciousness, you'll realize that it sometimes was the damsel who saved the prince. In a witch's version of the old story, the hotheaded prince goes charging into the dragon's den, creating a no-win situation where one or both of them must die. The damsel, on the other hand, knocks the prince off his horse, sits quietly for a minute, gathers her wits, then begins to talk to the dragon. She sympathizes with the dragon's anger and sees his loneliness. They talk about how he could get along with the prince, keep him warm, help vanquish his enemies. The stunned prince listens. If he is a true prince, he starts to get it. He and the damsel negotiate a truce and agree to a working partnership. Sound good? Yes, ma'am. So why not set your inner-witch free?

Take a minute to get centered and reach deep inside. Allow your ancient witch's wisdom and strength to bubble up and become yours. The witch can support you as you face your anger, fear and pain. Learn from her lessons and become a stronger, more compassionate person. She'll give you guidance and encouragement when you're confronting formidable obstacles. Seek her wisdom and strength. Valuing this part of you increases its power and makes it easier to access.

To learn more about witchcraft, check out *The Wicca Source Book: a Complete Guide for the Modern Witch* by Gerina Dunwich and *The Witch Book: The Encyclopedia of Witchcraft, Wicca and Neo-Paganism* by Raymond Buckland, which explores every aspect of the craft.

BLUES
FLASH!

A Little Stick May Do the Trick

Acupuncture, long used to help heal physical illness or injury, may also be able to remedy a blue mood.

Through the insertion of tiny, hair-like needles into specific points on your body (usually doesn't hurt a bit), you may be able to increase your energy or improve your state of mind.

According to Anne Mok, acupuncture supervisor at Brownsville Multiservice Family Health Center in Brooklyn, New York, "A specific point on the head, known as G20, has a lifting effect and, when stimulated, can leave you feeling more awake and alive."

PART THREE

Back to Basics

Bluesbusting solutions don't have to be unusual or complex. They can be as basic as breath, bed and bread. You'll look and feel better if you make some simple changes to your environment, inside and out. The chapters in this section offer an array of energy-boosting, mood-lifting activities that will get you back in touch with your best self—the part that knows without a doubt that what you *do* usually changes how you *feel*.

Chapter 27

Dustbusting

I may sound a little like your mother for a minute, but don't go away, you may need to hear this: Even when your life feels chaotic, the space you live in doesn't have to be. When you're in a funk, the simple act of cleaning something dirty or creating order from an unholy mess can put you back in control of at least part of your environment. Let's face it, being in control feels good. So does having clean, orderly, attractive surroundings.

Maybe it sounds like busywork to clean out the garage, organize a closet or vacuum the floor when you're down, but it can be much more than that. If you deliberately choose to change something for the better, then take action and quickly see the results of your action—well, talk about empowering! Taking charge like that helps you regain your ability to make positive change happen in other areas, too. Besides, physical activity is your first line of defense against the blues. As soon as you decide to do something constructive, you'll start to feel better; when you actually get up and going, you'll make a quantum leap.

If you think you can handle it, the dirtier the job, the more disorganized the project, the better. Taking on something big reminds you that even a seemingly overwhelming task can be mastered if you break the work down into small chunks, tackle one at a time and stick with it. My last blue-mood project was cleaning out the garage. The junk in it was so completely out of control, there was no place to park my car! I began in the morning and by noon my driveway was covered with piles of stuff, but the garage was still half full. I had forgotten that these projects sometimes get worse before they get better. I decided to clean half the garage that day, do the rest on my next free weekend and have a garage sale later. After lunch, I sorted through the piles one at a time, deciding what to keep, what to throw out and what to sell. Then I bagged the garbage and declared stage one complete. I rewarded myself with a trip to Starbucks for a double-tall vanilla latte and slice of carrot cake.

Three weeks later, when the project was fully and finally finished, I was so proud of myself! Bit by bit, I had mastered what seemed like an impossible job and made a couple of hundred dollars to boot at my garage sale. No more junk, no more blues and extra money in my pocket. Who could ask for more?

You don't have to start with something so daunting. Try cleaning or organizing a closet, dresser, bookshelf, filing cabinet or even your wallet or purse. Sometimes I restore or paint a small piece of furniture, clean out the refrigerator or simply wash and vacuum my car. Even the act of balancing my checkbook (a task I truly dislike and tend to put off) helps me feel that if I make an effort, I'll be able to restore balance to other areas of my life, as well.

Your opinion about your individual ability to solve problems, make good choices, triumph over adversity and control your own destiny is built slowly over time. You build it yourself, from experiences of all kinds that put you to the test. When you're feeling low, mastering anything can remind you of your ability to persist and make progress, to get big things done by taking small steps. So, rather than trying to take the giant leap of getting your entire life's act together, try getting your tool shed, basement, office or hall closet together instead. Believe me, your sense of accomplishment will spread to other areas of your life.

Who Ya Gonna Call?

Some moods are so blue that you can't get your cleaning and organizing act together. It's all you can do to keep yourself presentable, never mind keeping an orderly house. But there's no denying the negative effect of dirty, disorderly surroundings and you have to admit it would help if the place were spiffed up. So treat yourself to a visit from the Maid Brigade, the Happy Housekeepers, or whatever cleaning services are called in your neck of the woods. These well-trained, well-equipped clean-demons charge by the hour or the job, their rates are usually fair and there's often a one-time discount for new customers. You may like the results so much that you sign up for regular service!

Chapter 28

Breathing
Lessons

Breathe, baby, breathe! Besides being basic to survival, did you know that your inhalation and exhalation can release energy, decrease pain, reduce stress and improve your mood? It's true. In fact, the right kind of breathing can help animate and harmonize your entire being, even when a blue mood has the upper hand.

What's the *right* kind of breathing? Watch a baby. Babies breathe with their entire bodies, using their lungs, back, belly and diaphragm to inhale and exhale deeply and fully. But your breathing changes as you get older. Sedentary lifestyles and the stress of an ever-changing, overly busy schedule has conditioned you to take rapid, shallow breaths, using only your upper chest. This deprives you of precious oxygen and slows the flow of blood throughout your body. When you breathe like this, you're actually in a more or less constant, low-level fight-or-flight mode. Unless you're planning to run or do battle, this only creates more stress. It's a vicious cycle that undermines health and vitality, increases tension and interferes with your ability to feel calm, healthy and happy.

If you're skeptical, try a little experiment. Recall a joyful experience and try once again to feel those happy feelings, but do it while holding your breath. Doesn't work, does it? Less oxygen equals sadness and apathy. Here's another experiment you might try the next time you're crying. Put your palm flat on your belly and take in several deep, slow breaths, pushing your abdomen out as you inhale. As if by magic, your sobs will stop! Increased oxygen via full-bodied breathing equals positive energy and healing life force, which make it hard to feel sad.

The key to slowing down your breathing is focusing on breathing more deeply, using your diaphragm, rib cage, belly and lower back. My yoga teacher calls this "making bottles," because that's the shape your body takes as you breathe in—full at the bottom of the rib cage, narrower at the top. An easy way to practice full-bodied breathing is to make your exhalations longer than your inhalations. Notice your breath as you exhale. Feel the air moving smoothly through and out your nose, gradually emptying your lungs from the top clear down to the bottom. Gently push that last little bit of air out and then allow a natural pause.

Don't worry about inhaling. That will happen naturally, all by itself. Just be sure your tummy pooches out a little as you begin to breathe in and allow your lungs slowly to fill from the bottom to the top. That's all there is to it.

Try this for five to ten minutes, morning and evening, for the next week. I think it will astonish you that such a simple thing can do so much. You'll be starting a mind-body conversation that will improve your health, increase your energy and relax you, all at the same time. Your thoughts will feel clearer, you'll have a keener sense of your spiritual nature and it feels great!

Breathing Meditation

Sit quietly, spine straight yet relaxed. Rest your hands on your knees, palms up. Close your eyes. Sense your weight being completely supported by the chair or cushion, by the floor, by the earth. Tune in to the sensations in your body and your own aliveness. Notice your breath. Follow it with your awareness as you inhale and exhale. Don't change it. Just notice it. Notice the temperature and vibration of the air you bring into your lungs. As you exhale, breathe out tension. Notice how energy is released, then refreshed. When your attention wanders, gently bring it back to your breath. Do this for five to fifteen minutes a day. It's calming, grounding and deeply relaxing.

Though it happened years ago, I've never forgotten what Ian Jackson said after finishing an Iron man Triathlon: "It's like 140 miles of breath meditation. The last few miles of the run are like Champagne bubbles of bliss." You don't have to generate a distance runner's endorphins to get a taste of what he's talking about. Practice your breathing lessons for a week and see what happens.

Chapter 29

Make Your Bed
Like Mama Said

Okay, folks, here's more motherly advice: make the bed when you get out of it in the morning, even if you're not planning to leave the house. Be sure to change your sheets at least once a week.

Do these things whether you have the blues or not, but without fail when your mood is low. Sure, they're small things, but isn't most of your life made up of small things? Never mind those *Don't Sweat the Small Stuff* books, either. Small stuff can make a big difference. I believe that, over time, how you deal with the small stuff pretty much mirrors how you deal with everything. When you're blue, you have to start somewhere. Might as well start small.

I have to admit that part of the reason I'm sold on this idea is because my mother always did it. She believed that an unmade bed was a sign of illness or unforgivable sloth and always tidied her own before or shortly after breakfast. She also believed that there was something restorative about climbing into a bed made with freshly laundered sheets. For years, I resisted doing anything even remotely like my mother. Lately, though, I've found (as so many of us do) that I tend more and more to take after her. In this case, I really think she was on to something.

Besides, especially when you're feeling lousy to begin with, there's something about coming home to a rumpled, slept-in bed that makes you feel worse. On the other hand, there's something about coming home to a neatly made bed that says, "Well, you may not be wrapped up too tightly right now, but you're not falling apart at the seams, either." There is a sense of order and some degree of control over your personal environment.

When the bed is made, you can lie on top of it and daydream, doze or even snuggle under an afghan or throw and have a short nap without feeling as if you've "taken to your bed," which is altogether different—something you do when you're sick. Plus, it discourages major sleeping except when it's time to sleep—a very good thing (assuming you don't really need the rest) if you want to avoid low energy and lethargy.

Four-Poster Makeover

How inviting is the bed you make each morning and snuggle into each night? Is it a magnet for magazines, dirty clothes, tangled blankets and who knows what else? Does it look pretty much the way it did ten years ago? Maybe it's time for a change. Make it into the most beautiful, appealing thing in the room. Strip it and start from scratch: How old is your mattress? Could you use a new one? What about new sheets and shams, blankets, spread or duvet cover, bed skirt, even fluffy new pillows? Some comfy extras to consider: down comforter in a luscious shade; body pillow; thick chenille throw; backrest with arms for reading in bed, a really good bedside lamp. Or splurge big time and get all of the above plus a four-poster, with side curtains and canopy in a style that complements both your décor and your fondest bedroom fantasies!

Dirty dishes stacked in the sink fall into the unmade bed category. With our ubiquitous automatic dishwashers, soiled dishes and cups are not the eyesores they once were. Even so, they can pile up. Don't let that happen. Blues or no blues, wash them right after you use them or put them in the dishwasher. At the very least, wash them once a day, even if they need to soak. Who wants to walk around looking at a sink full of dirty dishes? Who wants to come home from a long day at work to that lovely sight? Who wants to feel so wretched they don't even clean up after themselves? Not me. Not you, either, right?

P.S. On the other hand, don't give yourself a hard time if you let the dishes pile up or the bed go unmade every now and then, especially if you're normally a neat freak. Sometimes putting your foot down and refusing to do what you're expected to do is an attempt to regain control over your life—a way of asserting your right to say "No!" without doing any real harm (see chapter 9, "Slob Appeal"). And sometimes you just need a break.

BLUES
FLASH!

Money, Honey

It's hard to be happy when you don't have enough dough to feel comfortable. Most people make financial management too hard. Follow these rules and watch your bottom line grow:

Budget. Write down every penny you spend for sixty days. Then make a budget and stick to it.

Keep meticulous records. Save receipts. This helps for taxes, too.

Ditch the plastic. If you must use cards, pay them off each month.

Pay yourself first. Even if it's only fifty bucks a month, take it off the top and save it.

Write financial goals. Do this at least once a year.

Create an emergency fund. Build it slowly until it equals six months' income. Use it only for true emergencies (a really bad hair day doesn't count!).

Chapter 30

Can You Dig It?
Gardening

Talk about getting down and dirty! If you've never tried it, you may not realize how absorbing and rewarding the process of growing plants can be. Don't think you need a large yard (or any yard at all). You can garden in pots on decks, patios or fire escapes. You don't need expert knowledge, either, although it never hurts to crack a book. Gardening can be as simple as mowing the lawn and raising a few geraniums or as complex as creating an elaborate theme garden. It can be as easy as bringing a bulb of paper-white narcissus into bloom or as exhausting as clearing rocky soil by hand. It can be as sensual as planting a night-blooming jasmine outside your bedroom window or as practical as growing your own vegetables.

I recently visited a friend I hadn't seen in quite a while and was astonished at the transformation in her yard. What had once been stubbly, weedy grass and overgrown shrubbery is now a thing of beauty, complete with trellised roses, a koi pond, stone statuary, a pretty gate, and a meandering path bordered by exotic grasses and flowers five feet tall. "I had a really bad year," she explained. "I decided to do this instead of seeing a shrink, although I didn't know that when I started. It all began with the rose bush, which I bought one day when I was feeling really stressed. It needed a trellis. The rest just mushroomed from there. It was hard work, but I loved every bit of it." She grinned. "Now, I'm researching my next project: how to build a gazebo!" She told me she thinks she's been blessed by her Garden Angel.

Gardening, of course, is a nice metaphor for life. For example, the quality of the process determines the quality of the results. If you start with a good foundation, provide nourishment, practice preventive maintenance and promptly tend symptoms of trouble, you'll enjoy an abundant harvest or a vibrant garden and many hours of pleasure. Like everything else worthwhile, gardening requires and rewards faith and patience. When you plant a packet of seeds and see them through to maturity, you'll feel proud, happy and maybe a little awestruck (how *does* a tiny, dried up speck of seed produce seven huge zucchini?). And, like life, gardening is a win-a-few, lose-a-few proposition. Everything you plant won't thrive, but that's okay. You'll learn as you go and if you plant a lot, there'll always be plenty that succeed.

If you live in a cold climate, there are ways to extend the growing season. You can even bring some of your gardening projects indoors. Urban gardeners work wonders in baskets, packing crates, barrels and window boxes on rooftops and balconies. Water gardens or fountains can be created in an afternoon. Salad baskets can be harvested in three to six weeks and a pot of chives on your windowsill will liven up your salads and scrambled eggs year round. Herbs are easy to grow and vinegars infused with them are so easy to make they should be illegal to sell. Flowers can be dried or pressed and used in a myriad of ways and many blossoms are edible. Nasturtiums, for example, require little space, food or water, seem to thrive on neglect and produce a profusion of bright blossoms that look and taste great. After the flowers fade, they develop seeds with a peppery flavor.

Every gardening activity is part of a larger generative process. Reading, planning, analyzing soil, researching plant varieties and going to garden shows all stimulate your brain. Clearing out sod, weeding, transplanting and tilling compacted soil work your body. Fresh air and sunshine are natural energizers. Sitting quietly with your senses wide open in the midst of the living, growing landscape you conceived and created is spiritual balm. All are good natural medicine for the blues. Dig it!

Green Theme

- **Create a mini-biosphere:** Plant a terrarium in a fish bowl or any large glass container. Put in some gravel, a few inches of soil and a bit of moss. Add miniature ferns, interesting stones and tiny statues. Water lightly, seal and watch what happens

- **Rent the film *Little Shop of Horrors*** starring Steve Martin, Rick Moranis and Dan Ackroyd. It's a wacky musical about a mild mannered clerk, sadistic dentist, a man-eating plant and the search for true love. Guaranteed to generate grins! (There's an earlier version with Jack Nicholson as the dentist that's every bit as good. Get both.)

- **Make an aquarium:** Fish are relaxing to watch and not hard to care for, if you keep it simple: a bowl, water, gravel or glass marbles, an underwater plant or two, etcetera. Of course, your fish will need names.

Chapter 31

Knead a Lift? Bake Bread

Get out a cookbook, preferably one with lots of color pictures, and turn to the bread section (unlike going to the supermarket, it always helps if you're hungry when you do this). What's your favorite kind? Sourdough? Rye? Cheese, challah, old-fashioned oatmeal, garlic or nine-grain? Ever tried to make bread yourself? Believe it or not, now, while you're down in the dumps, may be the perfect time.

One of the most heavenly smells in the world is bread baking, one of the most satisfying tastes is bread fresh from the oven and one of the best times to make bread is when you're blue. There's something about the process that mends your mood and puts you back in touch with things that are reassuring and reliable. So go ahead, break out the yeast, flour and mixing bowl, because you're in for a treat!

From the moment you pour warm water over the yeast, interesting things start to happen. First, that dry, dead-looking powder comes to life. It gets bubbly and fizzy, releasing a marvelous, pungent aroma. Then, after you stir in the flour and other ingredients, the dough has to be kneaded. Don't even think about doing this with a bread machine or food processor. Make it a hands-on experience.

Get your palms into the dough and use some muscle, pushing down and forward with the heels of your hands. As you fold the sticky dough back on itself, over and over, rhythmically stretching and folding, the texture changes. From a gluey mass that clings to fingers and the kneading surface, it becomes smooth and elastic.

Next comes an exercise in patience. Shape the dough into a ball, slip it into a big, greased bowl, put it in a warm place, cover it and wait. That's all for now. While you're being patient, the dough grows. When it's twice as big as it was at first, you get to do something very satisfying: punch it down! Just push the air out of it with your fist, reducing it to the size it was when you started. Whoosh! It deflates. (Know any people to whom you'd like to do this?)

Now it's time for the next exercise in patience: wait a while more. If you've done everything right so far, the dough is resilient and will grow again. Depending on what kind of bread you're making and the room temperature, this second rising may take another hour. Finally, after the dough has again puffed up with air, it's ready to bake. In thirty to sixty minutes, you'll have one or more loaves of crusty, aromatic, mouth-watering homemade bread. Talk about comfort food!

I should warn you that, especially if it's your first time, bread baking is not a sure thing. The first couple of times I tried, the results were less than perfect—loaves that were doughy in the center and far too dense. If you follow your recipe carefully, though, paying attention to water temperature (use a cooking thermometer) and making sure the dough has a warm enough place to rise, you'll be fine. If you aren't willing to risk failure, pick another activity. But remember, even "failed" bread smells fantastic and makes better-than-store-bought crumbs or croutons.

The Wonders of Bread

- **Start simple:** Bring home some Bread in a Bag or frozen dough in several varieties that you can bake yourself. Smells every bit as good (and tastes nearly as good) as the bread you make from scratch.
- **Get complex:** Make sourdough loaves, bagels, pita pockets, beignets, crullers or croissants. Stuff croissants with something yummy—almond paste, fruit preserves, chocolate chips, cream cheese, paper-thin prosciutto. Try making puff pastry for éclairs or whole wheat pizza. Bake cheese and onion biscuits. Gotta stop now. Drooling.

It probably hasn't escaped you that there are metaphors throughout this process. For example, given a favorable environment, dormant things return to life; you can have the air knocked out of you and still bounce back; good things sometimes call for patience and are worth the wait; you can provide for your own most basic needs. Baking bread is the little red hen and the little engine that could, for grown-ups. And it's you, doing something very ancient and traditional, making something brand new, creating both sustenance and pleasure. If that doesn't make you feel better, at least you'll make some fantastic toast!

Chapter 32

Enough Is Enough

What are you putting up with that you wish you could stop? It's surprising how many of us fail to say, "Enough is enough!" when we really want to, then chafe under what we have to tolerate as a result. But it happens all the time.

Tolerance is fine when it means recognition and respect for other opinions, beliefs and behaviors. Too often, though, tolerance means a grudging acceptance. You tolerate something because you believe you can't do anything about it. You put up with it, but you don't like it one bit. That's the kind of tolerance you may want to stop. Here's how, in three easy steps.

Step One: Make a List. Ask yourself, "What am I tolerating in my life?" Disrespect? Lack of affection or appreciation from your spouse or lover? A job that doesn't challenge you or pay what you're worth? Leaky faucets? Boring social obligations? Traffic jams or a long commute? Insolent teenagers? Low energy, poor health? Smoking, drinking, drugging, shopping or overeating? Bad weather? Bad hair?

Walk around the house and take notes. Sit down with a cup of something soothing and ask again: "What am I living with that I really dislike?" Write it down. Take all the time you need. Don't worry about sounding like a whiner; get it out.

Step Two: Analyze the List. Put emotion aside and approach this step logically. Divide your list into two groups: things you could do something about if you wanted to and things that are beyond your control. Next, pick the three that bug you the most in each group and rank them in order of gut-level importance. I urge you to actually write out this exercise. Doing it in your head isn't as effective.

Step Three: Commit to Action or Acceptance. Put the list away for a while to gain some perspective. After a day or two, come back to it. Think about what actions you could take to improve the situations you labeled possibly improvable. Write them down. Then, focus your attention on the top three things you earmarked as beyond your control and consider them as objectively as possible. Ask yourself, "If I were somehow choosing to have this in my life, what might the payoff be? What does tolerating this do for me?" Give yourself time with these questions. Look for the deepest answers you can find.

If this kind of inquiry feels too difficult, don't worry. Remind yourself that while this circumstance may not be within your control, your response is. What would it take for you to upgrade your attitude? Can you accept this circumstance in your life right now? Can you accept the possibility of benefit coming from it at some point? If not, is there some action you could take to try to lessen the negative effect?

For example, suppose one of the things I'm tolerating is the gray, wet winter weather where I live. The weather is out of my control. But I could buy wood or Presto Logs and build a fire in the fireplace to make the house cozy. Cozy works best in wet weather. I could plan a getaway to Hawaii. I could buy a full-spectrum lamp and bask in the next best thing to sunshine (see chapter 20, "Lighten Up"). I could hang up photos of beaches and flowers. I *could* actually move to a brighter climate and look for work in St. Thomas or Maui.

Or I could decide to simply accept the weather. I could stop putting energy into resisting something I can't control and make peace with it. Taking it one step further, I might even decide to see winter's beauty with fresh eyes. I could buy a bright yellow slicker, learn black-and-white photography, sing in the rain.

With a little thought, you'll come up with options for each item. Remember, the goal is to convert tolerance into either action or acceptance, which puts you in charge of your life in a big way. If you can't move to action or acceptance right now, that's okay. Put your list away and revisit it from time to time. When you're ready, it'll be there to help.

Ask for What You Want

Calling a halt to things you dislike is a step in the right direction. Here's one more. It sounds like a no-brainer, but it took me years to figure out. Other people can't read your mind and loving you doesn't mean they know what you want. So tell them. Whatever you want—more help with housework, more appreciation, less criticism, less arguing in front of the kids, time for yourself, better sex, better communication—ask for it. Of course, when, how and who you ask are important. To boost your chances of success, read *The Aladdin Factor* by Jack Canfield. It's all about how to ask for—and get—the things you most want.

BLUES
FLASH!

A Stress Rx

According to Dr. Andrew Weil, internationally acclaimed teacher and holistic physician, your body's need for B vitamins increases when you're stressed.

Vitamin B is especially helpful if you smoke, drink alcohol, don't eat a balanced diet or are overworked.

Dr. Weil suggests a daily B-complex formula that includes at least 400 micrograms of folic acid.

It's good for your heart and your head!

Chapter 33

Give Up
Put-Downs

Tether that wrecking ball! Put away that hammer! I'm talking about the ones you keep aiming at yourself—all those put-downs, criticisms and harsh judgments that you routinely beat yourself up with. It doesn't matter whether you do it aloud or in your thoughts. It doesn't matter whether you do it about your past, present or future, either. When you interpret the things you perceive and feel in ways that damage your self-esteem, you make trouble for yourself. If you do it a lot, you're probably used to feeling blue, because you're trudging in a vicious circle: weak self-esteem leads to put-downs and put-downs lower self-esteem. It's high self-esteem you need, however, if you're serious about wanting happiness.

When you were younger, the things you told yourself (your self-talk) reflected the way you were treated by mom and dad, grandparents, teachers, anybody who was an authority figure. If you got lots of approval, affection and support, your self-talk tended to be positive and why not? You were happy with yourself, for the most part. Happy with them, too. If you got a boatload of disapproval and criticism, your self-talk mirrored it. Unless you've made some big changes, there's probably still a demolition derby going on inside your head.

No big deal? Wrong! It's causing you a world of trouble. Negative self-talk is exactly like a wrecking ball or hammer. Every time you put yourself or others down, you take a little chunk out of the foundation upon which you're trying to build a happy life. No wonder it's so hard to feel centered, secure and in control.

Become a Build-Up Ace

Be ready with positive responses to your own chronic put downs. Call yourself "stupid" whenever you make a foolish mistake? Don't let yourself get away with that kind of self-disrespect. Respond with "Wait a minute. I'm not stupid. I'm smart! Everybody makes mistakes. Next time, I'll pay closer attention." Label yourself "ugly" a lot? Debate that nonsense. Say, "Beauty is in the eye of the beholder," and know that it's the truth. Start looking at yourself with generous, benevolent eyes. You're good and getting better. Make sure you think and talk like it.

Here's an enlightening exercise: Beginning right now and for the next twenty-four hours, censor yourself: let no negative judgments, put-downs or other critical remarks pass your lips about yourself, others, anything. Rein in any tendency to call yourself or anyone else names, especially when things don't go your way or your behavior isn't exactly flawless. Put a rubber band around your wrist. If you catch yourself thinking a negative thought, picture a big, red stop sign, snap the rubber band and shift your attention to something else. As you'll soon discover, this isn't easy.

You'll probably be amazed at how sore your wrist will be at the end of the day and the number of negative thoughts you caught. But just as hammers can be used to demolish or build, now that you're a grownup you can talk back to ego-bashing thoughts. After your twenty-four-hour experiment, stick with it. In fact, try to take it to the next level. Don't just stop the negative thoughts. Every time you interrupt and challenge a negative, exaggerated or distorted thought, put a rational, positive one in its place. As you do, be aware that you are strengthening the part of you that wants to be happy. Does doing this mean that you should ignore your problems? Not at all.

Instead, shift your attention from the problem to the solution. Stop pitying, shaming, blaming and criticizing yourself. Start imagining what it'll look and feel like when the problem is solved. Think and talk about what you want instead of what you don't want. When you make a mistake, instead of calling yourself names (stupid, idiot, loser), say, "That's not like me. Next time..." and finish the sentence with what you intend to do in the future.

P.S. Two terrific books that explain how to recognize and debate negative self-talk are Martin Seligman's *Learned Optimism* and Albert Ellis's *How to Stubbornly Refuse to Make Yourself Miserable About Anything—Yes, Anything!*

Chapter 34

Here's Looking
at You

Whether you're a fashion plate, set your own trends or take a casual approach to your appearance, it's still true that when you look good (whatever that means to you), you're more likely to feel good. According to some studies, attractive people often get preferential treatment, too. Do you remember Lorenzo, the Latin matinee idol played by Billy Crystal on *Saturday Night Live?* "Eez more important to *look* good than to feel good!" he told us, preening.

Of course, we all know that feeling good is the ultimate goal and attractive doesn't have to mean fabulous. Attractive sometimes just means clean and well groomed. I can still hear my mother advising, "Fix your hair, honey. You'll feel better," while I was down in the adolescent dumps. She was right. Bad hair days have a bad rap for a good reason. In fact, therapists are pleased when depressed clients take a renewed interest in their appearances; it's a sign that the darkness may be lifting.

Start with the basics: brush your teeth, shower or wash your face and hands, shave if you'd normally do that and shampoo or simply comb and arrange your hair. Choose an outfit that is both flattering and comfortable, clean and unwrinkled. Wear what you'd wear to lunch with a friend in a casual-but-nice restaurant. Do it even if nobody else will see you. Don't scold yourself if you don't feel like sprucing up, but if you usually slop around in funky, unwashed clothes when you're blue, try it. It really can make a big difference.

How about a professional manicure? Your hands are an exceptionally expressive part of your body that are always on view. Because they reflect a bit of who you are, making them look good can improve your mood. While you're at it, try a spa pedicure. Your tootsies will look terrific when you're done and you'll feel great while it's going on. Pedicures usually include a foot, ankle and lower calf massage, which can magically dissolve tension and relax your whole body. Men, this works for you too.

Think about getting a really good haircut or professional coloring and, if you wear makeup, have yourself "done" by a pro who'll teach you how to put on a face that flatters. If you're a guy, visit a top-notch stylist instead of a barber or find a barber you like and get a haircut and a shave. My father used to do this when we were on summer vacation; he said it made him feel like a million bucks.

There's nothing like a high-impact quick fix: If you hate your glasses, get new ones or get contacts. Get colored contacts. If you hate your yellow, crooked teeth, bleach them and get braces. If you hate that big old mole on your nose, have it removed. If you hate your spider veins, have them lasered away. Sure, these things cost money. Spend it if you have it or save for what you desire if you don't. It's worth it. How long are you going to walk around hating something about the way you look?

The Kindest Cut?

Cosmetic surgery is a risk that sometimes is worth taking. Straightening your nose, going back to just one chin or getting an eyelid lift won't make you a better person. It won't even make you happy. But it can improve your appearance, for whatever that's worth. If done for the wrong reasons, taken to extremes (Jacko, what *were* you thinking?) and/or botched, it can lead to pain and a world of grief. Done well, it can take years off your face and weight off your spirit. If you've been secretly longing to have some work done, make a couple of free or low-cost consultation appointments. Get at least two opinions from board-certified doctors, and make sure all your questions about risk, benefits, and costs are fully answered.

Consider longer-term projects, too. They can be worth the effort and patience. Commit to a reasonable, nutritionally sound diet and stick to it. Change your eating habits so you can keep extra pounds off. Exercise regularly and aerobically to burn fat, tone muscles, revitalize lungs and heart and generate mood-boosting endorphins.

Whatever you decide to do—major, minor or maintenance, take pleasure in it. Primp a little when you admire the results in a mirror: Lift your chin, give yourself a wink and say, in your best Humphrey Bogart voice, "Here's looking at you, kid."

Chapter 35

Become a
Glass-Half-Full Person

Family folklore says you got your green eyes from dad and your freckles from mom. That bump in the middle of your nose is definitely from grandma Ruth. But what about your tendency to see the glass as half empty? Could you have inherited that, too?

Recent research suggests the answer to that question may be yes. In 1996, scientists announced that they had located genes linked to anxiety, addiction, happiness and pessimism. Whoa! I'll bet that helps shed light on a few things. But does it mean you're a born loser in a biological game of chance? Definitely not. Parts of your personality may be inherited from your forebears, but biology is not destiny. Eye color and other physical characteristics are determined by your DNA, but personality genes are different; they simply indicate susceptibility. Whether you see the glass as half full or half empty, it turns out, is largely up to you and your worldview.

There is an endless list of good reasons to do the work of transforming yourself from pessimist to optimist (yes, it absolutely can be done; we'll talk about how in a minute). First of all, statistically, optimists do better in school, in their careers and in their personal lives. If that isn't enough reason, they are physically and mentally healthier. When optimists do get sick, as of course they do from time to time, they recover more quickly. And when adversity strikes, they bounce back faster and suffer less trauma. Please understand that these are not simply my opinions. There is a wealth of carefully conducted research behind these statements.

Words to Live By

As you continue reading *:60 Second Bluesbusters*, chapter 81, "Positively Speaking," will help you become more conscious of your current explanatory style and adjust it in an optimistic way. In the meantime, here's a quiz, adapted from one by Dr. Barbara Bruce at the Mayo Clinic, that can serve as a quick consciousness-raiser. Check the phrases that, in general, best describe your feelings:

- When it rains, it pours.
- Better safe than sorry.
- There's no such thing as a free lunch.
- Look before you leap.
- Every person for himself/herself.

- Every dark cloud has a silver lining.
- The best things in life are free.
- Seize the day.
- Love is the answer.
- Treat people as you want to be treated.

Checks in the left column indicate pessimistic leanings. Checks in the right column indicate that you do, indeed, look for the silver lining. A few in each means you're (I hate this word, but here goes) normal. In any case, unless you had all right-column checks, chances are you can benefit from fine-tuning your attitude.

One of the researchers is Dr. Martin E. P. Seligman, of the University of Pennsylvania. Seligman is probably the world's leading authority on learned helplessness and explanatory style, psychological terms for the thought patterns and behaviors that classify us as optimists or pessimists. In his book, *Learned Optimism*, he teaches readers how to become optimists. Here, easy as A-B-C-D, is Seligman's formula for learning how to be a glass-half-full person. I strongly recommend, however, that you get the book and read the full-blown version. It's lay-reader friendly and extremely eye opening. He suggests:

- When **A**dversity strikes, become aware of your automatic thinking. Do you generally blame yourself? Call yourself names? Exaggerate or catastrophize? ("This is a disaster and all my fault! I'll never live this down. I am so stupid! I want to die.")
- Identify the **B**eliefs you hold that are making you feel bad in this situation. ("I can't do relationships. I am such a fool. I never know what to say to authority figures. People just don't like me. You can't trust men. I should have seen this coming.")

- Now, identify the Consequences of those thoughts and beliefs. How do thinking these things make you feel? Fearful? Inadequate? Angry? Ashamed? Your beliefs and thoughts about events are the cause of your bad feelings, not the events themselves.
- Finally, Distract yourself (try to think about something else) or Debate your thoughts. Distraction may be all you can manage at the moment, but debating works better in the long run. How true and reasonable are your thoughts? What proof do you have to support them? Is there another possible explanation or conclusion you could draw? If so, what is it? Is there someone more objective you could ask to test the reality of your thinking?

BLUES
FLASH!

Jettison the Java

You don't have to quit altogether, but it's a good idea to stop at one or two cups, especially when your mood is blue. Why? Caffeine is the culprit.

Doesn't matter whether you get it in coffee, tea or cola, studies show caffeine interferes with the conversion of tryptophan (which makes you sleepy) to serotonin (which makes you feel good).

Try switching to green tea. It'll give you a little mood boost and it's loaded with antioxidants, which actually do your body good.

Chapter 36

Bust the
Burnout Blues

Overworked, overextended, overcommitted, overwrought? Feel like you're trying to squeeze two days of activity into every one on your calendar? If so, I'll bet you've vowed more than once to change things. But it hasn't happened yet. In fact, thanks to the "blessings" of technology (cell phones, pagers, laptops, instant messaging, instant cash, instant everything) it may have gotten worse and it can make you blue.

Small wonder. We're expected to be more competitive, active, accessible and successful in every aspect of our lives. If we don't take work home, we feel like slackers and, instead of resting when we happen to have a few free minutes, we try to cram in even more to catch up. Heaven help us if we have a spouse, kids, a demanding job, a desire to stay healthy and fit, a sense of community responsibility, friends and family and a high-maintenance hairstyle! Stress becomes our middle name and, sometimes, our claim to fame: "How do you ever manage to do it all?" people ask. The truth is, you don't. You can't. No one can, no matter what those high-achiever books and seminars tell you. What you *can* do is to start to take control of your time. Here's how.

Say no. It can be hard sometimes, but "no" is a boundary you just have to learn to set. Say it nicely, if it makes you feel better ("Thanks, I'd rather not; I'd like to, but my schedule won't allow it"), but hold your ground.

Track your time. For three days, keep an accurate log of how you spend your time. Not what you *guess* you did, after the fact, but what you actually do. Log in and out of every activity and note the time. Yes, this does mean one more thing to do, but when you're clear about how you really fill your days, it'll be easier to plan a strategy for change.

Attack the chaos. Read "Easy Does It" (chapter 51) and "Fire the Captain" (chapter 82). Then, plan an attack on your own clutter and disorganization as if you were an Army general. Start small and work up. Stop writing things on scraps of paper. Designate one and only one place to keep your purse and keys. Put receipts and other important papers in color-coded files. Make a master list of file names. Efficiency frees up time for things you really like—sleep, for instance.

Pay down your sleep debt. How many hours of sleep do you need each night to feel rested and alert? How many are you actually getting these days? Check your time log and see what you're doing from 6 PM to bedtime every night. Let go of some of those activities (television, phone calls, movies) in favor of more sleep. Adequate rest is not a luxury; treat it like the necessity it is (See "Don't Just Do Something, Lie There," chapter 47).

Take time out. Read "Take a Break" (chapter 10). Unions fight for breaks for their members, not because they're nice guys, but because workers are more effective when they don't work nonstop. You're no different. Take five minutes every hour or, if that's impossible, one fifteen-minute break each morning and each afternoon. Minimum. And for heaven's sake, stop eating lunch at your desk, in your car or standing in front of your fridge!

Stop negative self-talk. If you think you aren't good enough unless you're a superachiever, you'll drive yourself crazy. Take a look at "Give Up Put-Downs" (chapter 33). We're all works in progress and nobody (*nobody!*) is perfect. When you start letting less than perfect or even so-so be okay, you'll likely find you have a lot more time.

Get Physical and Metaphysical

People who exercise and/or meditate regularly aren't any less busy than you are. It just seems that way, because they tend to have a wellspring of balanced, calm energy. The benefits of exercise and meditation are legion and well documented. You'll find information about both in "No Place like Om," chapter 85, and "Turn on to a Natural High," chapter 42. If you make either (better yet, both) of them a regular part of your life, you can tap into that energy, too. So take up boxing or belly dancing, jumping rope or jogging, hit a bucket of balls, kick a soccer ball around or play catch with your kids (counts as both quality parenting time and exercise!). Then find a quiet place to sit, turn the volume on body and mind way down and do nothing but breathe for twenty minutes or so. Ahhhh. That's more like it!

Chapter 37

Blue Buyer, Beware

I'd be the last person to advise against a harmless bit of retail therapy now and then. It can be a nice little mood boost to come home with a new pair of running shoes, a couple of CDs, a pair of earrings or a lipstick. I'd also be one of the last to suggest that you steer clear of astrologers, fortune-tellers, card-readers and other relatively harmless pastimes that may give you a lift. In fact, we suggest a few of them in these pages, just for fun. The problem is that when you're blue, you may be vulnerable to influences and impulses you'd normally shrug off or reason away. You may feel inclined to look to them for definitive answers to your life's problems or for direction when you're adrift, and, as a result, you may find yourself more at sea than ever.

Keep your wits about you, especially when faced with extravagant claims for expensive health- or skin-care products (Face Lift in a Jar!), sexual stimulants (Libido of a Teen!), weight-loss aids (Lose 30 Pounds in 30 Days Without Dieting!), subliminal tapes (Reprogram Your Subconscious While You Sleep!) and anything else that promises amazing or instant results in return for your hard-earned money. If it seems too good to be true, it probably is. P.T. Barnum was right.

Subliminal tapes are a good case in point. Their manufacturers claim that imperceptible messages embedded into tapes of soothing music or nature sounds enable you to transform your life in countless ways, without any effort, without even paying attention. These tapes will, they claim, help you lose weight, enlarge your bust, become more outgoing and confident, get better grades, stop procrastinating, stop smoking, recharge a flagging sex life, eliminate stress and on and on.

It would be nice to believe that such things could help you, even a little, and it's true that humans can process certain kinds of information without being aware of it. But these tapes just don't work. Scientists— researchers who were genuinely curious about possible effects— studied them extensively. The results were consistent and conclusive: Zilch. Nada. Nothing. Even when the people who listened to these tapes *believed* that they had been helped, all the tests proved that it just wasn't so. Nothing changed.

Of course, the famed placebo effect can't be discounted. Placebos, remember, are inert substances (like sugar pills) that sometimes are effective due to a person's belief in their power. So, even though there's not a shred of scientific evidence that bee pollen, royal jelly or subliminal messages have any benefits, if you believe they do, you may find yourself feeling more energetic or prettier after using them. No problem there. But it's important to realize that the remedy isn't in the audio cassette or the bottle that cost fifty bucks. It's in the new hope in your head.

It's the same for every new "miracle" product on the market. You read impressive testimonials from people who may even believe them, along with some scientific-sounding claims. Next, real scientists test it to determine whether the product actually has any effect. It usually doesn't. Then the hucksters object, pooh-poohing orthodox science and touting anecdotal evidence. Eventually, the illusion fades, the product disappears and the hucksters move on, counting their money.

Seek comfort, by all means, but not at the expense of truth or you may find both your wallet and your heart feeling even emptier.

You Are Getting Sleepy...You Are Feeling Happy!

Because so much quackery and show business have been attached to it, misconceptions abound about what hypnosis can and can't do. It isn't a psychological truth serum and using it for "age regression" doesn't hold up under scrutiny. It doesn't enable people to perform superhuman feats, force them to act against their will or block sensory input. It does, however, have two therapeutic uses that reveal the mind's healing power. Hypnosis helps relieve pain. In fact, some ten percent of us can become so deeply hypnotized that even surgery can be performed without anesthesia. It also helps people harness their body's ability to heal. It's not yet clear how hypnosis works and certainly it offers no magic wand for happiness. But it can and does help us become more aware of how much our positive, focused beliefs and expectations matter—to mood, to health, to life.

Chapter 38

Happy Factors

Scientists study just about everything, from our sex lives to our preferences in the produce aisle, so it's not surprising that they've also studied what makes people happy. Some of the results of their research contain good news.

The best predictor of happiness has nothing to do with sex, age, race, marital status, where or how you live or even whether you have a job. The best predictor is...the past. People with happy dispositions tend to stay happy, no matter what life hands them, and people who are usually unhappy tend to say that way over time.

What, exactly, *causes* a happy disposition, besides genetics, which we can't do anything about? This is where the good news comes in. There are four inner traits, or ways of thinking, that create the "happy factor." None of is genetically programmed; all are learned behaviors, which means you can adopt them if you want to.

Happy people like themselves. In other words, their self-esteem is high. When the going gets tough, people with a strong, positive self-image keep going. In fact, when the University of Michigan studied well-being in America, the best predictor of general life contentment wasn't satisfaction with family life, friendships or income, but satisfaction with *self*. Happy people don't think they're perfect, but they have a reasonably high opinion of themselves. They are positive but realistic, because their opinion of themselves is based on the genuine achievement of realistic goals and ideals.

Happy people believe they control their destinies. They think that most of what happens to them is a result of choices they've made, not of outside forces over which they have no influence or control. They manage their time well, set short- and long-term goals, develop strategies to achieve those goals and, as a result, feel that they are in the driver's seat of their own lives.

Happy people are optimistic. They see the glass as half full, expect situations to go well and don't blame themselves when things plummet south. They aren't Polyannas who fail to consider the dark side of life, but they choose to focus on the positive and tend to feel hopeful rather than helpless. When faced with adversity, they persist confidently in their efforts to turn trouble around.

Happy people are outgoing. They are more involved with others, tend to have good social support systems (an important source of well-being) and find it easier to make and keep friends and get along with family. Because opposites don't really attract (we actually gravitate toward people who are like rather than unlike ourselves), outgoing people tend to hang out with other outgoing folks and usually end up having a pretty good time.

The bottom line. Even if you are not this way by nature, can you become more outgoing, build your own self-esteem, learn to see your glass as half full? Absolutely! A good way to start is to play Let's Pretend. Pretend you're an extrovert. An optimist. A confident, self-assured, happy person. Then, begin to act that way. This may be considered "faking it," but it's for a good cause. It's a psychologically sound, useful strategy for changing your point of view and, as a result, the way you feel. *Going through the motions can trigger the emotions.* You already know this. Have you ever been in a rotten mood when the phone rings and you pick it up and pretend to be fine? When you hang up, you often feel a bit better, right? Feeling happy can work the same way. William James, one of the grand old scholars of human behavior, said it perfectly, if a little stuffily: "If we wish to conquer undesirable emotional tendencies in ourselves, we must assiduously, and in the first instance cold-bloodedly, go through the outward motions of those contrary dispositions we prefer to cultivate." In other words, fake it to make it.

Go with the Flow

Between anxiety and boredom lies a middle ground where challenges absorb us and match our skills. This is the zone of "flow," a term coined by University of Chicago psychologist and best-selling author Mihaly Csikszentmihalyi in his book *Finding Flow: The Psychology of Engagement with Everyday Life*. To be in flow is to be one with what you are doing, without consciousness of self and without a blue mood. To experience flow, you need to find challenge and meaning in what you're doing. If the challenge isn't inherent in the task or in your job, you can challenge yourself. You can set goals, immerse yourself in ways to achieve them, pay attention to what's happening as you work and enjoy what you are experiencing at the moment. Say yes to things that interest you and no to things that bore you and waste your time. Use your leisure, not to kill time, but to engage and stimulate. Sometimes to lose yourself is to gain an enormous benefit!

BLUES
FLASH!

When women zapped their dietary fat in half, they ended up feeling more energetic, less anxious and less depressed than in the days when Cherry Garcia was a viable lunch option.

At least that's what happened to 555 women who took part in a study conducted by Fred Hutchinson Research Center. The 767 women in the control group saw no changes in their psychological well being.

The women learned how to avoid fat in small group meetings, at first weekly, then every month.

They also took off an average of nine pounds during that year. No wonder they were smiling!

Chapter 39

Love Those Lists

Too much to do? Overwhelmed? Out of control? Try making a list. In fact, try making several. Start with the old, standby To-Do list. It can help you visualize what needs to be done, task by task. Then, prioritize it. What will you do first, second and so on? This may not qualify as great fun, but it sure beats wallowing around in the land of the overwhelmed. Plus, if you're like me, you'll find that it feels really good to cross items off as you complete them.

I love lists. They help you remember details and go a long way toward keeping you organized and making sure every task gets done. I make them daily and depend on them as much as my watch or appointment book.

Don't stop at a To-Do list. Make a list of concerns in advance of visits to your doctor, lawyer or therapist; you'll avoid getting home and realizing you forgot to ask an important question. A shopping list is essential. Without one, I invariably leave something out. A daily gratitude list is a great way to stay mindful of what matters and a list of books you've read or movies you've seen and enjoyed will be lots of fun to look at in years to come. When your kids (or grandkids) are little, list the funny or sweet things they say and do. You think you'll remember, but one day you'll turn around, they'll be fifteen and you'll have forgotten so much!

How about making a list of your goals? Be as specific as possible. If you want to earn more money, come up with an exact amount. If you're longing for a love relationship, list your criteria. Then, list the steps you need to take to reach your goal. Set up time frames for the tasks and prioritize. Check your list periodically to revise and see how you're doing. Celebrate when you complete a goal and then establish a new one to keep you going and growing.

Before I Die

Like most fifteen-year-olds, John Goddard had a wealth of heart-stopping dreams, starring, of course, himself. One ordinary day in 1940, he went to the trouble of writing 127 of his life dreams on a pad of yellow paper. Most lists like that wind up with our report cards in the attic, but his became a blueprint for his life. In 1972, at age forty-seven, he had achieved 103 of his original quests, as reported by a *Life* magazine article entitled "One Man's Life of No Regrets." The article, detailing his Master Dream List, became one of the most requested reprints in the magazine's long history. Why not write your own Master Dream List? Let yourself go. Never mind money, time or other limitations. List everything you want to accomplish or experience before you die. How else are you going to ignite the spark? If you concentrate only on today, putting aside dreams that don't fit in with current needs, you'll be living a postponed life. Don't wait. Start now.

Probably the easiest inventory to make when you're down is a list of worries. When you're done, review it and ask yourself, "What little thing can I do right now to make this better?" Another way to cheer up is to record all your positive characteristics. If you have trouble thinking of many, ask your family, friends and colleagues. When you write down one of your attributes, it becomes more real and concrete. To further ensure that you allow yourself to feel the good things you are listing, take a deep breath and let each one in. It's not automatic. We're all likely to brush aside positives, especially when they come from others, yet we tend to take criticism to the grave! Change your perspective and savor the positives. Keep the list around to read next time you need a lift.

In personal growth workshops, we sometimes do an exercise called Behind Your Back. A group member turns his or her back while everyone else says good things about that person. Comments must be sincere and people can say as much or as little as they wish. The recipient writes down what's said as "I am" statements. For example, "I am friendly," not just "friendly." If you do that with your list, too, you'll be affirming as well as listing—a beneficial practice.

Think about making a list of important things you've accomplished or places you've traveled. A great feel-better list is one naming friends. Include everyone you've ever felt close to; it'll help you remember the good stuff. While you're at it, make a list of people you're close to now and those you can call on a bad day. Keep it by the phone as a reminder.

PART FOUR

Never Too Late to Rejuvenate

How long has it been since you felt as carefeee as a child? Believe it or not, this may be the perfect time to invite the uncomplicated kid in you to come out and play. Here are fourteen great ideas to help you regress, set your responsible grown-up free or just let spontaneity rule. When you do, your blue mood may melt faster than a popsicle on a summer day!

Chapter 40

Play's the Thing

Pretend you're ten again and listen to your mother: "Stop moping around! Go outside and play!" Okay, so you don't *feel* like it. But "Do I feel like it?" may not be the best question to ask. How about "Will it make me feel better?" Here are a few starter ideas for coaxing your inner child out to play.

Enlist the help of an expert. Kids can turn anything into a game. Borrow one for a while and start a game of peek-a-boo, horsey, tag, hop-scotch or hide-and-seek. Children love an appreciative audience, so let them entertain you. Better yet, join in. Get down on the floor and pre-tend to be an animal. Make silly faces and strange noises. Build a house from a cardboard box or by throwing a blanket over a table. Make a train out of a row of chairs. Play Captain Hook and Peter Pan; don't forget the crocodile. If you do your best to enter into the spirit of the game, you'll forget your troubles for a while and there's a good chance you'll find your mood lifting.

If no children are handy or if there are too many in your life as it is, take time out with a cat or dog. Dogs are less worry than kids and easier to please. Play fetch, can't-catch-me, tug-of-war or Frisbee. Roll around on the grass. Let it lick you and make you laugh. Like cats better? Tie the end of a string to a rubber band and dangle or drag it. If the cat isn't in the mood for action, just stroke it for a while. This kind of contact can improve both mood and health.

No kids, dogs or cats around or they're just not your thing? Play by yourself. What's going on outside? Snow is great, even if your grown-up self thinks it's a nuisance. When was the last time you made snow angels, built a snowman or took target practice at a tree? In summer, turn on the sprinkler and run through it as you did years ago or, if you can, take yourself to the beach. Build sand castles. Paddle around in a rubber raft. Or put on a straw hat and sandals and visit an amusement park. Buy cotton candy, go through the fun house and ride the roller coaster.

Spring is perfect for jump rope, bike riding, in-line skating or making yourself giddy on the merry-go-round in the park. It's also perfect for a trip to the zoo to see the baby animals. What blue mood can last while you're watching a fawn totter after its mom or a curious chimp grinning at you? Fall brings drifts of leaves to pile up and jump into (I really do this, at least once a year. So can you!). Collect some colorful leaf specimens, dip them in melted paraffin and make greeting cards. Cut branches to display in a vase.

If the weather is nasty or you're not comfortable outside where neighbors can watch you regress, stay in. Buy a new computer program or game and lose yourself in it for a while. Go on-line and visit an upbeat chat room or just follow your mouse (see chapter 58). With only a deck of cards, you can learn a new version of solitaire, teach yourself a trick or build a house. A set of watercolors, colored pencils, paints or markers transforms you into the artist you once were—one who doesn't give a damn about "good."

Fool Around with Ways to Play

- Play dates aren't just for kids. Make one with a friend. Go out to a club and try swing or salsa dancing. Go bowling at midnight. Visit an amusement or water slide park or a video arcade. Forget your dignity!
- Find an adults-only "camp" or learning center that teaches something you might enjoy: horseback riding, poetry writing, pottery, yoga, contra dancing, mask making, landscape design. Sign up for a day or weekend, more if you can.
- Invite a few pals over for a night of cards, board games or charades. Have potluck snacks and funny prizes for big winners. Videotape yourselves or take Polaroid snapshots.

Take your playful self into the kitchen and pretend you're that famous chef, Julia Childish. Whip up a batch of smiley-face chocolate chip cookies. Invent a recipe for your own personal version of comfort food. Bake bread (see chapter 31) and mix some things you love into the dough, just to see how it turns out.

If none of these ideas tickles your fancy, try to remember what you did for fun as a kid. Why did you stop? Too old? Too sophisticated? All you need to do the activity again is the desire. Even if you don't feel like it, even if you're not sure it'll do any good—lose your dignity, lace up your sneakers and take mom's advice.

Chapter 41

Paint Your Mood

Got a case of the blues so solid you could slap a coat of paint on it? Hmmm. Maybe that's not a bad idea.

Talent be damned, it can feel exhilarating to express your feelings—especially the darker ones—through art. Cameron, who describes himself as self-taught, has a fascinating collection of drawings, collages and paintings he created during what he calls his "black period." I think they're wonderful. A local gallery agrees, because he's about to have his first show. Each work is related to the others, yet each is different—swirling masses of chaotic shapes, inky images, angry swaths of color. You can't help but sense some of his emotions at the time. They are visually compelling, carefully crafted works he can be proud of, whether anyone buys one or not.

I don't think of myself as an artist, but I have a kind of autobiographical art collection in my journal. I began it with a 12"x20" blank book so I'd have plenty of room to play. At first, those big blank pages felt intimidating and overwhelming, so I made small drawings in little boxes. I suppose these early efforts reflected my insecurity about doing something so out of character. Gradually, though, I expanded my drawings to fill a whole page, even two pages. These days, with a few painting lessons under my belt, I feel right at home with broad, sweeping strokes and vivid colors. In fact, I've come to love this creative part of myself and am as proud of my amateur artwork as Cameron is of his.

Why not try? It's relaxing, revealing and fun. Start with a few jars of poster paint, some dime-store brushes and a pad of newsprint paper, the bigger the better; or start small and work your way up. Finger paints are great, too (the sheets of shiny paper that come in the box aren't nearly big enough; buy a roll of shelf paper with a nice, slick finish or use poster board). You can become an instant calligrapher with a jar of India ink and a big, pointy brush; or experiment with a box of watercolors.

It doesn't matter what you paint on (canvas, cardboard, wood, glass, paper, fabric, plastic), what you paint with (paint brushes, tooth brushes, knives, fingers, cotton swabs) or even whether you paint at all (try drawing, cutting and pasting, sculpture, pastels, crayons, fabric collages). It doesn't matter if the finished product pleases anyone or looks like anything you can name. All that matters is that you get your feelings outside your head, into your hands and onto or into something else.

If you're tempted to trash the final product(s), don't give in. Save it. Scribble the date and a few notes about your creation on the back. Mat and frame it, if you want to see it take a big step up in eye appeal and importance, or just tuck it away to look at again when you're feeling better.

Making Faces

Life mask kits, available at hobby stores and on the Internet, are relatively inexpensive and easy to use, or you can experiment with plaster of paris, Vaseline and a couple of straws for breathing. It doesn't take long and when you're done, you'll have a perfect 3-D impression of your face. With any luck, you'll look blissful rather than terrified that the plaster goop will never come off. Speaking of which, this is something you should do with a friend; it's messy and, if done carelessly, can be dangerous (well, not terribly). The plaster impression serves as a mold from which you make the mask. Why not make several and decorate each as a different facet of your personality. Paint the faces, add hair and get creative. Mount and hang them.

Another kind of painting also offers stress release and a mood lift as byproducts. Not usually called art, it is nevertheless a creative act: Paint a room, a piece of furniture, a fence, even the whole damn house. This kind of project shifts your attention away from yourself and your mood toward something you can feel good about, both during the process and afterward. It's work, no doubt about it, but sometimes manual labor is just what the doctor ordered.

It's also a deliberate act of transformation, conceived and engineered by you personally. When it's done, stand back and say, "This is better, because of me. I created this transformation myself!" It's a soul-satisfying feeling. No case of the blues is solid enough to stand up to that for long.

Chapter 42

Turn on
to a Natural High

Naturally high. Sounds pretty good, doesn't it? Like something you could use right now? Luckily, your body is ready to generate it for you. Endorphins, as you've probably heard, are chemicals produced whenever the body has to work harder and longer than usual. They cause runner's high, the famous second wind and surge of euphoria that kicks in when a long-distance runner pushes past the desire to quit.

Producing endorphins isn't something only long-distance runners and other athletes can do. Whenever you exercise aerobically, you make endorphins. And whenever you make endorphins, you feel good, which seems like an excellent of reason to do it. Of course, if you do enough aerobic exercise, it also builds lung capacity, burns fat and tones muscles, including your heart; but when you've got the blues, you may not care much about those things. Almost any kind of physical activity may seem like paddling upstream—the idea of aerobic exercise downright laughable. Even if exercise is a regular part of your life, there are days when it may feel like a Herculean effort.

Do it anyway. If you're not used to being active, launching any kind of exercise program in the middle of a case of the blues can be a hot ticket to an immediately improved outlook. Really. As soon as you actually start it, good feelings begin to stir. First, though, make sure your doctor thinks it's okay, especially if you have serious health problems.

The key is to start small. In his book *Spontaneous Healing,* Dr. Andrew Weil outlines an eight-week program for developing optimum physical health and a strong immune system. The exercise he recommends is brisk walking, starting with ten minutes a day during the first week, gradually building to forty-five minutes a day by the end of week eight. One of the best things about walking is that no special equipment is needed. Just comfortable, weatherproof clothing and a good pair of walking shoes.

If even ten minutes seems like too much at first, start with five. That's where I began. Even dedicated couch spuds like I was can walk briskly for five minutes a day! Do it for a week, then increase your time in increments. Aim for an ultimate goal of thirty to forty-five minutes each outing. Get a cheap pedometer at a sporting goods store and monitor your progress, adding a hundred steps each time out.

The most important part, though, is *persistence*. Walking for a day or two here and there may temporarily help your mood, but it's obviously not enough to build a bluesbusting habit. Do it no matter what, every day for at least a week and you'll start to feel a lot better. Do it for the full eight weeks and you'll have built a new habit that will help you feel and look good far into the future.

Sound good? If so, take the *:60 Second Bluesbusters* challenge: Lace up your walking shoes and march right out of your mood. Fair weather or foul, by yourself, with a pet or a friend, in the park, around the block, at the mall or on a treadmill: turn a deaf ear to your excuses and go for it.

Step Lively

Join a hiking club. You'll meet lots of others who like to walk and you'll get out to some beautiful and interesting places. Walking clubs are common, too. Members often meet at shopping malls. Bring a Walkman or portable CD or MP3 player and some upbeat music.

Walk with a furry friend. Exercising Fido is good for him and good for you. If you don't have a dog, I'll bet you have neighbors who do. Borrow theirs. They'll love you for it!

Sign up for a walking tour. Most major cities have them. So do many tourist destinations. Summer garden tours or fall foliage walks can be a delight. Art walks are common wherever there are shops and galleries, or how about a docent-guided walking tour of your nearest museum? After you're done with the leisurely stroll at which most tours are paced, go back over the route moving quickly. See what you notice that you missed the first time around.

P.S. While we're focusing on walking, if you'd rather get your aerobic high some other way—swimming, bicycling, roller or ice skating, exercising the dog, playing tennis or racquetball, salsa dancing, raking leaves—go to it. Walking, however, is easy and easy is good when you're blue. Anything that gets your heart beating a little faster for a while is good medicine for a bad mood. In case you're wondering, as long as it's hot and heavy, that definitely includes making love.

BLUES
FLASH!

"Take two aerobics classes and call me in the morning" may just be an antidote for the blues.

According to *Psychology Today*, exercise not only beats the blues (including mild to moderate depression), it is four to five times more cost-effective than traditional forms of psychotherapy!

Recent studies also indicate that exercise can keep the blues at bay. How this works is unclear, but, like antidepressants, it may alter brain chemistry.

Chapter 43

Hot Mamas
in Pajamas

There are lots of ways to have a good time in bed. If the first thing that comes to mind is "napping," you're overworked, under-rested or blue, baby. So go read a book and stay in your jammies all day if you want to. Wallow in it. In fact, why not throw a pajama party?

Not like the ones in 4th grade, when someone always ended up in the closet, crying. Remember the times in high school you got together with friends and stayed up all night, talking and laughing until your stomach ached? Maybe you styled each other's hair, painted nails, pierced each other's ears, tried on false eyelashes. For sure you gossiped, mostly about boys, but about other girls, too. You ate junk food and pizza. You drank coke or beer or anything else you could get your hands on. Once you got tipsy on someone's parents' peppermint schnapps. You made movies of each other.

Whatever you did, it was fun and that was the point. It still is, right? Just planning this shindig can cheer you up. So, who do you want to invite? Old friends, new friends, a little of each? What about asking a few close friends to come, each bringing another friend you don't know well? New ideas and new people might be just what you need.

Think about how much work you want to do, too, not just who you want to hang out with. If you want to take it easy, ask guests to bring their own bedding and a dish for a potluck meal; add a twist to the potluck— specify that it's gotta be comfort food (see chapter 1). Or just order out after your guests have all arrived. Go Asian and get egg drop soup, pad thai, crab cakes, shrimp satay or anything yummy. If food cheers you up, you may want to go all out and cook something yourself or just break out the crackers and Brie.

What about creating a theme? Ask each guest to bring a secret to tell or old pictures of themselves to share. Have a spa night, giving each other French clay facials and paraffin hand dips. Maybe it would be a kick to play dress-up (see chapter 15) or make it a bluesbuster marathon (see chapter 3). Ask each guest to bring an all-time favorite movie, then stay up all night, watching and knoshing.

Glam Mamas, Lounging Pajamas

Throw an afternoon Pajama Tea. Wear your most glamorous lounging outfit. Take it over the top with feather boas, elbow-length gloves, gold lame mules, little hats with veils, flowing kimonos. Brew several kinds of exotic tea. Serve assorted pastries and yummy little sandwiches with the crusts cut off. Get out your best china or pick up some delicate cups and saucers at a thrift shop (no mugs allowed). If you'd rather make it a cocktail party, serve manhattans, martinis with sake or flavored vodkas, or Perrier with a twist in martini glasses. Sit around and gossip, or gather in the kitchen and cook a communal dinner. Too many cooks won't spoil this broth; they'll make it a gas.

House too full or too small for a pajama party with pals? Chip in and rent a room or, better yet, a suite at a local hotel. Business hotel/motels often have great weekend deals. You can still bring in food and fun and you'll all be on a mini-getaway from your everyday homes and lives. What the hell, why not go all out and rent the bridal suite or the penthouse? It won't cost much split several ways and they have outrageous bathrooms!

I went to a PJ party recently, only we called it a retreat. That sounds so much more grown-up and important, doesn't it? It was really a big pajama party. We slept on the floor, ate, drank a little wine, talked and laughed for a good part of the night. The food was simple—brownies, chips and dips, Ben and Jerry's—but it tasted great, because we were having a good time, eating what we wanted when we wanted. We talked to each other about our problems, our hopes, our fears and frustrations. We told jokes and funny stories about each other and on ourselves. We prayed. We sang and danced. We hugged each other and lent each other things and had a great time. Even though we didn't sleep much, we came home refreshed and revitalized.

If you need more convincing, ponder this. A pajama party is the best kind of party there is, not only because things relax so wonderfully when the opposite sex is nowhere in evidence, but because the food is usually terrific, no one cares if you pig out (in fact, it's encouraged) and you get to talk about things you actually like.

Chapter 44

Spoil Yourself— You're Worth It!

Doesn't everyone like receiving a gift? It just feels good. It can feel even better when there's no special reason. It carries a silent message: "I care about you...you're special to me...I want you to feel happy." Sweet, huh? So, what about this: Don't wait for someone else to give you this mood-lifting attention. You could wind up waiting a long time. Instead, when you're blue, send the same message to yourself, special delivery, with a gift.

What kind of gift? That's up to you. It can be costly or free. It can be gift wrapped or too intangible for a box and bow. It can be something you've always wanted or something you've never thought about before. Does anything come to mind right now? What would you like to have that you've been denying yourself? If someone else were to offer you a gift, what would you choose? Any desires you haven't fully admitted to yourself?

The gift of time can be wonderful. Time to concentrate on yourself, give to yourself, take care of yourself. You could take time for a long walk, or you could take a Hollywood bath (see chapter 2). Watch a movie, go to a museum, visit the library, drive into or out of the city, read a novel (chapter 11), write poetry—whatever you feel like and can do with no thought for anyone else. Arrange to have an hour, a day or even a weekend off, but be sure that what you do with it feels good and is for you alone. Don't give yourself time only to end up balancing your checkbook, cleaning the garage or pulling weeds in the garden, unless these activities are truly fun and/or restorative for you. Remember, this is a present. It's supposed to delight you.

Purchase a gift, if your budget will stand it and you're in the mood for a little retail therapy. I often buy myself flowers, especially when I'm feeling low. A bouquet of lilies, tulips or dahlias gives me a lift as soon as I pick it out and the pleasure lasts for days. A massage, steam bath, or sauna is great, too, or, every now and then, a full-service visit to a day spa. If it's not something you do routinely, a manicure, pedicure or facial can help dissolve a blue mood (trust me, this works for men, too).

If you have the money and are in the mood, consider a serious splurge. What about a trip to a place you've always wanted to visit or the purchase of a piece of fine jewelry? I once bought myself a bluesbusting ring that I fell in love with the moment I saw it. I had never spent that kind of money on a piece of jewelry before, so it wasn't easy to write the check, but I've never been sorry. I wear it often and it gives me pleasure every time I see it. I love it when someone asks, "Who gave you that beautiful ring?" and I get to say, "I did!" It's a special gift from someone who loves me, which, in this case, means me. What a great feeling!

Hold a Yankee Auction

A Yankee auction isn't really an auction and no one seems to know how it started. Regifting is giving a gift you got from someone else. Combining the two can be great fun. Get a group together and ask each person to bring a wrapped regift. Pile them in the center of the room. Have everyone take a number. Number one has first choice of the presents, unwrapping it in front of the group. Number two can either take number one's present (whereupon number one picks a replacement) or select something from the pile. Number three has two unwrapped gifts to choose from, or can pick from the pile and so on. Instead of regifts, you can do the same thing with new items, used CDs, even food.

Here's another trick that, assuming you can remember where you put them, works well and costs little. Buy five or six small gifts, the kind you'd choose for special stocking stuffers. Wrap them up and put them away, out of sight. If they're the kind of gifts that can lead to other activities (a box of watercolors, a jar of pesto sauce, a gift certificate for a massage), give yourself extra points. The next time you need a lift, pick a present from your personal grab bag. Go ahead, pick two. Remember, the message is not "stuff makes me happy," but rather, "I can make myself happy." As dear Mr. Rogers used to say, "You're worth it—just because you're you." He was right. Especially when you're blue.

Chapter 45

Take a Hike

When you were a kid, you probably spent a lot of time outdoors. Whether you grew up in a city as I did, in a small town, on a farm or in a tenement, your mode of transport was feet or bike and you knew your neighborhood intimately. Many of your games and much of your socializing happened outside, unless you happened to be sick or were pressed into some family activity, like dinner. Outside was where life happened, at least the part of life that interested you most.

Slowly, over time, all that's changed, hasn't it? You get where you're going these days in an automobile, subway, bus or plane. The bulk of your life happens inside a building. Outdoors is that thing you walk through to get from your house or office to your car. Okay, maybe not that extreme, but close. Being outdoors now is what happens when you go to some trouble to make it happen.

But you are a natural animal living in a natural world; the rest of the stuff—the billboards and shopping malls, skyscrapers and parking lots—people made because they thought...well, who knows what they thought. The point is this (and it's likely you already know this but have lost touch with it): it's not good for you to live in ways that cut you off from the natural world. Sure, you can do it. You'll survive. But something inside withers.

There is magic in the mountains and valleys, oceans and rivers, forests and beaches, the marshes and rolling hills. I greatly admire the organizations and people who make it possible for inner-city kids to get at least a little time in the natural world. They do it because they understand how being a part of the natural world for even a short period of time can touch and affect children. These charities and philanthropies do it for the same reasons I recommend it to you.

For one thing, it gets your feet walking on something besides concrete or some other perfectly flat surface. Walking on soil is good for you in a primal way that is hard to describe. It literally grounds you. For another thing, the sounds in the air are entirely different. If you can get far enough away from cities, all you'll hear are natural sounds. Birds chirping, creeks burbling, twigs snapping, frogs croaking, coyotes howling, the wind rustling the leaves in the trees.

It smells different, too. Most of our houses and workplaces have an artificial, neutral smell—a mix of the materials that make up the structure, plus all the things we eat, use, decorate and wash with, spray into the air, etc. Air conditioners and dusty heating ducts offer the underlying base notes and the "perfume" we inhale is an unnatural, manmade hybrid. Sometimes, the windows of our office buildings don't even open! On the other hand, the smells of the natural world are so keenly wonderful, they dilate your nostrils: pine, cedar, moss, damp earth, decaying wood, saltwater, beach grass, charcoal, wet kelp, wildflowers.

Doing something different is good when you're down in the dumps. Doing it in the middle of a natural setting, even when you're alone (sometimes especially when you're alone), is doubly good. Doesn't matter where you live; you can get to and back from some place naturally beautiful within a day or two, in most cases. Within a few minutes, for some of us. But it's not about how close the natural world is to you. What matters is how close you are to it. If you can't get out of town, find a place that'll do almost the same thing for you: a city park, conservatory, roof garden, aviary or other urban oasis. Then go take a hike.

Nature as Art

Bring the natural world into your living room. Rent the astonishing documentary film *Rivers and Streams*. It's about an artist who painstakingly creates beautiful, three-dimensional art from things he finds in nature—fallen leaves, twigs, rocks and stones, even icicles. All his creations are temporary and none use paint, glue or other manmade materials. Equally amazing is *Winged Migration*, which follows migrating birds all over the globe. This is no ordinary documentary. I don't know how they did it, but in many scenes you have a literal bird's eye view; it seems as if you are part of the airborne flock. It made me very sorry I can't fly, except in dreams, and very glad birds can.

Chapter 46

Gray Matter Matters

To shrink a case of the blues down to manageable size, there's nothing like learning something new. Whenever you set out to learn something new or expand knowledge you already have, you're putting yourself into a growth mode. It's a rare blue mood that can exist alongside your own growth.

Beyond increasing your supply of knowledge and skills, when you learn something new you do something else important. You boost your self-efficacy, which is how you view your own effectiveness. When your self-efficacy is high, you believe that, sooner or later, you can learn whatever you need to learn and do whatever you need to do to make your life work. When your self-efficacy is high, blue moods visit less often and leave sooner.

One of the best ways to build self-efficacy is by having mastery experiences. You take on something challenging and, with persistence and time, master it. You've already undergone lots of these. You mastered crawling, walking, running, riding a two-wheeled bike. You learned to read, write and express yourself in your native tongue. Maybe you've even learned another language. You've acquired an incredibly broad base of information and skills that helps you earn a living, manage a household and care for yourself and others. As long as you're alive, you never stop learning—but you sure as heck may slow down.

If your learning curve has gone flat, this is a perfect time for some new experiences. Remind yourself that you are a person who can persist in the face of difficulty and learn whatever you want to learn. Speaking of which, it doesn't really matter what you choose, except that the subject should meet all three of these standards: (1) It should be something in which you're truly interested, not something someone else thinks you should do; (2) It shouldn't be so hard that you have doubts about your ability to do it; and (3) it shouldn't be so easy that it won't take some real effort. Goals that fit these guidelines have better chances of success.

A Little Learning

Going into a growth mode doesn't have to mean committing to a class that last weeks or months. A myriad of one-day, half-day and one-session classes offer plenty of options. Check local newspapers, your city's parks/recreation department, YWCA, JCC or community college continuing education departments, as well as community bulletin boards. In a few hours, you can hone computer skills, learn to cook gumbo, tune up your car, maintain your bicycle, find out how to play blackjack poker, make scented soap, teach your dog to obey or flirt with strangers. What's your pleasure?

Maybe you're thinking that when you have a bad case of the blues, you won't feel much enthusiasm for becoming a student. Objection duly noted, but it's important to understand that enthusiasm isn't necessary. All you need are the desire to do something that has a good chance of making you feel better and the willingness to make a good-faith effort.

Find a teacher who will be glad to serve as guide on your learning adventure. Colleges, universities and community colleges all offer continuing education classes. You can enroll on a noncredit basis without formal admission, you won't have to worry about exams or papers to write and you can pay with plastic. Beyond the campus, many communities offer adult learning courses. Check yellow-page listings under adult education, as well as specific subjects of interest. Newspapers and community bulletin boards are good sources, too. Many parks and recreation departments offer adult classes in everything from yoga and co-ed volleyball to computer skills and haiku.

Keep your eyes open and do a little homework; you'll find something that piques your interest. Then, take the leap and sign up. Don't worry about whether you'll like it. Don't worry about how well you'll do. Don't worry about anything! You're not getting married, just taking a class. In fact, expect to feel a little lift as soon as you commit to the process. As you build self-confidence and become more involved with your studies, you'll learn a few things about yourself, too. Maybe one of them will be that you haven't got time for the blues!

Chapter 47

Don't Just
Do Something, Lie There

When you're sleeping poorly, your body's resources diminish quickly; mental and emotional resources soon follow. Maybe you're sleeping badly because you're blue; maybe you're blue because you're sleeping badly. Either way, you lose. Get help. White-noise machines, sleep masks, earplugs, herb- or grain-filled pillows, Sleepytime tea, room-darkening shades, warm milk, audios of breaking waves or guided relaxations—all can smooth your journey on the Morningtown Train. So can medication, if lack of sleep becomes an ongoing problem. Nonnarcotic sleep facilitators can be a great help and several fairly effective herbal sleep remedies are available over the counter, too. Talk with your doctor or naturopath before using either or both, but don't wait.

Wake-Up Call

I used to have an alarm clock with such an abrasive, unpleasant ring that I unconsciously trained myself to wake up before it went off. It was a wretched way to come back to consciousness after a nap or long night's sleep. I now have a clock that calls me back from the Land of Nod with the sound of chimes. At first they are spaced about ten or fifteen seconds apart; after a minute, they become more frequent and a little louder. Even though the chimes are gentle, I don't sleep through them, as I feared I might. I am so attached to this clock that I take it with me when I travel, even though it's much bigger than my travel alarm. Shaped like a triangle, it is featured in lots of mail-order catalogues, but many other kinds can wake you with a smile, too. Search for one you like. Don't let the first sound you hear in the morning be anything but pleasant!

In your quest for healing rest, remember that putting yourself into motion is as important as laying yourself down. You need both—an oscillation between activity and rest—every day. Each enables the other. Each nourishes the other. Rest can come in the form of a nap, too. Of course, in a culture that worships high achievers, nap is a bad word and nappers are seen as slackers: "What, asleep in the middle of the day? Are you sick or something? If you snooze, you lose. Quit wasting time!"

Wrong. Some of the most productive people in the world are confirmed nappers. Napoleon napped between battles. Winston Churchill said he napped to cope with his wartime responsibilities. Eleanor Roosevelt and Golda Meier napped. So did Einstein and JFK. Jim Lehrer of public television's *News Hour* closes his office door every day at 12:30 PM for an hour's nap. He says it's the best habit he ever developed. The Bible tells us that on the seventh day, God rested and a day's rest in that time frame probably equals a very short nap.

Napping makes sense, especially when you're stressed or blue. All of us have an internal biological clock called the circadian rhythm, which regulates temperature, metabolism and sleep. Typically, circadian rhythm dips around the middle of the afternoon, right about the traditional time of siesta. For those who can and do, like me, a midafternoon nap is a kind of daily renaissance, a reliable time-out for rest and renewal. Often, twenty minutes is enough to do a world of good. If sleeping during the day makes you feel groggy, a cup of green tea upon awakening can bring you back gently. Try simply lying still with eyes closed and mind quiet for half an hour.

When I spent my workdays in the corporate world, I often skipped lunch in favor of desktop snacking and used my lunch break for napping (behind an office door that closed and locked), like Jim Lehrer. For a while, I told people I was meditating, but later I came out of the closet. I went from being a secret napper to an outgoing, up-front napper and many of my colleagues said it gave them courage to do the same.

These days, I like my naps either short (thirty minutes or less) or long (an hour and a half), depending on my mood and what's happening. Many days, I don't nap at all and don't miss it. On blue days, it's a respite I welcome without guilt. If you're still not convinced that napping should be indulged in guilt-free, track down "The Art of the Nap" by Aristides, originally published in *The American Scholar*. Then, get hold of a delightful kid's book by Audrey Wood, *The Napping House*—a cumulative story, like *The House That Jack Built*, that begins with Granny taking a snooze on a rainy afternoon. Next, check out *Change Your Life without Getting out of Bed: the Ultimate Nap Book* by Sark.

Finally, at www.napping.com, you can order *The Art of Napping* by William A. Anthony, Boston College professor; buy signs to hang over doorknobs (Working Nap in Progress); T-shirts (Nappers—Lie Down and Be Counted!); or a Vocabulary of Napping bookmark. Check them out. It might change your *nattitude* (feeling proud about napping).

BLUES
FLASH!

A 30-second nap? Yes, indeed. A nap as short as half a minute can give you a quick energy refill. It may sound unbelievable, but it won't leave you feeling groggy, as a longer nap might.

Sit in a comfortable chair, feet firmly on the floor. Rest your elbows/lower arms on your knees, while holding your key chain loosely.
Let your head hang down. Try to "shut yourself off."
With practice, you'll fall into a brief sleep.

The key chain is your alarm clock. As soon as you fall asleep, the keys will drop to the floor, waking you up. You'll get a burst of energy
until you can get the longer rest you need.

Chapter 48

Get Pumped

Sometimes you gotta get tough with the blues! A few years ago, I turned into the Queen Mother of Lousy Moods. Who could blame me? A major relationship was on the rocks, my career was stalled and after twelve years of abstinence I was smoking again. I felt so lonely and helpless I could barely drag myself out of bed. Underneath it all, I was angry. Underneath that, terrified. I was having trouble staying clear and centered with my clients, too and my energy level was in the basement. Even my reliable spiritual connection had come unplugged.

Then, I forced myself to take a weight training class. I did it because I knew that, unless I wanted to end up living in a tent, I had better do something to break out of my miserable funk. Plus, the idea of lifting weights was appealing. Even if it didn't help my mood, I figured it would help my body, which could certainly use some help. Because body and mind are connected, I also figured that if I did the exterior some good, the interior would benefit.

Well, it worked. Better than I had hoped. I'm still amazed at how quickly I began to feel and look better. From the first session, my troubles took a back seat for a while as I worked to learn how to raise and lower dumbbells, use a Nautilus machine, stand and breathe.

Breathing is an important part of lifting weights. Interestingly, it's also an important part of many martial arts and spiritual practices. (A yoga teacher I know says, "Control your breath and you control your life." Think about that next time you're stuck in traffic.) So, when they teach you to lift weights, they also teach you to breathe in a way that builds endurance and keeps your muscles nourished with oxygen. The calming, centered feeling was a bonus I didn't expect.

There's also something terrifically satisfying about overcoming these heavy, physical weights that transfers to other, less tangible, obstacles. I began to see that if I was patient and persistent, I could do more than I had at first thought. So can you. You can put sleek, sexy muscles in place of flab and you can grow stronger than your problems, even though they may seem invincible right now.

For me, working with weights became a kind of meditation, a way of turning off my brain for an hour every other day and letting the repetitive motions be all I thought about, all I did. If it wore me out sometimes, it also made me sleep like a baby. Best of all, it helped me feel strong, clear and calm. Even with such fine feelings to recall, it was still a struggle to go back to the gym after a few days away. I did go back, though, often enough to develop a routine and the rewards were always there.

Get rid of your muscle-bound stereotypes, if you have them. Weight lifting isn't just for men, bodybuilders or athletes. With the right instruction, anyone in almost any physical condition can do it. People in their eighties can do it. Kids can do it. There are classes for women, seniors, teens. It doesn't build big, bulging muscles in women, because females don't have enough testosterone. It doesn't require a lot of expensive equipment or a lot of time, either. Three thirty-minute workouts each week can work wonders.

Circuit City

If weight training doesn't sound like a good time for you of the female gender, try Curves or Shapes. These women-only programs offer circuit training, which means you alternate weight-bearing and aerobic exercise. With a dozen or so hydraulic weight machines and "jogging pads" placed between them, you can get a good aerobic workout in thirty minutes. Don't expect big muscle tone improvement, as you use the weights for only thirty seconds at a time, but it's a beginning. Each circuit lasts about fifteen minutes; you go around twice. It's fast. It's easy. It's done to upbeat music and clear, recorded instructions about when to move to the next machine. And it really is fun.

In addition to those who lift, individuals who box tend to be pretty upbeat people. Maybe it's all that aerobic exercise—skipping rope, working with speed bags, endurance running. Or maybe it's the primal satisfaction of landing a few powerful (and padded) punches on an opponent who could be a surrogate for, well, all sorts of things. In any event, along with weight training, traditional as well as kick-boxing classes for women and men are everywhere, too. Call your local YW/YMCA or check the yellow pages for health clubs and gyms. Find out why smart men and women *love* dumbbells!

Chapter 49

Nouveau Age

Feeling bummed by the aging process? Noticing sleep creases when you wake up? Do you sag or bag where you once were firm? What about those five or ten extra pounds? Weight seems to be one thing that doesn't follow the rule "What goes up must come down." Although aging isn't a picnic, consider the alternative. Then smile, because you're still around and starting to look like you have some character. Dig your heels in. Refuse to be tyrannized by a youth-worshiping culture!

Our life span is fast approaching one hundred years, which means that people between fifty and seventy are now considered middle-aged. It also means that forty to fifty-year-olds are still young. Cases in point: Goldie Hawn. Tom Hanks. Oprah. Susan Sarandon. George Clooney. Diane Keaton. Sean Penn. Diane Sawyer. Pierce Brosnan. Michelle Pfeiffer. Denzel Washington. "So what?" you may say. "I *feel* old."

Maybe that's because you're dissatisfied with who you are, not how you look. Do you consistently put other people's needs before your own? Are you getting enough sleep? Enough feedback that you're valuable? Caring for babies or young children can drain your energy, sap your sleep and isolate you. Nothing like being tired and alone to make you feel old. Older children and teens can do you in, too. Teens especially are likely to remind you of how little you know and how ancient you are. How about at work? Does it seem like younger coworkers are hot on your heels, breathing down your neck? Is keeping up with them exhausting you?

Fight back. Take some time for yourself every day. How about a Hollywood bath (chapter 2)? Join a group, take a hike (chapter 45), get a makeover or have a pajama party (chapter 43). Set up a weekly or monthly girls'/

guys' night out. Spend more time with friends old or new, sharing issues, ideas and fun.

Plan, Prioritize, Play

The people who most feel (and look) like they're over the hill are the ones who are least active. Waking up knowing you have a full day of interesting activity in front of you is energizing, but those activities won't come knocking at your door. You have to plan for them. Check out the continuing education department of your local community college or university. Most offer a wealth of skill-developing classes and many have special programs for folks over fifty. Senior centers usually have a pretty good lineup of classes and social events, too. "Experimental" colleges often have an even broader array of classes, some ongoing, some one-time only. Plan your days to be full but not hectic. Is physical fitness important to you? Helping out your church or community? What about opportunities to make new friends and socialize? Or keeping your mind agile? Plan your time to reflect your priorities. Then create a calendar of activities that are both fulfilling and fun!

You're not finished at fifty, sixty or seventy. Far from it. You may have at least thirty years or more after retiring or emptying your nest to do whatever you like, without worrying about what's expected of you. Those years mean time to stop being an extra in other people's movies. Instead, you can become the star of your own. What will you do when it's your turn to stand in the sun? What have you always wanted to do? What's your passion, your purpose, your gift? Discover it. Use it! What did you once want to be when you grew up? There's still time.

I've heard it said that grandchildren are the reward for not having killed your children. I don't know about that, but they certainly are a reward. When I became a grandmother, I quit my corporate job and decided to follow my bliss. I still needed to support myself, but now I do work I love, at my own pace, on my own time.

Lynda, who is eighty and whose goal is to live in a world of peace and harmony, has very little money and loves to dance. She heard about an international dance for peace organization, investigated her options, got a scholarship that included plane fare and accommodations and off she went. Not only did she dance her shoes off, she met many other like-minded people; they now live communally, travel together and dance for peace.

Think of all the knowledge, experience and skills you've developed over the years. How would you like to use them? Would you like to learn, teach, travel, write, paint, contribute or all of the above? The possibilities are endless. You could travel around the world in eighty months, instead of days and when you finish there'll still be time to do lots more. The world is your oyster. Open it up.

Chapter 50

Get Scrappy

Do you have shoeboxes, plastic bags or bureau drawers filled willy-nilly with memorabilia: photographs, greeting cards, programs, ticket stubs, postcards, letters, dried flowers from your senior prom corsage? Have you thought, from time to time, about doing something with them someday, maybe even organizing them and putting them into a scrapbook? Go to it! Once you do, you may be surprised to find that it isn't the chore you thought it would be. In fact, it may turn out to be pure pleasure—the kind of activity that seems to make time—and your blue mood—melt away.

For a decade or so, scrapbook making has enjoyed a national renaissance. Its origins are lost in the mists of history, but the reasons for doing it probably haven't changed at all. From the time your cave-dwelling ancestor slipped a bone from a memorable meal into a fold of her or his bearskin blanket, people have been saving souvenirs. Like journals and photograph albums, scrapbooks are a way to capture and preserve part of the past so it can be revisited, remembered and passed along to others.

Scrapbooks have come a long way from bones in blankets or even from pasting ticket stubs, letters and greeting cards into a blank book. Today, just about every arts and crafts store has a section featuring scrapbook supplies. There are scores of Internet sites and even entire stores devoted exclusively to supplying and stimulating scrapbook artists. All over the country, scrapbook circles—something like quilting bees—meet regularly to encourage each other and share equipment, supplies and tools. And, as you might expect, several scrapbook craft magazines (*Memory Makers* is one of the oldest and largest) and how-to books have sprung up, too. A quick keyword search for "scrapbooks" in the book section of Amazon.com turned up more than 6,000 entries!

"Scrap Books" is now a category in the Yellow Pages. My local directory includes more than twenty listings, including several scrapbook consultants. These, it turns out, are experts in the craft—accomplished scrapbook artists who will meet with you and either help you come up with ideas or take your memorabilia and create a unique, stunning scrapbook or collage for you. I visited one of these pros in her studio, where I saw a leather-bound book created for a fiftieth wedding anniversary that was so gorgeous and sweetly sentimental, I had to reach for a tissue! I also visited a scrapbook store and came away amazed by the vast array of special papers, fancy scissors, colored pens, decorative borders, clever cut-outs and assorted scrapbook paraphernalia one can buy—most of it acid- and lignin-free, meaning it is of archival quality and therefore less likely to deteriorate over time.

Specialty scrapbooks have become all the rage. Entire volumes are dedicated to celebrating the births of babies, the antics of toddlers, elementary-school, high-school or college years, weddings and honeymoons, grandparents and great-grandparents, athletic or musical endeavors, home-improvement projects, family vacations, seasonal holidays, pets, hobbies…you name it. At the consultant's studio, I also looked through a beautiful scrapbook she was putting together for a memorial service.

Never mind making yourself miserable. Make memories, instead. Check out www.scrapbooks.com for ideas and inspiration.

Plan a Trip Down Memory Lane

If you're going to create a photo-based scrapbook, the first thing you'll need to do is sort through your pictures and categorize them. When I decided to make my first scrapbook, devoted to family Christmas celebrations over thirty-plus years, it didn't take long to come up with the concept. It took much longer to go through all the boxes and envelopes of snapshots, separating Christmas photos from the rest. As I progressed, I began to see possibilities for other scrapbooks and, as a result, a need for other categories. This may happen to you, too, so before you get started, round up several small- to medium-size boxes with lids. Separate your photos into piles: kids, family, pets, pals, travel, etc. When you're done, stash them in the boxes. Label each so you'll know what's in each box when you're ready to make your next scrapbook.

Chapter 51

Easy Does It

These days, many of us live fast-paced, extremely demanding lives with very little down time. We juggle multiple roles and responsibilities while trying to cope with the resulting stress and maintain some sort of balance. No wonder we find ourselves feeling blue and longing for slower, simpler times. If this sounds like you, why not let go and slow down? It's not as difficult as you might think.

To begin lifting yourself out of the too-busy, overwrought blues, farm out some of your tasks. Sure, you have a lot to do, but you don't need to do it all yourself. Make a list of chores someone else could take care of. Housekeeping is a good place to start. Hire a cleaning service or enlist the aid of your family. They probably won't love the idea, but fair is fair. Everyone can help, even little kids. Limit the job to two hours and assign age- and strength-appropriate tasks. Make a checklist for each worker, put some upbeat music on the stereo and get busy cleaning, cutting the lawn or clearing out the garage. When the work's done, take everyone out for pizza or ice cream.

If they're not already helping, ask family members to take a share of the daily chores, too. Make a weekly list, including completion dates, and post it on the refrigerator. Assign someone to do the laundry or send it out. Get a regular once- or twice-weekly sitter or arrange an exchange with another parent. Car pool instead of being the lone chauffeur. You get the idea. Start slowly, letting go of one thing at a time. You'll be delighted by how this lightens your load.

Maybe this is a good time to get rid of some of your clutter, too. Less stuff means more time for you. Change is often difficult, so start small. Discard or store things that no longer improve your life, please your eye or reflect who you are now. Cancel subscriptions to magazines and news-papers you seldom read. Check closets, drawers, cupboards, nooks and crannies. If you haven't used something in a year, consider throwing it out or at least putting it into storage. Clean out the medicine cabinet, the junk in the back and top of your closets and anything you just stuck someplace because you didn't know where to put it. You'll be happy to hear that uncluttering seems to perpetuate itself. Once you realize how much simpler and more pleasant life is without all that stuff, it becomes easier to let go of more.

Go All the Way

Look over your home and identify the room with the most clutter—the one that seems most out of control and overwhelming. Then, call in a professional organizer. If you don't know any in your area, contact the National Association of Professional Organizers at 512-206-0151 or *www.napo.net*. These pros will come in (with a friendly, nonjudgmental attitude) and help you sort through and make keep, store or toss decisions about your stuff. After these decisions have been made, they'll help you put the room back together in an attractive way that works for you and your lifestyle. They'll also help you set up systems that will keep things running smoothly and your space clutter free. Once you've done this to your worst room, you'll have the know-how to do it to the rest of your space.

After the clutter is gone, you might want to feng shui your home. Feng shui is the ancient Chinese art of arranging a harmonious environment to promote well-being. Hire a consultant to analyze your home and make rec-ommendations (often expensive) or do it yourself. Feng shui is popular, so lots of courses and how-to books are available. For more information, con-tact the Feng Shui Guild at 303-444-1548, or visit www.fengshuiguild.com.

Here are a few feng shui basics to get you started: Be sure all doors open and close easily, completely and quietly. Face beds toward the door and maintain an unobstructed view. This is said to encourage positive energy flow. If your bathroom doesn't have a window, place a mirror opposite the medicine cabinet mirror. Green or flowering plants bring the outdoors in and freshen the air. Eliminate as much untidiness and clutter as you're comfortable with. Finally, arrange furniture so that traf-fic flow is smooth and efficient. Then sit back, feast your eyes and smile.

Chapter 52

Heat Up
Your Lust Life

We're talking about S-E-X. Having it. Doing it. Reveling in it. Think physical pleasure, pure and simple: getting it on, getting off and getting out from under a blue mood. There's nothing quite like red-hot, lusty sex to take your mind off your problems for a while. Well, okay, it doesn't have to be red-hot, exactly, but it should at least be pretty darn warm and pretty much fun. Here are a few suggestions to get your motor running.

If you're married or partnered and have been for a long time, it's entirely possible that hot sex is something you used to have, but not lately. It's also possible that it's something you never really had at all. Sigh. If that's the case, it doesn't have to continue. Take a trip to the library or bookstore and pick up a copy of *Hot Monogamy*, by Dr. Patricia Love (her real name), because sex shouldn't be boring…or worse. Love's book, also available in audio, is totally nonjudgmental. It won't make you feel like a failure or a freak. Instead, it offers an enormous amount of useful information and proven-effective, friendly advice about how to keep the physical part of your love life both interesting and satisfying.

Trust me, you can have this if you really want it and if you're willing to patiently do the work of creating change. In fact, you can have it even if you're not sure you want it. Even if you're pretty sure you don't! I counseled a couple of high-school sweethearts who'd been married for eight years. They came to see me, at the husband's insistence, because their marriage was at risk and they had two young kids they both loved enormously. They loved each other, too. The wife just wasn't interested in sex. She was willing to do whatever he wanted to please him, but didn't like anything much to happen on her end (no pun intended) and never had orgasms. He felt inadequate, confused and angry. She felt pressured and

128

defective and admitted that there were about a hundred things she'd rather do than make love, including grocery shopping. But listen to this. By the end of a year, she was a different woman, he was a happy camper and they were having a really good time. So can you. Get the book and get help.

If you're not partnered, don't just go out and pick someone up. It could be dangerous and is likely to lead to worse feelings the next day. Consider a friend who'd be willing to fool around, if you're not worried about upsetting the balance of the friendship. Many people don't need a lot of convincing in this area, but you still need to consider this option very carefully. When sex enters a friendship, the friendship can get complicated.

Thank goodness for solo sex, which can be great fun, whether or not you're married or partnered. It has the great advantage of being, as so few other things are, all about you. You get to imagine anything you want, the wilder and more outrageous the better, without actually having to do any of it. And you get to experiment a bit, try a few new things—a vibrator, maybe, or some other sex toy, without any embarrassment or performance anxiety.

On the off chance that you think there's something wrong with solo sex, even kinky solo sex, I'm here to tell you otherwise. It's not disloyal to your partner and it certainly won't make you go blind. We humans are made with our arms just long enough to reach our genitals, a body part that has the function of making us feel good. Isn't that wonderful?

What Do Women Want?

Ever since Freud asked that famous (and really stupid) question, women have been shouting, "Just ask us!" When it came to porn, females starred in it, but were usually bored by it. It featured improbably stacked twenty-four-year-olds who made women feel old and ugly and glorified the hard-on. Not anymore. There's a wealth of female-produced erotica and soft porn out there. Try www.sensualempire.com and www.cakenyc.com, for starters. Then follow your nose.

Note #1: Be careful where you point your browser. Entering most traditional porn sites causes a barrage of unsolicited e-porn, unless your computer has an anti-spyware program that protects it.

Note #2: In the movie *The Piano*, director Jane Campion gets more erotic mileage from one square inch of skin and a hole in a black stocking than most directors get from frontal nudity (there's a great full frontal of Harvey Keitel in this film, by the way). *The Piano* is sexy, smart and strange and it has a happy ending (sorry, I just had to tell). If you haven't seen it, rent it. Then do it.

Chapter 53

Get Help
from Herb

Unless you're suffering from clinical depression (see "Dealing with the Big D" at the back of the book), treating your low mood with prescription drugs is not appropriate and won't be effective. Don't even *think* about borrowing a few pills from a friend's bottle of antidepressants or tranquilizers! You could do yourself real harm. On the other hand, the use of certain herbal products and/or nutritional supplements may be worth considering. If you're contemplating a so-called "natural" remedy, be aware of a few cautions and limitations before you try or buy.

First, not all over-the-counter products are safe and none are regulated or monitored by the Food and Drug Administration. Plus, there are no uniform standards for quality or strength. If you're going to try one, buy it from a reputable health-food store, a well-established pharmaceutical company (many well-known drug or nutritional supplement firms have added herbal products to their lines during the last decade) or a naturopathic physician.

Second, don't take more than one at a time and be careful about mixing them with other drugs; there can be serious, sometimes dangerous, reactions and interactions. Consult your doctor while taking herbals with other medications or see a naturopath and bring along a list of the medications and/or supplements you currently take.

Third, herbal medicines may take quite a bit longer to work than prescription drugs. Three to eight weeks is not uncommon; so don't stop if nothing seems to change right away. Give it a fair chance.

Finally, don't let herbal remedies keep you from seeing a counselor or other professional, especially if your blue moods seem to be increasing in frequency, lasting longer than usual or intensifying.

Okay, you've been properly cautioned. Now, here's a list of the leading over-the-counter products purported to ease symptoms of mild to moderate depression. I'm not recommending them; I'm just giving you options to consider.

- **St. John's Wort:** Generally takes six to eight weeks before mood improvement is felt. Non-habit forming, few side effects, well tolerated. Usual dosages are 900 to 1800 mg/day. Don't take with prescription antidepressants, with drugs used to treat AIDS or migraine headaches or with warfarin, theophylin, digoxin or birth control pills.
- **SAM-e:** Non-habit forming, few side effects, well tolerated. Dosages range from 400 to 1600 mg/day. Mood improvements begin to be noticed after about four weeks. Always take with a vitamin-B complex supplement.
- **5-HTTP:** We don't have much research on 5-HTTP, but it makes some people feel better. Non-habit forming, few side effects, well tolerated. Typical dosage is 300 mg/day. Symptom improvement may be seen within two to three weeks.
- **Kava Kava:** Can reduce anxiety and insomnia. It's generally well tolerated, but can (at high doses) cause intoxication, drowsiness and reduced alertness. It may be habit forming, though the research on this isn't adequate.
- **NOTE:** Two over-the-counter products to avoid are valerian root (can aggravate depression; should never be used when you feel blue) and melatonin (0.5 mg taken at 6 P.M. can help with sleep, but most melatonin products come in 1, 2, or 3 mg sizes; at these dosages, it can worsen your mood.) Again, if you decide to use any of these products, be sure to tell your doctor, therapist or pharmacist.

Fork Up the Fish

According to recent scientific and clinical evidence, it looks like omega-3 fatty acids are a gift from the gods. They not only help keep your heart healthy, they also help boost your mood! Many studies have shown that when consumption of omega-3 goes up, depression rates go down. How come? It's thought that they may raise serotonin levels (the brain chemical that's directly responsible for elevating your mood). Supplements are relatively inexpensive and highly recommended. In addition to taking omega-3 capsules, go right to the source: at least once a week, preferably more, eat salmon (not the farm-raised kind; get canned or line-caught wild salmon), sardines, anchovies, tuna or striped bass. Other useful sources are flax seeds and flax seed oil (always keep refrigerated).

**BLUES
FLASH!**

**The Best News from England
Since The Beatles**

If you find yourself going round and round with the "28-day blues," otherwise known as PMS, try 50 mg. of vitamin B6 once or twice a day.

According to a report published in the *British Medical Journal*, B6 helps relieve overall premenstrual and depressive symptoms.

Get B6 from a supplement or load up on whole grains, nuts, fish and white meat.

PART FIVE

Reach Out
and Touch Someone

Lonely and blue often go hand in hand, but you don't have to sing those lonesome blues any longer. Stop isolating yourself. Instead, start to restore the human connection you need to speed through your low mood and come out happily on the other side. The chapters in this section are full of suggestions that will help you reach out to others for the support, comfort and understanding you deserve without sounding desperate or needy.

Chapter 54

Make Someone's Day

Does a blue mood make you behave as if the world revolves around you? It's natural to feel self-absorbed when you're in a funk. In fact, it's natural anytime. Who do you look for first in a group photo that includes you? Researchers say we think about ourselves roughly 95 percent of our time. But, as mom said when she toilet trained you, what's natural isn't always best.

Making a conscious effort to do something good for someone else does something good for you at the same time. Even the first time you do it, it shifts your attention away from yourself for a while. Next thing you know, something amazing starts happening to your eyesight! You begin to see all kinds of people who could use some cheering up or a helping hand. Everywhere you look, you'll see more. Soon, you'll be able to see a whole world of opportunity.

Next, you'll start feeling an urge to do more, to make a positive difference, even if it's a small one. Offer a smile and a friendly word or two to a toll taker. Pay the toll for the car behind you. Put quarters into other people's expired parking meters. Give the panhandler of your choice a ten or twenty instead of something paltry or nothing at all. Make arrangements to pay anonymously for a stranger's lunch. Surrender your window seat to a kid or help someone stow their stuff in the overhead compartment on a bus, train or plane. But, I warn you, be prepared to see some amazed smiles. What's more, every time you perform an unexpected act of kindness, you'll probably feel a spark of genuine joy flare up in your heart. Doing good feels good. Isn't that fortunate? Maybe that's why our species has survived as long as it has.

Surviving in a public service job can be tough, so I especially enjoy complimenting salespeople, clerks and servers on their attitudes or skills. It always seems to please and that makes me happy, too. To add major impact, get the person's name and tell his or her manager, on the spot if possible, or mail a note. Of course, your words have to be sincere. Most of us can spot the difference between empty flattery and honest praise in a heartbeat. If you're faking, it won't make you or anyone else happier.

Corny as it sounds, causing someone else to smile or feel good really does make the world a better place. It's also contagious. Once, while driving in heavy traffic on a rainy winter day to meet with someone I didn't like, I stopped to pay a toll and the toll taker handed me a long-stemmed rose. What a stunning, delightful surprise! His gesture transformed my mood, which was as nasty as the weather. This happened more than fifteen years ago, but I still think about that toll taker from time to time and his act still generates good feelings. I wish he knew how much it meant to me.

A few years later, I tried to pass his gesture along. I took a big bouquet of roses to a nursing home and gave them away one by one, stopping for a few minutes of conversation with each recipient. I dare you to try this. It's a heartwarmer (and heartbreaker), an immensely gratifying experience that still chokes me up when I think about it.

Flirt with a Nerd

During a recent lunch with my daughter, who has a handsome boyfriend, she flirted shamelessly with our server, a pleasant young man with a weak chin, bad skin and crooked teeth. During our drive home, I asked what was going on. After trying to deny the flirting, she confessed: "Good-looking people get hit on all the time," she said. "But how often do guys who haven't been, shall we say, blessed by nature get to feel admired? So maybe I did a little something for his day. Does that seem arrogant?" she wanted to know. It didn't.

Neighbors, friends, co-workers and family deserve kindnesses, too. Let them know that you appreciate them and don't take their presence in your life for granted. Send a handwritten note or card, baby-sit their kids, share homemade treats, run errands, do yard work, wax a car, wash a dog, make a special gift that speaks to shared history.

To inspire yourself, pick up a copy of *Random Acts of Kindness*. It'll open your eyes, your hands and your heart. No matter how you feel, no matter how blue you are, you have something to give. So, go ahead— today, tomorrow, maybe even for the rest of your life—make someone's day. Your own will start to look much brighter.

Chapter 55

Dial Up
a Connection

You're hurt, confused, frustrated, furious or low-down blue. You could use a sympathetic ear. So pick up the phone and call a friend. That's one of the things friends are for, right? It doesn't have to be a long-time bosom buddy. A sibling, close neighbor, relative you're tight with or anyone you trust will do. Sounds simple, doesn't it? Sounds almost too obvious to mention.

Simple and effective, too, but it's amazing how many of us don't always do it. Me, for one. When I feel miserable, my first impulse is to withdraw into an emotional cocoon—the grown-up equivalent of pulling my blankie over my head and sucking my thumb. But I've learned the hard way that I have to shake off the urge to isolate and push myself to make a caring human connection.

If you're feeling incompetent, unloved, unimportant or terribly sad, you may stop yourself from calling, because you think nobody in their right mind would want to talk to you. Not true. Remember, we all fall into the clutches of a low mood from time to time. Once they know what's going on, people understand and sympathize. Telling someone isn't being a wimp, either. It's being honest and real. And it's taking action on your own behalf.

Remember, too, that words aren't cold germs. Talking to a friend about how you feel won't make him or her catch your case of the blues, no matter how much your pal empathizes. What it does do is send the message that you think enough of this individual to want his or her help. What's more, being willing to admit that you're less than together at times gives your friend tacit permission to do the same. It'll deepen your friendship, too. While we admire and respect each other for our strengths, it's often our human frailties that generate tenderness in others.

Besides, who wants to be friends with someone who never seems to need anyone else, never struggles with self-doubt or sadness, never reaches out for help? Of course, if cries for help are the only sounds you hear in a friendship, it probably won't last long and if it does manage to survive, it won't be much fun. On the other hand, if help is never wanted and support never needed, the friendship will likely remain superficial. Who wants that?

Ask if your friend has a few minutes to listen. If so, describe how you're feeling (crummy) and what's going on (nothing good). If it's hard for you to get the conversational ball rolling, start by saying you want to talk about something that's difficult for you. If you can figure out what your friend could do to help you feel better, ask for it, as specifically as possible. If you're not sure what you want, just make the connection anyway. Sometimes that alone is all you need. If you can't think of anything specific to say, just plunge in with the truth, any way you can. Let your friend know you're feeling low and just wanted to hear a compassionate voice. She or he will probably take it from there.

If you've caught your pal at a bad time, explain the reason for your call and arrange a callback, as soon as possible, or just try the next person on your list. Which leads us to a few other suggestions that at first seem too obvious to mention, but may not be: Don't call people you barely know or friends you're not currently friendly with. Don't, for heaven's sake, call ex-lovers, unless both of you have truly made that rare transition to friendship and you're not kidding yourself. Don't call anyone so self-absorbed that he or she can't hold an entire conversation about you. And don't call anyone so busy that you will feel he or she is doing you a favor by taking your call.

Home Alone, Too

Can't come up with even one person you can call? When you feel more like yourself again, think about some things you could do to make new friends. People with strong friendships and other support systems tend to handle life's trials better and bounce back more quickly. A good therapist can help you recognize behaviors that may have prevented you from forming friendships in the past, come up with ideas for how to do it now and support you in the meantime. And listen: If you can't reach a friend or therapist and you'd really like someone to talk to, call your local Crisis Hot Line. It doesn't have to be an emergency. The folks who answer crisis lines are well-trained, empathetic and always willing to listen.

Chapter 56

Give Your
Face a Lift

When you're feeling blue, you might as well wear a sign. You're broadcasting your state of mind to the world via body language—walking around with shoulders slumped and head bent, avoiding eye contact. You sigh more often. Your eyes lose their sparkle and the corners of your mouth turn down. You look exactly the way you feel—as if the weight of the world were on your shoulders. "Leave me alone," your face and body are saying. "It's a lousy day…Life sucks…What's the point?"

If the message you're sending isn't intentional, well, the people watching don't know that, do they? So they respond predictably: They avoid you, ignore you, may even become insulted, hurt or angry with you. Needless to say, these responses are not likely to improve your mood. In fact, they'll probably weigh you down with even more gloomy feelings.

You can change all that with a smile. It's true. Try it: Stand up, smile as if someone were taking your picture and say this out loud, if you can: "Mr. Rogers likes me just the way I am and *so do I!*" Now you'll really be smiling and that smile will lift your sprits. Maybe just for a second, but it'll happen. The more you smile, the better you'll feel.

Take your smile out into the world. Sure, you may have to fake it for a while, but sometimes that's how it works. Fake it until you make it. Lift your chin, straighten your shoulders and look other people in the eye. Imagine that it's actually pleasant to see them. Smile at them. They're very likely to smile back, which always feels good.

Worthwhile Smiles

Why reserve your smiles for other people? Every time you catch a glimpse of yourself reflected in a shop window, mirror or any shiny surface, smile! Smile because you like the way it makes you look. Because you like the way it makes you feel. Because no matter how you feel or look right now, you've chosen to be happy. When asked what ordinary people could do to improve the world if they couldn't go to India and help the poor as she did, Mother Teresa said, "Smile more." No matter where you want to go or what you want to do, a smile is a good place to start.

Once, when I was feeling unattractive and unloved, I tried this exercise, though I was sure it wouldn't work. I looked up, made eye contact and smiled at a nice-looking man coming toward me in the grocery store. He looked a little uncertain at first, as if he were trying to place me; then he returned my smile with a big grin of his own. It felt so good, I almost laughed out loud! I finished shopping and, as I was checking out, the man stopped me at the cash register and, blushing a little, politely asked if I'd like to join him for a cup of coffee. I declined, although later I wished I'd accepted and went on my way feeling ridiculously pleased with myself. What a nice ego boost!

Here's another true story about the power of smiles. A woman I worked with for a while had been feeling unhappy with her husband for a long time. She complained that he was always grumpy, especially in the morning. It was making her grumpy, too. I'm not sure where she got the idea, but she decided to try an experiment. Every day, she greeted him with a warm smile, a few cheerful words and a light touch: "Good morning, my dear! How are you today?" Two weeks later, she could hardly contain her delight as she told me what happened. At first, there had been no response, but after several days she began to notice a subtle change. One morning, he gave her a grudging smile in return. The following Friday, he bought her a bunch of flowers, because, as he put it, he was "just feeling happy!"

Everyone wants to feel happy and just about everyone likes to be greeted with a smile. You may not get dramatic responses, but smiles beget smiles just as frowns beget frowns. Plus, it's probably the easiest thing in the book to do: no special equipment, it's instantaneous and you're already an expert. No sweat. If you have trouble remembering to do it, draw a smiley face on your hand or wear a colored rubber band on your wrist.

P.S. Did you know that smiling changes your voice? Customer service phone representatives are taught to answer while smiling, because it softens the voice and makes them sound friendly, warm and welcoming. Try it yourself. See what happens.

BLUES
FLASH!

Pets Can Be Purrfect Bluesbusters

In his book *Love & Survival,* Dr. Dean Ornish discusses results of a study that showed the positive effects of pets on heart patients. After a year, 28 percent of those who didn't have pets had died, but only 6 percent of pet owners had passed away.

These days, pets pay regular visits to (or take up permanent residence at) many health care facilities, because their cuddly, unconditional love cheers people up and speeds healing.

Although they take time and energy to care for, a kitty, pooch or other pet can make you smile and boost your mood.

Chapter 57

Shake a Leg, Lend a Hand

You've heard about it. You've probably even thought about it. Smack in the middle of a blue mood may be the perfect time to actually do it: Become a volunteer. It'll give you some mood-lifting social contact, help you reconnect with your own unselfish nature and may also shine your personal spotlight on some problems that are even worse than yours.

Without question, you're needed and no matter how busy or blue you feel, you have time. We're not talking about a major commitment, only a couple of hours here and there. So, which of your skills or hobbies might you share? With what kind of people would you like to work? What social problems move or disturb you enough to want to pitch in and help? Hospitals, hospices and nursing homes always need volunteers. You could deliver flowers, bring around the book cart, read to those who can't, give hand/foot massages, stroke and rock babies. Jack dresses as a clown and makes balloon animals for the kids. Sometimes he has funny conversations with them through Sesame Street hand puppets. My mother, bless her heart, got great satisfaction from bringing wine and cheese "picnics" to patients on oncology wards.

My cousin, Susan, remembers feeling very sorry for herself the first Thanksgiving after her divorce. Her kids were spending time with their dad and although she'd been invited to join married friends, she declined. Her mood was too low and she thought she'd feel like a fifth wheel. I don't recall exactly how she ended up volunteering at a soup kitchen, but she told me that it was one of the best Thanksgivings she'd ever had.

After helping prepare and serve a complete turkey dinner to hundreds of her city's homeless, Susan returned to her life feeling grateful for her comfortable home, full refrigerator and steady job. She liked the people she worked with and the people she served, too. What's more, she discovered that most homeless people are not crazy, alcoholics or addicts. Women and children, she told me, are the fastest growing segment of the homeless. She now volunteers one Saturday a month to a local women's shelter.

Maybe you'd rather work behind the scenes. You could collect food for a food bank, raise money for community projects, drum up supplies for relief efforts, distribute donations to shelters or drive AIDS patients or seniors to medical appointments. If you know how awful it feels to be too sick to do housework, become a member of the Chicken Soup Brigade that cleans houses for those unable to do it themselves. How about reading to the blind or to preschoolers at your local library? Helping developmentally disabled folks learn living skills? Giving your clerical talents to an organization that provides a service you think is important? Supporting a political candidate you admire?

The opportunities are endless and, as Susan discovered, the need is immense. In my city, several organizations provide free tutoring for GED and citizenship tests and to help adults learn to read. Some give free Internet lessons to those who are elderly or disabled. Others arrange one-on-one help for kids having trouble keeping up in school. And that's just the beginning.

Who, Me?

- Mow your neighbors' lawns some afternoon when they're not home.
- Leave homemade goodies at a shut-in's door.
- Offer to take an elderly neighbor grocery shopping.
- Babysit a friend's or neighbor's kids for no special reason and no charge.
- Send flowers (or pick them yourself and deliver) to an elderly neighbor.
- Mark a box of second-hand toys, books or art supplies "Free!" and drop off at a playground.
- Pick up the litter that's blown into the street or the garbage in the vacant lot.

Think about what you have to offer and whom you'd like to help. I don't care who you are, you have something to offer. I once had the privilege and delight of a conversation with Alec Dickson, the Englishman who invented the volunteer agency after which John Kennedy modeled the United States Peace Corps. He said, "You don't have to *be* good to *do* good. All you have to be is willing." If you are willing, choose an organization and make the call. Volunteering will make the world a better place. It will also make you a happier camper.

Chapter 58

Get Lost
in Cyberspace

If knowledge really is power, then the Internet is probably the most powerful tool on which you've ever had your hot little hands. It's also fun and the greatest thing since…well, since the silicon chip for taking your mind off your mood. In cyberspace, the world is literally at your fingertips. You don't have to be a computer buff to feel at home. You don't even have to own a computer. The wonders of the World Wide Web are available free through most public libraries and at minimal cost through the urban computer cafes that have sprung up everywhere.

From aardvark to Zimbabwe, it's all out there on the information highway—in living color, streaming video and stereophonic audio. You can explore any topic under the sun, pop into universities and libraries all over the country, all over the world. I once spent a fascinating hour looking at Civil War photographs from the Smithsonian's Matthew Brady collection. Later that week, I exchanged e-mails with the rare books curator at a museum in Amsterdam.

If things like that bore you, don't worry. You can follow your favorite celebrity, soap or sitcom, download games, solve puzzles, play poker, read jokes, check out your horoscope, download an electronic book or peruse an electronic advice column. If you're itching to travel, you can learn more about possible destinations; shop for the best fares; check out local maps, hotels, rentals, bed-and-breakfasts, campgrounds or hostels, including photos; see what special events are scheduled when you're going. My son used the Internet to plan a trip to Denmark. He found inexpensive lodging, followed the currency exchange rates, changed his money when the rate was good and electronically "met" several Danes before he left. He was even able to arrange for someone to pick him up when he arrived. Not bad.

I booked a month-long European jaunt, from airfare to museum tickets, including a farmhouse B&B in Provence, on the Net and recently watched via a Webcam as the ship my daughter works on went through the Panama Canal. Also not bad.

Want to know more about your family's history? Genealogy research is easy and incredibly fast on-line. Feel like shopping? You can order just about anything from on-line retailers, or browse and bid at electronic auctions. The Internet is a tremendous boon for anyone with health problems, too. It offers an incredible array of resources for every aspect of physical and mental health, nutrition and fitness.

If your blues are the lonesome kind, the Internet can reconnect you in minutes. Look for a long-lost friend or a brand new lover. Add your two cents or just eavesdrop on a chat room conversation. Make new friends or business contacts. Find fellow enthusiasts (games, collectibles, music, sports, gardening, needlework, antiques) or hook up with an e-pen pal from a place about which you've always been curious. Arrange to swap houses or exchange students. If you're hankering for a real-life, 3-D place to have fun or meet people close to home, go on-line and check out your local newspaper. Which movies, concerts and sporting events are in town? What's happening in the club and music scene? Anything there to tempt you?

If you're a computer novice and the information highway feels more like a cul-de-sac, get help. Ask a cyber-literate pal to teach you the basics, buy a beginner's book (I like *Internet for Dummies*), take a class or experiment until you start to get a feel for it. All browsers/Internet Service Providers have help menus and technical service numbers to call. Any computer store employee will be glad to give you a hand, too. If it feels a bit confusing at first, hang in there. It's fun, fascinating and can rocket you past your mood (and into cyberspace) as easily as you can click a mouse.

Only a Few Clicks Away

Create your own Web page. Windows comes with a program to help, you can buy cheap software (DreamWeaver is terrific) and there are now so many on-line resources and books to explain how, that what used to be a big job has become a virtual snap.

Surf for freebies. It's surprising how many samples, discount coupons and just plain free things you can find and order on the Net. Become a discount detective and see what you can turn up.

Visit the guilty pleasures department. For many people, playing Free Cell is reliably entertaining, sometimes even challenging: If you don't know what I'm talking about, it's time you did: Go to Start, Programs, Games, Free Cell. Enjoy.

Chapter 59

Forgive and
Don't Forget

Has your mood turned blue, because someone has done something cruel, punishing or hurtful to you? Whatever the scenario, you think you've been wronged somehow. Cheated. Mistreated. Lied to. Betrayed. And you feel so angry, bitter, resentful and sad that you could inspire a whole album of country-western songs.

You already know you can't change others or relive history, right? That individual did what he or she did, it happened and you feel like hell. You're in a miserable mood because of it. So now what?

Here's what I think: What you do now is try to forgive. To let go and go on. Forgiving is one of those things that's easier said than done, but if you want to live happily ever after, sooner or later it's necessary. You forgive, not to help the other person, but to help yourself. You do it to get rid of the oppressive weight that being a victim lays on you—the baggage that acts like a ball and chain and keeps you tied to the past. You do it to get rid of the grudge that has you linked to someone you no longer like and with whom you are angry. You do it to become a bigger, better soul. And you do it so you can free yourself from this dark mood and get on with your life.

No, it isn't easy to forgive some things and, yes, it often takes time. At first, it seems easier to condemn the person who has wronged you, to invent fantasies of revenge and vindication. This can be a grim kind of fun for a while. But, far from empowering you, these feelings take a tremendous toll on your ability to grow as a compassionate, resilient person. Not only that, they compromise your health.

As you begin to think about releasing these feelings, remember: Forgiveness doesn't imply that you condone the behavior, deny the damage or take it lightly. It doesn't necessarily mean you're willing to continue in a relationship with the person you're forgiving, either. And you certainly aren't going to forget what it's taught you.

But you need to put it behind you if you want to resume living fully. Why hold on to negative reactions that serve only to diminish and deplete you? While you're at it, why not shed your fantasies about perfect people. Each of us is imperfect, vulnerable and capable of doing real harm; that includes you and me.

Blow the Blues

Imagine that you are blowing up a blue balloon. With each breath, blow out anger, pain and resentment. Blow out every negative feeling you have for the person you haven't forgiven. Imagine tying off the balloon, letting it go. Watch it float up, up and away, out of sight. As it does, imagine that it is taking all your bad feelings with it. Or buy a package of latex balloons, choose a blue one and do it for real. Take big, deep breaths and blow out all the bad stuff. When it's as big as it can be, pop it with a pin and say so long to the past.

Shakespeare's character Portia described the quality of mercy perfectly: It *is* twice blessed. As important as your willingness to forgive others is the fact that doing so makes it easier to forgive yourself. After you start feeling better about what happened, see how far you can go in forgiving, not just that person, but anybody who's ever done you wrong in a way that still stirs pain or anger. Then, see how far you can go in forgiving yourself. Be aware that you're choosing happiness over moral superiority, a wise and generous choice. And, when you're ready, here are two activities that can ease the process:

• Write a letter about the behavior and what it meant to you. Express forgiveness and describe the kind of relationship you want in the future. Ask forgiveness for any role you played in creating the situation. You can choose to send the letter or burn it and release your painful feelings as it goes up in smoke.

• Take yourself to a place of worship or a natural setting that has a special spiritual meaning for you. Once there, conduct a ritual of forgiveness: pray, read something inspiring, light a candle, release a helium balloon, tear up a letter and scatter the fragments, make a boat, fill it with your emotions and set it adrift on a stream—whatever feels right. What you do isn't as important as your heart's intent: to let go and move on to better feelings.

Chapter 60

Write from the Heart

Imagine that your best friend is feeling really blue. We're talking navy blue. Midnight blue. It's been going on for several days now. Maybe your pal has reasons for these feelings, maybe not a clue. Doesn't matter. Sit down, gather your thoughts and write a letter to try and help this person feel better. But the best friend you're going to write to is you.

It probably won't do much good if you try to complete this exercise in your mind. You need to actually put pen to paper or fingers to keyboard and create a document. So get out your nicest stationary or letterhead and turn off your phone for a few minutes. Write logically, clearly and persuasively, but speak from your heart.

Reach inside for the words you'd seek out and find for a friend who's struggling with despondency. Maybe you'll want to express your distress at her/his sadness and your confidence that a better mood will come soon. If so, explain exactly why you're so confident. Does your friend have experience getting through tough times and coming out on the other side? How about strength of character? A good support system? A thoughtful nature? A kind and loving attitude? Resiliency, vision, faith? The kind of optimism that eventually will find the silver lining? Remind him/her of these things.

Remind your friend, too, that you are there, ready and willing to help. Offer a different perspective, if you can come up with one. Mention some specific things you'd be happy to help with—no faking; they should be things you really would be glad to do—and ask to be told if there are others. Tell her/him that your affection is absolutely dependable, assuming that's how you'd feel if your best friend was in trouble. Say everything that you'd have on your mind or heart, honestly and openly, with the goal of helping your friend crack a smile and break through the blues barrier.

Include an inspiring or relevant quotation, if you like, or a photo or souvenir that might trigger pleasant memories. Dig through your memorabilia or your mind and tell again the story of the time you had to change that tire in the dark, without any help and how absurdly good it made you feel afterward. Or fish out that old photo of your pal, grinning to beat the band and wearing the leg cast that everyone signed after the skiing accident.

Then, put it all into an envelope, address it to yourself and mail it. I know this sounds a little silly, but do it. In a day or two, it'll come back to you. Maybe you'll feel a lot less blue by then, maybe not. Regardless of how you feel, open the letter and read it carefully. Recognize it for what it is: an expression of love and offer of support from someone close to you, a person who knows you better than anyone. Someone who truly cares about your happiness and who sees more in you than you can sometimes see in yourself. Just the kind of friend you want to be to yourself, right?

Read it again and take heart, because the part of you that's blue is probably still lurking around, but now it's having an interesting encounter with another side of you—a side that is able to see things a bit differently. A side that has a great deal to give. And it's beginning to look like all the love, empathy, optimism, problem-solving ability and wisdom you would offer a friend may be readily available to you, too. That is, whenever you're ready to take yourself up on your own offer.

Write a Dear John Letter to Your Addiction

If you don't have an addiction, skip this. But if, like so many of us, you struggle with an addiction to tobacco, alcohol, a drug (including caffeine), shopping, gambling, sex, on-line chat, sugar, compulsively checking e-mail or anything else that's doing you more harm than good, here's a useful idea. Borrowed from Henriette Klauser, author of *Writing on Both Sides of the Brain* and *Put Your Heart on Paper,* it is both simple and powerful: Write a kiss-off letter to your addiction. Tell it everything you feel—what you hate about it, the good times you'll miss, the reasons you're calling it quits. Although the letter alone won't be enough to release you from the compulsion, it can be a catalyst that leads to freedom and a brighter future.

Chapter 61

Don't Bug 'Em—
Hug 'Em!

Sometimes giving or getting a big hug is all it takes to lift your spirits. Human contact is essential for an infant's normal growth and development. You're not a baby anymore, but it's still important—especially when you have the blues. Hugging is a wonderful way to get the close-up touch you need.

The language of hugs is universally positive, although this kind of major body contact is more acceptable in some cultures (and some families) than in others. With a hug, we talk to each other on basic emotional and physical levels. This is good for us. It calms the heart and lowers blood pressure. There's also plenty of evidence that loving touch has a positive effect on the immune system. When he directed the Pain Control Unit at UCLA, Dr. David Bresler wrote:

> We can all benefit by learning to express and meet our physical needs in a loving, caressing way. Thus, I give many of my patients a homework assignment: During the upcoming weeks, they are to get and give four hugs a day...don't underestimate how powerful this therapy can be and the role it can play in the healing process.

Some of us are uncomfortable with hugging. If that's you, I'm not suggesting you must change—but you certainly can if you want. A couple I counseled had no trouble showing physical affection to their children, but neither was able to indulge in the same sort of nonsexual touching with the other. As a rule, they touched each other only when they had sex and—no surprise—their sex life left a lot to be desired. They learned to change, though. They began by getting very clear about how change would benefit them. Then, together they developed a step-by-step change strategy. They started with pats, then moved up to hugs, a little at a time. Was it comfortable? Not always. Was it worth the discomfort? They said it changed their lives and saved their marriage. Think what it could do for you!

While a hug conveys acceptance and caring when words don't come easily, it's not the only way to send a loving message. A pat on the back, a gentle squeeze or rubbing on the arm, a touch of the hand—these can also say what you want to say. If you'd like a hug, but aren't sure about the other person, use your intuition. Don't be afraid to take a small risk. Of course, there's nothing wrong with asking, "Is it okay if I give you a hug?" or stating, "I need a hug."

Listen to your heart and you'll find a way to do what the old phone company commercial recommended: Reach out and touch someone. It's also fine to ask for a hug for yourself, as often as you like. Offer them, too. Don't hold back. I don't know how many times I have said, "You look like you could use a hug," to someone who has then gratefully reached out for an embrace.

Give Great Hugs

Wear an "I Give Great Hugs!" or an "I Need a Hug!" button. Never mind that it's corny. Set a goal to give and/or get at least four hugs every day. Hug friends, parents, children, spouses, sweethearts, pets. If huggable people are temporarily in short supply, hug yourself, a pillow or a stuffed animal. Don't end the hug until you feel ready. As you embrace, summon your most loving, compassionate feelings. Try to really feel them. Mentally send those feelings to the person you're hugging, whether it's yourself or someone else. Send them to every human being in the world who, like you, feels low right now.

Believe it or not, you don't even need a partner for a good, healing hug. One night, shortly after my daughter had left home for college, she phoned me in tears. "There's nobody here to hug me and tell me it's all going to be all right!" she wailed. I said maybe she could hug herself. She didn't think much of the idea, but I convinced her to try. It worked. Maybe it'll work for you, too. Close your eyes, cross your arms over your chest and reach as far around as they'll go. Then squeeze long and hard, with lots of love in your heart. Sound silly? Sure, but only because it's a new idea. Go ahead, try it. It really does feel good! And it's a good reminder that you can usually find a way to give yourself whatever it is you need.

BLUES
FLASH!

Kiss Me, You Fool

Kissing feels good and can lead to things that feel even better. But did you know that kissing lifts your spirits by releasing endorphins into your system?

Kissing has other health benefits, too: It exercises facial muscles, which helps keep them toned and you looking youthful.

And passionate kissing burns up to two calories a minute, which isn't gonna pare off any pounds, but is a nice fringe benefit.

Pucker up and enjoy!

Chapter 62

When You're Down,
Listen Up

Funny thing about the musical kind of blues: A blues singer always performs solo. You just never hear the blues sung by a group. Sure, there may be musicians and backup singers, but a blues song is essentially a one-singer gig.

Funny thing about the moody kind of blues: It's the same story—a one-person gig. A blue mood moves you away from other people. You pull back from social contact, focus your attention on yourself and become not only the center of the earth, but of the entire universe. If you get an invitation to go out, you decline—partly because, while misery may love company, nobody who isn't miserable likes to be around it and partly because you just don't feel up to it.

But, listen: Try not to isolate yourself when you're blue. This is so important that, though I normally hate these words, I'm about to say "have to." If you've essentially been in isolation for a few days, you have to get out and mingle! You must spend some time around other people anyway, at work or obligatory social events, right? Since you're forcing yourself to show up in the first place, go one step farther. You don't have to talk a lot if you don't want to, but why not decide to be an attentive, genuinely good listener while you're mingling? It'll help time pass faster. Maybe your mood will do the same.

Don't wait for people to come to you. Seek them out. Look for the folks with whom it might be fun to hang out if your own mood were better—the ones you'd most want to sit next to at a dinner party. Then, ask simple questions designed to encourage that person (or persons) to open up. It's always a good idea to lead with a sincere compliment, followed quickly by an open-ended (as opposed to yes-no) question. Keep it positive: "You really look great! Life must be treating you well. Tell me, what's going on these days for you?" Or, "Every time I see you, you look like you've just had good news. What's your secret?" Use your own words, tailored to the situation.

Now comes the hard part. Listen, really listen, to the answers you hear. Stay focused and tuned in. What is this person feeling? What is he leaving out? Is she happy with this topic? Should you redirect things? Go deeper with this? Ask more specific questions ("What was that like? How'd that come about?") and make comments to encourage the information flow. It's fine to offer information about yourself, if you want to, but keep it light. Don't go into detail about your plight or throw yourself a pity party in public. And don't let the conversation shift to being all about you. Remember, your job, just for this little bit of time, is to listen: to empathize, get outside yourself and be concerned, for the moment, only with the person you're talking to. To really hear them. To make sure they feel heard.

Why does this help when you're in a low mood? First, pure and simple, it connects you to another human being in a direct, compassionate way. It distracts you from your preoccupations, gives your head a chance to clear and reminds you that there's a whole world to care about outside that space between your ears. It may also offer unexpected, useful information or a path to another connection that will benefit you in the future. Networking rocks—this book probably wouldn't be in your hands without it. What's more, moods are contagious, especially good moods. Spending a few minutes with someone in high spirits can start you smiling and laughing in spite of yourself. As you connect with his or her good mood, there's a good chance that you'll also reconnect with your own.

For Your Ears Only

Find a place where you can sit for a few minutes without being disturbed. Indoors is okay, outside is preferable and it doesn't have to be a gorgeous natural setting, though that's always nice. Make yourself comfortable and close your eyes. Now just listen. What can you hear? Does what you hear change as soon as you close your eyes and pay attention? Does it change after a few seconds? A few minutes? Are there layers to sound? Do certain sounds affect you emotionally? When your attention wanders, just bring it back to listening. Do it for five minutes, more if you can. Interesting. Refreshing. Fun.

Chapter 63

Make a Deal

When you're down, you tend to be more self-critical than usual. When you heap criticism on yourself, you spiral down even farther. It becomes a vicious cycle, prolonging your blue days and darkening your mood. Like most of us, you probably have plenty to pick on yourself about. These are all those things you were going to do, but didn't—losing weight, quitting smoking, cleaning out the basement. No doubt the list is much longer, but we'll stop there. Then there are the things you meant to start, but haven't gotten around to—going back to school, exercising, meditating, learning how to back up your computer files, salsa dancing.

Of course, it's not just you. We all waste time and energy resisting, postponing and "forgetting" to do the things we say we're going to do. Then we waste even more time and energy getting down on ourselves about it. It's amazing we have time left to accomplish anything at all.

While not ideal by any means, procrastination and the accompanying guilt do seem to be part of the human condition and we are all, thank goodness, human. But you certainly don't need any more guilt. You don't need any more aborted goals, either. Finishing the worthwhile projects you start and persisting enough to achieve your goals are two great ways to build self-esteem and banish a blue mood. If you'd like to boost your chances of achieving your goals and have more fun doing it, why not hook up with another procrastinator and try the buddy system? Talk with your friends and see who wants to accomplish the same types of things that you do. Then, make a deal to do it together.

Once you've chosen your partner, spend some time talking about your respective wants and needs, defining your goal and working out the fine points of the deal. Be as specific as possible. "We're going to run five miles three times a week around the track at the high school, rain or shine" is better than "Let's run a few times each week." Make your goal realistic, neither too easy nor too hard—something you know you can accomplish with effort. If it's too hard, you're likely to become discouraged and quit. If it's too easy, you'll feel that you haven't really done anything worthwhile.

Make sure, too, that you have time to honor this commitment. No matter how well-meant or noble, a goal that means you'll have to increase your stress level significantly or stop doing something you really don't want to stop or cram something else into an already over-busy schedule has the proverbial snowball's chance in hell of being realized.

Finally, plan a celebration for each short-term goal you achieve—after one month of success, for example; again after three months. Make it something you both really enjoy. Dinner out is one of my favorite rewards for achieving goals in tandem; my friend and I alternate choosing the place. As our accomplishments get bigger, the restaurant becomes pricier. We figure we deserve it...and we do!

By the way, it's a good idea to put your commitment to each other in writing. Draw up a contract and make a ceremony of signing it. At the very least, say it out loud; it'll improve your chances of success. It's also helpful to agree to turn to each other for encouragement or a gentle kick in the pants when the process starts to seem difficult and to decide how and how often you'll check in with each other.

That's really all there is to it. Write a starting date on the calendar, tell each other how much fun it's going to be and go for it!

Up the Ante

Set up a competition with your pal and make a bet. Be sure the stakes are high enough to motivate both of you: "I bet fifty bucks (or a month of dog-sitting or whatever you can afford but don't want to lose) that I can shed ten pounds faster than you, by eating only healthful food." Years ago, when a friend and I decided to quit smoking, we got a big screw-top jar, cut a slot in the top and pledged to each put in three dollars a day for a month. Our deal was that at the end of the month, we'd open it. If one of us had smoked even a puff, the other would get all the money. If neither of us had smoked, we'd split it. If both of us had smoked, we'd give the money to the American Cancer Society. It worked for us and it can work for you. Get creative, get competitive and get going!

Chapter 64

Relationship on the Rocks

If the title of this chapter were a mixed drink, it'd be something sweet, like Chambord or Crème de Cocoa, mixed with plenty of bitters, served over ice. But we're talking about real relationships and if you're past the dating or newlywed stage, you know the terrible truth: you aren't going to live happily ever after, like in fairy tales. There are lots of up and downs in intimate relationships, plenty of days when you can't even remember why you thought being with this person was a good idea. It's even possible that the one you thought would give you a daily dose of happiness for the rest of your life has left you disappointed, lonely, trudging listlessly along, feeling like a failure. If that's the reason you've been slipping in and out of blue moods a lot lately, no wonder. Who wouldn't, given the death, or at least the chronic illness, of romantic love?

What is romantic love, anyway? Definitions differ. One of my favorites comes from University of Minnesota social psychologist Ellen Berscheid, a veteran researcher of close relationships. Berscheid says that if she were asked "what is love?" and "forced against a brick wall to face a firing squad that would shoot if not given the correct answer," she would whisper, "It's about ninety percent sexual desire as yet not sated." She's speaking about romantic love and may be overstating things, but her wit contains wisdom.

Romantic love isn't what makes long-term relationships thrive, no matter what Hollywood, novelists and *People* magazine would like you to believe. Sure, sex in relationship matters a great deal, but it is the *quality* of sex far more than the quantity that predicts happiness and the quality increases when the level of intimacy is high.

Intimacy means, among other things, that you freely share private feelings—hopes, dreams, worries, fears, likes, dislikes, proud accomplishment, embarrassment, shame, clay feet. It means trust, coming and going; you each make it safe for the other to tell and to hear the truth. It also means equity and equality. Both partners in a relationship need to feel that they are getting, on balance, about as much as they give and that neither one has a better deal. These things usually don't happen automatically, not for long, anyway. They require persistent effort, skill and time.

Both of you can learn how to create trust, build intimacy, listen with open hearts and share your thoughts and feelings with honesty and kindness. You can also learn how to resolve conflict and talk to each other on a daily basis in ways that shore up rather than chip away at the relationship. Here's a good place to start: Let go of the idea that if your partner would only change, everything would be fine. Then start thinking about yourself. It's more important to be the right person than to find (or have) the right person. Work on being the person you wish your partner would be. Set a good example. Do it to improve the relationship (trust me, it will), but do it mostly for you.

Finally, get help. In my opinion, the top counselors for relationship skills training are Dr. John Gottman and his wife, Julie Schwartz Gottman. They're world-class researchers as well as therapists. As far as I know, no other approach to couples' education and therapy has relied on such intensive, detailed and long-term scientific study of why marriages succeed or fail. The Gottmans are based in Seattle, at the Gottman Institute, but they work all over the country and offer excellent video workshops, books and self-help materials. Check out their Web site, www.Gottman.com, to learn more about the work they do helping couples develop and maintain healthy, satisfying relationships. Of course, there are many excellent marriage/relationship counselors and therapists everywhere. Do some local research and find a professional with whom you and your partner can work.

Sooner is Better

• Fact number one: The average couple waits six years before seeking help for a relationship on the rocks. • Fact number two: Half of all marriages that end do so in the first seven years. It doesn't take a math major to figure out what these facts add up to: Most people wait too long. Don't be average. Be proactive. If you're having problems, seek help now. • Fact number three: Happy couples have high standards for each other, even as newlyweds. The most successful couples are those who refuse to accept hurtful behavior from each other, right from the get-go. The lower the level of tolerance for bad behavior in the beginning, the happier the couple is down the road. But even if you're past the early stages, there's still hope. Stop waiting. Stop settling. Get help.

BLUES
FLASH!

When your mood is blue, you may tend to be over-sensitive. Use the "Teflon Technique" to strengthen your immunity to negative input.

Whatever happens, don't take it personally.

Insults and unkindnesses are about the person dishing them out, *not* about you. Develop a good nonstick attitude and they'll slide right off.

Don't let other people stop you from enjoying life. Just smile and turn your attention toward something else. (The smile will drive them nuts!)

Chapter 65

Make the
Street Your Beat

Ever have journalist fantasies? See yourself as Diane Sawyer, Peter Jennings, Katie Couric, Dan Rather or Barbara Walters interviewing someone famous, getting the straight scoop, the inside dope? While your chances of anchoring the national news or recording a tête-à-tête with movie stars Al Pacino or Catherine Zeta-Jones are slim, there's no reason why you can't shake off the blues by doing something almost as exciting and maybe even more fun: go to a busy place for an hour or two, tape recorder in hand and conduct your own Man in the Street interviews.

When I was in college, I worked for the campus newspaper. They gave me a badge and I. D. card, a tape recorder and a job description. One of the things I had to do every Monday was ask a random sample of students the Question of the Week, a prospect that, before I gave it a try, made me break into a cold sweat. I was afraid people would be annoyed by someone walking up to them, sticking a microphone in their faces and asking them to stop what they were doing and answer an off-the-wall question. With one or two exceptions, they weren't annoyed at all. On the contrary, most of them seemed pleased.

Because I'm normally a borderline introvert, I thought I'd probably be tongue-tied if I tried to talk to strangers. That didn't happen either. After the first time or two, when I was too nervous to smile, I was as smooth as any pro. In fact, it turned out to be the part of my job to which I most looked forward. Not only was it fun and fairly interesting, I met tons of people, many of them cute guys, to whom, left to my own devices, I would never have spoken. It's how I met Frank, the man I went out with for the next two years. It's also how I met Yvonne, one of my all-time best women friends.

Of course, if you decide to try it, you won't be wearing a little badge that says "Reporter" and the publication's name, though you can invent one if it makes you feel better. I think it's always best to tell the truth or, at most, a little white lie, i.e., "I'm researching public opinion (which you are; you don't have to say for whom unless they ask. If they do, you can reply by saying, "For an article I'm considering writing," or "Don't worry, it's not for publication," or simply, "Just to satisfy my own curiosity."). Would you give me sixty seconds of your time to answer a question?" Some people will refuse. Expect it. They're the same ones who won't take a flyer or a free sample if you hold it out to them and they probably won't smile back at you, either. Don't worry about them. Just tell yourself they're too busy, keep smiling and ask the next person.

American Idol, Street Style

If you really want to push the envelope of your own nerve and other people's comfort zones, try asking them to sing into your microphone! Since the karaoke craze has turned so many of us into instant pop stars and American Idol has taken "amateur" to a new place, you may have better luck than you think. If your question for people on the street or at the mall is, "What's your all-time favorite rock and roll song?" and you then ask them to sing a few bars, you'll get a few takers. To add variety, ask for favorite show tunes, love songs, lullabies or songs to sing in the shower. P.S. There's something magical about a microphone, so make sure you have a real one to hold out.

People won't necessarily want to give their names and you probably don't want to ask. If they volunteer, fine, but be careful about giving yours. If you meet someone you really want to connect with later, take his or her name and number; you make the contact. As I'm sure you know, it's unwise to do it the other way around.

Finally, serious questions are fine and can net some thoughtful replies, but the more lighthearted your queries, the more fun the answers and the more likely you'll end up laughing yourself right out of your low mood. Here are a few suggestions to help you get started: What's your favorite way to break out of a blue mood? What things to eat do you think they should sell in movie theatres that they don't already have? What's the one television show that always makes you feel good and why? Who do you think is the funniest person on the planet? Do you think dogs really smile and if so, why?

Chapter 66

Build Bridges

Human beings are herd animals, not meant to live alone. Infants and children need to be touched (stroked) if they are to thrive. As adults, we need stroking too, but once you're grown, stroking can be both physical and verbal. Listening, encouraging, celebrating and empathizing are all forms of verbal stroking or support. Verbal support can also involve analyzing failures and giving a gentle push when necessary. Lack of sufficient support from others can bring on a prize case of the blues. On the other hand, ongoing positive communication and connection can help you bounce back from bad times more quickly. One way to get these things is to join or create a support group.

Scores of specialized support groups are available and many have been around for years. These groups are free. Twelve-step programs are no longer just for alcoholics or substance abusers. They offer support for recovery from a wide variety of other problems and compulsive behaviors, too, including overeating, out-of-control anger, gambling, shopping, even sex addiction, and Adult Children of Alcoholics (ACOA) is for anyone with problems traceable to childhood. There are groups to support and encourage families of (and people suffering from) various long-term or serious diseases. Self-help groups also abound, including groups for singles, couples, gays and lesbians, new or single parents, widows and widowers and those who are divorced. Check your phone book for hotlines and referral agencies that will help you find a group to meet your needs.

If the idea of an already established or problem-centered group has little appeal, start your own group or look around in your community to see what other types of groups are already in place. Those that focus on spirituality may support practical matters, too. You can get together with friends or acquaintances for almost any reason, then transform it into a support group, if that's your intention. Or you can put together a group to encourage personal growth and self-awareness, or simply to support and bear witness.

Any group develops its own set of norms eventually, but to ensure a positive atmosphere, it's a good idea to discuss desired behavior and expectations in advance. Support groups work best when members are committed to being there and to letting others know if they must miss a meeting. If you set this up as an expectation, it's important to contact folks who don't show or call. Remind them of their commitment and let them know they were missed. It's also a good idea to set a time for beginning and ending meetings and stick to it.

Frequency of meetings will depend on what members want and can accommodate, but try not to over-schedule (more than once a week) or people won't attend regularly. Avoid under-scheduling (less then once a month), too; a certain amount of regular contact is necessary to build the trusting, concerned relationships that make these groups work. Size of the group is also important. Ideally, they can be as small as three, but not larger than eight to ten. You need enough people for liveliness and diversity, but not so many that each person doesn't have a chance to share.

You might want to begin meetings with a check-in period, so members can let each other know what's been going on. It's usually best to let this move around the group without cross talk. This way, people can feel heard and share as much or as little as they choose. Discussion of what's been said during check-in can happen later. Other ground rules to consider are confidentiality, nonjudgmental listening, avoiding interrupting and, of course, treating each other with respect.

Make a Group Charter

A great way to encourage group members to maintain certain desired behaviors is to work together to create a group charter. Have a discussion about what each of you wants the group to accomplish. Consider behaviors that facilitate the trust, confidence and security it takes to encourage openness and to allow people to be vulnerable. Some things you might include are nonjudgmental listening, sharing similar experiences rather than giving advice, accepting each other's fallibility, being emotionally available, keeping things confidential, being open and sincere, handling conflict and accepting disagreement. Once the group has decided on the behaviors you'll each commit to and expect, write up a charter and have each member sign it. Make the signing a celebration with food and wine or sparkling cider. Give each member a copy as a reminder.

Chapter 67

What's Cooking?

Cooking something special and sharing it with others is a tried-and-true way to brighten your mood on a blue day. Because of demanding schedules and perennial time crunches, many people spend very little time in the kitchen. Even if you do all the meal preparation for yourself or your family, fast food, frozen pizza, microwave meals and even gourmet takeout have all but made cooking a lost art. You may not miss it or maybe you feel that you already do more than enough, but if you let yourself really get into cooking, it can be creative, satisfying, fun and nourishing for your soul.

A young mother I know loves cooking with her kids. She says that during the long winter months, when she and the children are often indoors, cooking is one of the few activities they all enjoy. "We make simple foods that they like and can put together with minimum help. The kids learn patience and self-discipline as they clean up together and wait for the food to cook. They end up feeling proud of what they've done and for me it's a wonderful bonding experience. Plus, lunch or dinner is taken care of."

Another friend, who enjoys cooking but usually doesn't have time to prepare multi-course meals, occasionally puts aside an entire day to cook up a storm. She says that spending her day in a kitchen full of terrific aromas and yummy food to sample reminds her of her childhood and makes her feel creative, caring and happy. It also gives her a freezer stocked with appetizing food.

A Class Act

Take a cooking class. Learn to whip up fabulous Chinese, French, Mexican, Thai or vegetarian dishes. Want to learn how to make tapas, puff pastry or roast a pig, Polynesian style? Maybe you'd just like to learn how to bake a perfect apple pie or make pasta from scratch. Check out local food co-ops or community colleges for class offerings and schedules. Perhaps you're knowledgeable enough to teach a class. What's your specialty? My friend Mario makes to-die-for biscotti. A few of us persuaded him to share his secret recipe. We brought the ingredients from a list he provided, as well as lunch and lots of enthusiasm. Everyone had a good time and took home Mario's recipes, along with a box of almond, orange and hazelnut biscotti. We humans have a special connection between heart and stomach!

I recently attended a recruitment meeting for a volunteer group. Members of the organization prepared a fabulous "Thanksgiving" meal to welcome potential new members while they described their program. Our hosts talked about the joy of preparing the food and sharing it with us. It was easy to feel comfortable and part of this group as we ate and talked. The meeting was a smashing success; almost everyone who attended also joined.

My Wild Women support group wanted to do something for others in our fellowship, especially those who are shut in because of illness, surgery or disability. We decided to cook and freeze meals to donate when they're needed. Several cookbooks and a lively discussion later, we agreed on what to make. All seven of us went shopping to buy the ingredients. What a kick that was! Then, we all trooped over to Nancy's, who has a big, fully-equipped, airy kitchen.

We cooked and ate, cooked and talked, cooked and laughed, then ate some more. We made enough of one of the casseroles to have it for dinner. Someone brought a belly dancing tape, so we drank wine and belly danced as we cooked. We produced eight dinners and two big pots of soup, enough for eight more meals. It was a great day. We were productive, charitable and enjoyed ourselves, all at the same time.

Another way to cook your way to happy is a progressive dinner. Each person or family makes enough of one course for everyone and the group moves from house to house for cocktails, appetizer and salad, the main course, dessert and coffee. Or try a "cook your specialty" barbeque. Everyone brings their favorite barbeque fare, you fire up several grills, play upbeat music, have lots of beer and soda and you've got yourselves a party! However you do it, cooking and feeding others is a great way to move from blue to rosy.

Chapter 68

The Coach Approach

Whether you have the Bad-Boss or Boring Job Blues or simply want a better career or life, a personal coach can help. According to one of the most respected senior coaches in the field, Robert Hargrove, author of *Masterful Coaching*, the coach is a "vision builder and value shaper." Which means a coach helps you clarify your values and discover what you really want. Once you know what that is, a coach works with you to set appropriate goals, then helps you to reach them. He or she will also help you create subgoals or objectives and break them down into tasks that need to be accomplished. But that's not all coaches can do for you.

Coaches are advisors, cheerleaders, nonjudgmental listeners and mentors. They help you identify and articulate problems and find hidden opportunities. They know what questions to ask to uncover concealed issues, encourage creativity and help you stretch and grow. Your coach might suggest research, give you homework or help you come up with action plans and timelines. Coaches support and encourage growth in the ways you most want to grow.

It's amazing how much more you can accomplish when you make yourself accountable to another person, especially when you're paying that person to help! If you aren't meeting your goals or doing your homework, your coach will discuss problems and obstacles and help you come up with remedies, but will never force you to do anything you don't want to do or urge you to promise more than you can deliver.

Like me, many personal coaches started out as therapists, but coaching isn't therapy. Although coaching is centered on your wants, needs and helping you create the life you want, it assumes that you are healthy and functioning well and makes no attempt to deal with deeper psychological issues. When coaching is going well, it's exciting, energizing and rewarding. Your coach is one hundred percent on your side, never an adversary. He or she is someone to whom you can talk honestly and openly, someone who really listens.

Are You Coachable?

To get the most out of your coaching experience, you need to be at a place in your life where you are coachable. To find out how coachable you are, circle the number closest to representing how true these statements are for you right now.

Least True 1 2 3 4 5 Most True

1 2 3 4 5 I can be relied upon to be on time for all calls and appointments.

1 2 3 4 5 This is the right time for me to accept coaching.

1 2 3 4 5 I am fully willing to do the work and let my coach do the coaching.

1 2 3 4 5 I keep my word without struggling or sabotaging.

1 2 3 4 5 I'll give my coach the benefit of the doubt and "try on" new concepts or behaviors.

1 2 3 4 5 I'll be open and honest.

1 2 3 4 5 If I'm not getting what I need or expect, I'll say so and ask for what I need.

1 2 3 4 5 I am willing to stop/change self-defeating behaviors that limit my success.

1 2 3 4 5 I have the funds to pay for coaching and see it as a worthwhile investment.

_____ Total Score (add all numbers)

10-20 Not coachable now
21-30 Somewhat coachable
31-40 Coachable
41-50 Very coachable, high likelihood of success

The feedback you can get from a coach is usually better than anything you're likely to get from friends or family, because the coach is there only for you. He or she doesn't want or need anything from you, except that you honor your agreements and treat the relationship with respect. The only agenda is your success and happiness. Even your mother is not usually that selfless!

Coaching is most often done by telephone and coaching sessions take place anywhere from one to four times a month, depending on your needs and budget. Be sure to interview several coaches before you choose one. Many people have hung up Personal Coach shingles these days, but no universal standards for certification or accreditation yet exist, so be cautious. An online search using the key words "personal coach" or "coaching" will turn up slews of Web sites.

Take your time checking out prospective coaches and know what you're looking for. Do you prefer a man or a woman? Someone who has successful business or entrepreneurial experience? Someone with a therapy background or other special training? Ask about education, experience, coaching philosophy, ground rules and, of course, costs. Some coaches offer a free first session or give free teleclasses to help you get to know them. Take them up on the offer, but don't feel obligated to continue if it doesn't feel right. While you're doing your research, take a look at the book *Personal Coaching for Results,* by Lou Tice and Joyce Quick. It's full of interesting stories and proven-effective techniques for mentoring yourself and others to amazing growth.

BLUES
FLASH!

Misery Loves Company

This old saying may be true, but hanging out with
other sad sacks when you feel miserable isn't a good
idea.

You're likely to drag each other down until you're all
lower than a snake's belly.

For a mood lift, surround yourself with upbeat, optimistic, fun people. They'll help you to see the bright
side and encourage you to laugh. Sometimes that's
all it takes to banish the blues.

PART SIX

Dig a Little Deeper

You'd probably prefer to prevent low moods in the first place, right? Getting to know (and like) yourself better is an important part of avoiding the blues. This doesn't have to be a white-knuckle experience. It can feel exhilarating, expansive and even be fun. The chapters in this section are designed to help you excavate the true you and live more authentically and positively.

Chapter 69

Hocus Pocus,
Change Your Focus

Did you ever have one of those days...? You know how the rest goes. Emotionally speaking, you just can't seem to get out of your own way. No matter how hard you try, you keep tripping over old stuff. It's called baggage. And it feels like baggage—a whole planeload of it, strewn all over your living room, bedroom, office, your entire life.

Maybe part of the problem is that you're trying too hard. You're full of self-criticism, bumping into your own negative image every time you turn around. You can't do anything right, even though you're not really doing anything differently. So maybe this is a day when you *need* to do things differently. Maybe this is a day when you should try changing your perspective. Deliberately. Literally.

Artists and photographers understand that when you change your perspective—your point of view—what you're looking at changes, too. A rose is not a rose is not a rose. Sure, it might be a posy that says, "I love you," but, depending on who's looking, in addition to a thorny flower, a rose could also be a tattoo, a painful memory, a wood carving, a painting, the face of a woman, the name of a song, the name of a war.

When you're blue, try to see the world from a different perspective for a while. Stand on your head. Pretend you're someone else. Pretend you're some*thing* else: a dog, cat or bird; maybe a robot, car or computer. Stretch your mind and test your assumptions.

Just for a while, let go of your limitations, your traditions, your habitual ways of being and doing. If you normally depend on logic to solve your problems and plan your life, try being guided instead by your feelings. Stop struggling to figure things out, to find definitive answers. Look for synchronicity and coincidence. Exercise your intuition. Pretend you have ESP. Consult the I Ching, the Tarot or a psychic. On the other hand, if you're normally very much in touch with and guided by your feelings, try to be purely objective for a change. How would Sherlock Holmes approach your problems? Test your assumptions. Ignore your feelings. Employ only deductive reasoning, logic, facts and figures and see how that works.

Shake up the routines of your everyday life. Put your shoes on before you brush your teeth if you always do it the other way around. Take a different route to work. If you always use the elevator, take the stairs. Go to a different supermarket. Order something you've never tried for lunch. Shower at night instead of in the morning. Read the *National Enquirer* instead of the *New York Times*. Skip the six o'clock news and go for a walk. Stop wearing your watch. Put your habits into a kaleidoscope, shake the tube and see what new patterns emerge. Take some small risks and approach the world with a sense of adventure.

Trading Places, Trading Faces

Have you seen *Freaky Friday, Trading Places*, or other movies where characters switch bodies or personas? Imagine trading physical bodies with Halle Berry, Jackie Chan, Uma Thurman, Tiger Woods, The Rock, Venus Williams. What would you do differently if you had that other body to live in and care for? Would it be more work or less? More fun or less? Why? If it were a conventionally beautiful body, would there be any down side? What would it be like to inhabit the body of a child for a while? In the film *Big*, Tom Hanks did it the other way around. Finally, here's a stretch for your spirit: If you feel particularly upset with someone, imagine being that person, with all his or her history, all their experiences. Don't approve or disapprove. Just imagine.

Trust me, this is not pointless activity. You're trying something new, just to see how it feels. You're experimenting with change, deciding to take control over how you do things. Small things, at first. But small things matter and control is a lot like exercise — the more you do, the more you *can* do. Maybe you won't like the change, maybe you will. Maybe you'll learn something about yourself. Maybe you'll learn something about other people, while you're at it. What is certain, however, is that you'll be stimulating your own creativity. That's what happens when you put old things together in new ways or new things together in old ways. And that's good, because it's hard to feel blue while you're being creative.

Chapter 70

Take a Chance, Make a Choice

Some people believe they have little to say about their futures. "Things just happen," they say. "I have no control." Of course, if you think something is beyond your control, you probably won't try to change it. If you do, your efforts will be half-hearted and you'll soon give up. Other people think, "While I can't control everything that happens, I can certainly control my response." This is more empowering, because it allows for choice. Finally, a few people maintain, "I decide what happens in my life and I can change anything I want." This is a high-choice, action-based point of view—the most empowering belief of all.

Feel like trying an experiment? See what happens when you adopt a high-choice viewpoint: "I choose my own life. I always have. I choose it all—thoughts, feelings, behaviors, responses, even my body and my experiences." If you decide to try on this point of view, it's important to realize that only some choices are conscious, meaning you make them thoughtfully. The majority are unconscious. Maybe they're unconscious because you learned to do certain things to be safe, approved or accepted when you were a kid. Now, when similar situations arise, those old behaviors automatically pop up. Maybe they're unconscious because they involve feelings so painful you don't want to deal with them. When they leave your awareness, they don't go away; they go underground.

Whatever the reason, if you want to make your life work better, try to bring your unconscious choices into awareness. That's the only way you can control or change them. Here's a process that can help:

Look for the payoff. You don't make choices just to make your life miserable, even though that may be the result. There's always a good reason. Here are some common payoffs attached to low moods: You get to stop cleaning your house. You get to complain and maybe gain extra attention and sympathy. You get to let your appearance go. You get to make other people (with whom you may secretly be angry) miserable. You get to cry. You get out of some responsibilities. You feel like there's drama in your life. You get to indulge yourself. What do *you* get?

Look for the fear. Ask yourself, what could I be afraid of here? How might I be trying to protect myself with this choice? Keep asking, gently but firmly, until you get answers. Are you afraid you're not competent? Afraid you'll be shown up as a fraud? Afraid you're unlovable, ugly, deficient, dependent, selfish, stupid?

Give yourself a break. When taking a high-choice point of view, *be gentle.* No shame, guilt or blame. Looking at the choices you've made isn't about right or wrong, good or bad. It's about what works. It's about making useful choices in the future. When you're in distress or pain, it isn't helpful to say, "Well, you made this stupid choice, so just handle it!" Neither is it helpful to try to impose a high-choice point of view on others. *Use it if and only if it helps you.* If you are ill, injured or in danger, don't question yourself about deeper motives. Get out of the situation and get help. Later, when you're ready, you can quiz yourself about the fears/payoffs that made those choices attractive.

It's also fine to ignore a blue mood and wait for it to blow over. Until it does, you may not feel that you have many choices. Wait until you're feeling better. Then, experiment with taking a high-choice point of view.

Go to Extremes

If looking at life from a high-choice vantage point makes you a little dizzy, see what happens when you take the low road. Sounds nuts, but trust me. Put on the gloomy mask of tragedy for a while. Play the role of Major Victim: Woe is you! You have no control. You are completely helpless and hopeless! You might as well sell yourself into servitude, wear manacles and leg irons! Did anyone ever feel as wretched as you do? Will it ever end? No! You'll feel like this forever! Throw a major hissy fit (see chapter 6). When you deliberately take it over the top like this (best done in private or with a sympathetic audience cheering you on, no little kids allowed), it actually helps you come back down, put things into perspective. In fact, it works so well it can tickle a fit of the giggles. Better blatant than latent!

Chapter 71

Battle Scars
and Gold Stars

If you've had blue periods before, you got through them, right? This is a good time to look back and recall how you did it. What worked for you in the past? Was it simply the passing of time? Remember that time will pass for you again and in a few days, you'll probably begin to feel better. Was it help and comfort from family or friends? Call on them again. That's what friends and family are for (see chapter 7, "Baby Yourself"). Was it purposeful activity, some project that captured your energy and enthusiasm? Time spent with a therapist? Your religious faith? A vacation to clear your mind and shift your perspective? Those things are still available and what worked before may work again.

If this is your first serious bout with the blues, be aware of the purpose of problems. As human beings, we are problem-solving animals. We grow by meeting and mastering difficulties. It's how we develop resourcefulness and resiliency and it's how we learn to see ourselves as people who can get through tough times. Every now and then, we face a problem that seems bigger than we are. We feel intimidated, inadequate, helpless and hopeless. But the beauty of a situation like this is that we don't have to remain frozen in our inadequacies. We can deliberately choose to grow.

One of Sir Edmund Hillary's team members died in a failed first attempt to climb Mt. Everest. When he returned to London, many of the most powerful people in Great Britain held a banquet to honor him. Behind the speaker's platform were giant photos of the mountain. When he stood to receive the applause of the audience, Hillary turned his back to them, faced the photos and said, "Mount Everest, you have defeated me. But I will return and I will defeat you, because you can't get any bigger...and I can!"

Hillary was right, of course. We can learn what we need to learn and change ourselves, even when we can't change the problem. Problems always—yes, always—present opportunities for growth as well as obstacles. Your willingness to see the opportunity inside the obstacle is sometimes all it takes to stimulate growth. If you look for and find the seeds of your own development within your dilemmas, you're likely to struggle less and move more quickly toward solution and resolution.

While you're analyzing your past, take a look at the good times too. Your entire life hasn't been painted in shades of indigo. Remember the moments, hours and days of pleasure and contentment you've experienced. Remember the triumphs as well as the tragedies. Take a few minutes now to reminisce: Return mentally to some of your most treasured times. Relive them. Imagine them, as vividly as you can. As you do, feel again the feelings they evoked. Remind yourself of the role you played in creating them. And remember that you're still as capable of joy as of sorrow.

Tales from the Trenches

Hard to remember your own history right now? Talk to siblings, parents, grandparents, cousins, favorite aunts or uncles. Ask them to tell you about their own battle scars and gold stars. What was it like for Grandma during the Great Depression, with a husband out of work and four mouths to feed? How did she survive after Grandpa died? How did she put three kids through college? What was it like for Aunt Mary when they diagnosed her cancer? How did Uncle Bud build his business from one person to twenty in only five years? When your older sister quit drinking, what was the hardest part? Where did her strength come from? Questions like these not only make for fascinating conversation, they may reveal some things about your family that you never suspected. They may also give you a new perspective on your own blue moods.

Your ability to be happy hasn't been destroyed; it's just hibernating. There are dark times in our lives, just as there are winters. There are seasons of growth and of dormancy, times of things coming together, times of things coming apart. All pass, all are valuable. Can you accept blue times as a natural part of the cycle of your own growth and know that you *will* feel happy again?

Believe me, there are good times ahead. There is joy in your future, just as there is joy in your past and in the present. When you're ready and willing to look for it, to create it, to make the transition into a new phase, you'll find it.

BLUES
FLASH!

Get It in Writing

For speedier healing of both body and spirit, get your feelings down on paper.

A British research study of people who wrote about hurtful emotional events for twenty minutes once a day, indicated that they healed faster than subjects who simply wrote about trivial matters.

Researchers theorize that writing about your feelings lowers internal stress levels, results in improved comfort levels, increased immune system activity and facilitates healing.

Chapter 72

Censor Your Sensibilities

What you see is mostly that for which you're looking. For example, as soon as you decide to buy something—say it's a new television—you start noticing all sorts of ads for televisions on sale. When you're driving, you see signs in store windows advertising televisions. In department stores, the television display leaps out at you. At a friend's house, you take note of the kind of TV they have for the first time. Television sets seem to be everywhere you look. Of course, they were there all along, but you didn't notice them, because they weren't important to you. You weren't looking for them, so you didn't see them.

It's the same with feelings. When you're blue, all you can see are reasons for your low mood. You are, in effect, looking at the world through blue-colored glasses. And, sure enough, you see plenty of evidence that supports and reinforces your sad state of mind.

Even when you're in a miserable mood, however, there are moments when you feel a tiny spark of joy, hope, gratitude or other positive emotion. Because of those blue-colored glasses, though, you barely notice them. They come and go quickly—so quickly they don't register. They don't fit your present blue-tinted picture of yourself and the world and since you're not looking for them in the first place, you don't see them. Then, sure enough, the spark goes out, almost instantly.

But you want that spark to catch fire, not go out. You want it to grow big enough to keep your spirit warm. So when you're blue, remember this: Be ready for these happy moments. Be on the lookout. Decide that you *want* these pleasures, that they're important to you. When you do this, it automatically changes your awareness. You begin to notice more and more joyful moments studding your dark mood like little stars. Don't let them get away quickly. Comment on them—silently or out loud. Try describing them in a little notebook. You see a kid in frog boots and a yellow rain slicker jumping in puddles with both feet and your heart smiles. You smile at a Molly Ivins interview on the radio. You hear a song you used to love and your feet feel like dancing. You smell spring in February and your heart takes a little leap. You never know what's going to do it for you, but whatever it is, don't let it go without taking note of it. Focus your attention on it.

After it passes, remind yourself that you are still capable of feeling happy. Remind yourself that there are still many reasons to feel happy, that the world is still full of beauty and curiosity. An interesting thing happens when you do this. The more you notice your happy moments, the more happy moments you'll have.

Everything You Love

Create a big (posterboard size, no smaller) collage of everything that makes or has ever made you happy. Collect magazines, catalogues, newspapers. Cut out every picture that rings your feel-good bell, no matter how slightly. Try to find images of all the things you love. For the real people, places or critters in your life, scan or photocopy favorite photos. Glue them together in a way that pleases you. Add poems, letters, tickets, programs, stickers, stamps or other small objects. Decorate with anything that shows or symbolizes what you really care about. Make it fast or slow, plain or fancy, but make it from the heart. When you're finished, display your creation where you'll see it every day. It'll help you remember what really counts.

Happiness isn't a matter of luck. It isn't a matter of hard work. It isn't even a matter of great timing, though all of those are useful. Happiness is a choice you make...and make...and keep making.

When you're blue, happiness can be a tough choice, sometimes possible for only moments at a time. That's okay. Recognize those moments for what they are—small tastes of joy—and applaud them. Recognize the next moment, too, when it comes. Welcome it. Invite it in. See how long you can make it last instead of how quickly you can squash it. Replay it in your memory. Collect your happy moments like photographs and paste them into a mental album. Open it often and look through it. Share it with other people, if you like, or keep your mental album as a private pleasure. Either way, you'll be getting better acquainted with your own capacity for joy.

Chapter 73

Get Past
the Nasties

When you cling to angry or resentful feelings, they grow. You try to justify your own behavior and complain about others. You talk to anyone who will commiserate with you. You may fantasize about revenge or actually try getting even, adding fuel to the fire. Eventually, though, you will be the one scorched by these bitter feelings. They will stop you from growing. Spiritually, they're deadly.

Carrying anger and resentment around is like poisoning your own well. Plus, sooner or later you're going to figure out that, no matter how angry or upset you are and no matter how wrong you think they are, you can't change other people. But you can change how you feel and how you behave in the future. The more you practice, the easier it gets to make the switch.

Use the blues as a tool for greater self-awareness. Here are some steps to help you spot and defuse bad feelings:

Accept your feelings. It's almost impossible to move on and let go if you've denied or ignored what you feel. When the nasties show up, don't pretend. Acknowledge them. Wallow for a while, if you feel like it. There are situations when you need wallowing time because you're so sure you are a victim. After all, Jennifer did betray you by going out with your boyfriend and Jason was promoted after he badmouthed you to the boss. You have a right to feel upset, don't you? Absolutely. And, for a short time, anyway, that's not a bad idea. You have the right to be angry and to blame those awful people, if you must (see chapter 6, "Throw a Tantrum"). But the goal is to get it out of your system, not make it a way of life. A few hours, at most a day or two, should be all you need.

Get past the nasties. Remember that you give power to whatever you focus on. As long as you focus on pain and anger, you'll feel more of these emotions. All that negativity is bound to make life worse, not better. Blaming may feel good for a while, but as long as you feel like a victim, you give away your power. In the long run, reclaiming your power is how you move on.

Learn from the experience. Whatever is happening in your life can be changed by changing your choices (See chapter 70, "Take a Chance, Make a Choice"). What did you learn about Jennifer? About your boyfriend? About yourself? How might you behave in the future to improve the odds of avoiding a similar situation? What criteria have you been using to determine who to trust with your feelings? What coping skills can you develop to handle this with less pain if it happens again? What about Jason? What did you learn about him, about your boss, about the culture in which you work? Do you want to keep working in such an environment? What are you willing and unwilling to do in order to advance your career? These so-called bad experiences can be marvelous learning opportunities. They can help you clarify your value system and provide a reality check regarding your expectations.

Try an awareness short cut. Ask yourself, "What did I want from this person that I am unwilling to give myself?" If this yields nothing, try "What did I want that I feel unable to give myself?" Go forward from there. This short cut won't work every time or in every situation, but it's a great way to use a negative experience to increase your awareness and your options.

Taking Care of Business

Byron Katie, spiritual teacher, author and wise woman (thework.com), says there are only three kinds of business: God's business, other people's business and your business. God can run things without us. Other people's business is not our affair, either. We don't know, she says, how important what's going on may be to their growth, even if it looks bad right now. Our own business is more than enough to occupy us. "Who would you be without that thought?" she asks people who are troubled by ideas of how things "should" be. Often, the answer is "a happier person"!

Chapter 74

Stretch
with a Shrink

Are you one of those fiercely independent souls who think that people should handle their problems without help? Do you believe that consulting a mental health professional is okay…as long as you're crazy? Are you convinced that counseling is completely out of your financial reach? If any of these notions is holding you back from seeing a therapist for depression (see appendix for symptoms) or a case of the blues that's becoming a way of life, trade in your creaky, old idea for a new, improved point of view.

What would you say to someone with a severe toothache who wanted to handle it alone, without help? A friend who believes that only spoiled, rich people or the insane ask for legal advice? Someone who didn't get treatment for a life-threatening illness because she/he thought it was too expensive? You get the point. Professional help, whatever package it comes in—psychologist, clinical social worker, licensed counselor, clergyperson, psychiatrist, community mental health clinic—is available and affordable. The quality of the help you get, however, can make a huge difference in how quickly you find your way back to comfort and clarity, so choose carefully.

The best way to find a good therapist/counselor is to ask around. Ask friends, family members and your family doctor. In the city in which I live, there are counseling referral services. Maybe your city also has them. If you're stuck, try looking in the phone book However you get the name, aim to feel good about the person you choose.

When you call, ask about education, experience, fees and insurance reimbursement. Many therapists offer free or low-cost first sessions. After chatting for a bit, you'll have the information you need; you'll also have a sense of whether you like this person, which is important. You won't get much done if you don't feel comfortable.

If you haven't seen a therapist before, you'll no doubt have questions. Ask them during the phone interview or first session. Here are some of the most common, along with my answers; your therapist may answer differently.

How long will it take? Individual sessions usually last fifty or sixty minutes, but how often you meet and how long you continue depends on the size of the dragons you need to slay and how much you feel you're benefiting.

How expensive is it? Your health insurance will probably cover all or part. Some therapists are expensive. Others cost less or offer a sliding scale. Price tag isn't necessarily an indicator of effectiveness, so do some shopping.

Do I have to be mentally ill to see a therapist? All you have to be is a person trying to live a happier, more satisfying life.

Isn't therapy painful? Why would I want to subject myself to it? When it's working, therapy is liberating, stimulating and encouraging. It expands your horizons, gives you more options, helps get you unstuck and heals old wounds. Sure, it can be painful at times. It can also be full of humor, warmth and new wisdom.

What goes on in sessions? That's up to you and your therapist. The goal is to help you see how your problems developed, learn new skills for coping with them and keep them from recurring. Sometimes, your therapist will listen as you describe your experiences. Sometimes, he/she will offer insights, ask questions, help you explore thoughts/feelings, suggest books or behaviors. Whatever the methods, what you can expect from stretching with a shrink are growing feelings of self-esteem and hope.

Silver-Screen Shrinks

Sometimes going to see a for-real shrink is the right thing to do. Sometimes seeing a fake one works, too, especially if you exit laughing. Start with Billy Crystal and Robert DiNiro fooling around in *Analyze This* and its almost-as-funny sequel, *Analyze That*. Then watch Kevin Spacey as patient and Jeff Daniels as shrink in *K-PAX*. Switch to the small screen and catch a few *Frasier* reruns (David Hyde-Pierce is the best on-screen shrink ever), or see if you can get the old *Bob Newhart Show* on DVD or video—the one where he plays a psychologist, opposite Suzanne Pleshette. Billy, Bob, Frasier, Niles—all experts at shrinking big blue moods and their hourly rates are fantastic!

Chapter 75

Sort Out
Your Shoulds

Stop with the "shoulds": "I should exercise more. I should be nicer to my mother. My husband should stop smoking. I should get a better job. My boss should give me more approval. I should spend more time with my kids." No matter how reasonable they may sound, shoulds are troublemakers. When you have an army of them telling you what to do, it's like letting a critical parent run your life. You'll hate it and you'll try to get out of your shoulds whenever you can. Maybe you think you "should" have at least a few, but not so. Here's why.

Shoulds are unwritten rules about how you and others are supposed to feel, think and behave. The trouble with having these kinds of rules for other people is that it doesn't take reality into account. People aren't always going to conform to your expectations, no matter how reasonable they may be. Besides, they're largely unaware of your shoulds. Even when they are aware, it may not matter. They have their own sets of rules, which are likely to be very different from yours. Shoulds for other people make you a victim. They cause angry, disappointed, bitter, resentful feelings because people keep letting you down and don't do what you think they should. If it weren't for their screwups, selfishness and bad behavior, you'd be so much better off!

See what I mean? Next thing you know, you're blaming others for your problems and feeling angry and helpless. To skip that trap, simply decide what behaviors you prefer and let others know. If that doesn't help, avoid their company, if you can (explain why you're backing off, when that makes sense) and focus your energies elsewhere. When you stop feeling like a victim, you subtract self-pity from your blue mood, which is like taking the congestion out of a cold: You breathe easier and it passes more quickly.

Aimed at yourself, shoulds are just as sneakily harmful. Many are leftovers from childhood that no longer suit your current value system or beliefs. If some still do, it's a good idea to upgrade them to choices or preferences. If they no longer make sense, but you keep them anyway, it's a safe bet you'll disappoint yourself. You may even unconsciously punish yourself for failing to honor them. It's a no-win situation, because you're putting you and yourself into an adversarial relationship!

Why not sort out your shoulds? Make a list with these four headings: I Should, My Family Should, My Friends Should, Everyone Should. When you're done, honestly consider each group of shoulds. Could any of them be a tad unrealistic? Do any make you feel victimized or disappointed? Do some express important values? Do some simply mean "My life would be better if..."? How many can you get rid of—just cross off, either because they no longer make sense, because you're minding someone else's business or because the truth is, you don't want it on your back anymore?

Shoulds Up in Smoke

For a week, pay special attention to your inner should-demon. Write down every should, have-to and ought-to as it comes up. Start each entry with the phrase "I should" and record them in a notebook or on separate index cards. At week's end, see how many you can convert into new sentences beginning with the words "I want to" or "I choose to."

Have a ceremonial burning of the rest. Put those you couldn't change into a fireproof container, set a match to them and, as they go up in smoke, release yourself from every last one of these self-imposed obligations, until further notice. That lightness you feel is freedom!

With too many shoulds in your brain, it's like trying to walk through a beautiful park on a path six inches wide. Others can't walk alongside you; they'll always be ahead or behind. You won't enjoy yourself or see much of anything, because your focus will be on staying inside that narrow boundary. Your soul can't expand under such restrictive conditions! Broaden your path by getting rid of your shoulds and operating from a choice-based philosophy. In fact, without shoulds, you get to leave the path altogether, if you want. You can kick off your shoes and walk on the grass. After all, it's your life we're talking about, your grass. And the liberating truth is that, if you're willing to stake your claim, the whole damn park belongs to you!

BLUES
FLASH!

Map Your Mood

Create a one-to-five scale: 1 = just fine, thanks; 5 = bottom of the pit. You decide what 2, 3 and 4 mean.

For the next month, take your "mood temperature" three times a day: morning, midday and just before bed. On graph paper, write the days of the month across the bottom (using three squares for each day) and write the scale (1-5) down the left side.

Make a dot at each day's mood numbers and connect the dots. Your graph will answer three questions: Is there a pattern to my moods? How much time do I spend feeling miserable? Do I need to think about getting help?

The very process of measuring often improves symptoms!

Chapter 76

Inspiration
without Perspiration

About five years ago, I was given a ticket to a conference on human potential. I was feeling lousy, because a project I had worked long and hard to develop had just fallen through. I almost decided not to go. I had spent the night before trying to figure out what had gone wrong, slept badly and woke with a backache and the urge to bawl. I forced myself to go anyway and arrived just before lunch.

The keynote speaker was a man in his thirties who was born without arms. I don't remember his name, but I'll never forget his face or what he did for me that day. He was one of the most dynamic, witty, persuasive speakers I've ever heard. His message was simply that all of us are limited by our beliefs about ourselves far more than we are by things like appearance, physical ability, economic status, education, race, sex and so forth. Nothing he said was news to me, but he really brought the message home. I came away feeling grateful, energized and inspired, my blue mood completely gone.

I'll bet similar things have happened to you. You were feeling absolutely crummy and then someone lent you *Chicken Soup for the Soul*, or you rented *Dead Poet's Society*, or you were channel surfing and happened to catch an Oprah show on real-life angels. Suddenly you were so unexpectedly moved and inspired that your mood turned around. I hope this will happen to you as a result of reading this book. After all, its whole premise and purpose is that *what you do can change how you feel*. The important thing to remember is that you don't have to just sit and wait, hoping that something inspiring will happen. You can arrange some inspiration for yourself.

If you can remember a movie that once did it for you, track it down at a video store and watch it again. If you once read a book that lifted your spirits, get it off the shelf or from the library and read it once more. If it worked in the past, it has a good chance of working now. Ask friends and family for the names of books, movies, recorded music, audios and videos that inspire them. Try a few of their suggestions. Visit a bookstore and ask for names of best-selling or personal favorite feel-good works.

In the world of computers, Garbage In/Garbage Out means that you can't get an outcome or result that is any better than the data you program in. It's no different for you. If you want to feel happy, put some happy programs into your system. To start you thinking, here are my Top Ten Most Inspirational Books and Films:

Movies:	Books:
My Left Foot	*Kitchen Table Wisdom* by Rachel Naomi Remen
Enchanted April	*The Dragon Doesn't Live Here Anymore* by Alan Cohen
The Color Purple	*Henderson, the Rain King* by Saul Bellow
Groundhog Day	*Jayber Crow* by Wendell Berry
Dead Poet's Society	*The Road Less Traveled* by M. ScottPeck
Forrest Gump	*Unconditional Life* by Deepak Chopra
Mr. Holland's Opus	*I Know Why the Caged Bird Sings* by Maya Angelou
American Quilt	*Oh, the Places You'll Go* by Dr. Seuss
It's a Wonderful Life	*The Little Prince* by Antoine de Saint Exupery
As Good as It Gets	*The Prophet* by Kahlil Gibran

Create your own Top Ten. Create a Top Hundred! Store your ideas where you'll have easy access to them next time you need an updraft to help your spirits soar. Mine started out in a file folder, but have moved uptown to a rosewood box with "Inspiration" carved into its lid. Include quotations that move you, touching sacred passages, letters, cards, photos and keepsakes. Throw in ideas for inspirational things you can do, like watching a sunrise, going to midnight mass or climbing to the top of the tallest building in town. It doesn't matter what it is. You're creating a treasure chest to open when you need inspiration, so anything that works for you qualifies.

Inspire Someone from the Future

Would you be interested in reading stories written a hundred years ago by a woman in your family? Who wouldn't! What if these stories contained neither fiction nor facts about her grand adventures, because she led a fairly ordinary life, but did have lots of details of her day-to-day existence—good times and bad, ups and downs, what caused them, how she dealt with them, her hopes and dreams? You'd love it, right? Think about writing your own stories. What would you tell a young descendent one hundred years from now? How would you describe your life? What would you say about blue moods? Any advice for dealing with dark times to pass along?

Chapter 77

Write On

You may not be a published author, but when you keep a journal, you become something even better. You become your own *author*-ity. It could hardly be easier. All it takes is something to write in, something to write with and a little time. Keeping a journal isn't necessarily a quick fix for the blues, but starting one certainly qualifies. And, if you stick with it, journal writing not only helps hold the blues at bay, it'll help you learn and grow.

Try making a unique, personal journal. Begin with any kind of notebook, binder or blank book. You'll need glue and a few do-dads to decorate the front: construction or gift paper, ribbons, stickers, rubber stamps, fabric, glitter, stars, photos, dried flowers—whatever strikes your fancy. Let your imagination run wild as you design and create your journal cover.

When it's finished, take up your pen. On the first page, enter your name, the date and briefly describe what you hope to accomplish by writing. As you write, remember: anything goes. Don't censor yourself, write what you think you should write or feel you have to write every day. If it feels strange at first and you're not sure what to say, begin by saying just that.

Keep your journal in a safe place, well hidden or under lock and key if you're concerned about privacy. For inspiration, read some books about journaling or take a look at a few that have been published. Your library or bookstore is sure to have many fascinating journals kept by soldiers, pioneers, explorers, writers, artists, people in crisis or working through grief and spiritual seekers.

Treat your journal as something important and it will become important. Write about your intentions, hopes and plans each morning or about your accomplishments, feelings and thoughts at night. Review your activities and speculate about what you might have done differently. Record and applaud the things you're glad you did. Talk about the things to which you're looking forward and the things of which you're afraid. If you feel stuck around a particular issue, try dividing a page and looking at pros and cons. Imagine the consequences of each decision and describe your ideal outcomes.

If you use affirmations, record them too. Draw and sketch as well as write, if you're so inclined and glue in photos, pictures, poems and inspiring quotes. Remember the past, put the present into perspective and plant seeds for the future. Blow off steam, try out plans and fantasies, gain a bit of distance from your daily life and organize your experiences into something meaningful. Express feelings, thoughts, wishes, hopes or fears that you aren't ready, willing or able to share with anyone else.

Reading about Writing

Check out some books about the journaling experience. Some excellent reads include *Keeping a Journal You Love* by Sheila Bender, *Notes from Myself: a Guide to Creative Journal Writing* by Anne Hazard Aldrich and Natalie Goldberg's *Writing Down the Bones.* Peruse some published diaries or journals, while you're at it. There's plenty of great fiction in the form of diaries too. If you've only seen the film, check out the hip, funny best seller *Bridget Jones' Diary* or revisit the true and extraordinary *Diary of Anne Frank.*

Make your journal into a trusted friend. Try keeping a gratitude journal: Record at least five things you're truly grateful for at the end of each day. Stick with this and you'll be vaccinating yourself against depression; the blues and gratitude can't coexist.

Over the long haul, your journal will help you understand yourself and your strengths. When you're feeling low, turn back to entries made during other hard times for a reality check. You're likely to come away thinking, "If I could get through *that*, I can certainly make it through this!" What's more, you'll have your own personal record of the fact that feelings transform themselves over time. Dark moods eventually brighten; dilemmas become resolved. Your journal will remind you of your resilience and strength. And it will help you get your dark thoughts out of your head, where they can brew trouble, and onto paper, where they can be described, dissected and even laughed off.

Chapter 78

Tie Up
Loose Ends

Ever feel like you need a cart to help you carry around all that baggage? If so, you're not alone. We're all lugging around unresolved guilt, anger and pain and we continue to carry it until we work out the feelings. Why not lighten your load and settle a few things right now? Unpack some of those heavy bags and free up more energy to live productively and happily. Doing this may not be as hard as you think. In fact, it can be downright easy. Try these three simple steps:

1. List Unfinished Business. Write down everything about which you feel guilty, angry, hurt or resentful. Think back; aim for as many as possible. They don't need to be earth-shaking: The condolence call you were going to make but didn't; the money your sister borrowed but never paid back; your friend who won't leave her dog home when she visits, despite your allergies; last year when your husband forgot your birthday; the punishments you got as a kid.

Do you have any positive unfinished business? The teachers and coaches who had such an impact on your life; the boss who saw more in you than you saw in yourself; the baby-sitter who was so caring and creative with the kids; your favorite uncle, who came through with that loan. Have you told them how you feel?

There'll likely be a few blockbusters in there, too—hanging around your neck like an albatross. Don't be afraid. Remembering them may stir up pain, but if you're expecting it, it'll be more manageable. Besides, you're about to deal with these biggies in a healing way, so take heart.

Making your list won't be as hard as it may seem. It'll take some focused thought to get started, but once you do, things will begin to bubble up. If you run dry, stop and start again later. When you think your list is complete, put it away and let it rest for a couple of days.

2. Review and rate it. Use a one-to-five scale, with one the most troubling. Then, transfer every entry that received a one to a new priority list, with which you'll work first.

3. Decide how to handle it. What about contacting some of these people to explain, confess, apologize or reconnect? If you do, remember that your goal is to finish things, not continue them or make them worse. As you think about each one, ask the wise, gentle part of yourself what might help you be done with it. If you can't or don't want actual contact with the person, try this: Sit facing an empty chair. Pretend the other person is sitting in it, paying close attention. Then say whatever you want to say. If that feels too strange, write a letter. Here's a sample:

Dear (name): Thanks for...(*almost all relationships give us something; how did you benefit from this one?*). I'd like you to know... (*apologize, explain, express anger, forgive or say whatever it takes to close the book.*) In the future, I'd like...(*describe how you want/intend to interact with this person from now on.*) Thanks for hearing me out.

Sign the letter and put it away, throw it away, burn it (burning is such a dramatic symbol!), or use it as a model for one you'll write and actually send. Do whatever feels best—whatever it takes to unload your baggage. Afterward, notice how much lighter you feel.

Of course, there are other kinds of unfinished business. They may not involve as much emotion, but can still clutter up your life and weigh you down. I'm talking about those phone calls and appointments you need to make, that giant pile of paper waiting to be filed, the chaos in your closet, the bathroom that desperately needs paint, the mess in the yard or the backseat of your car. If you list, prioritize and tackle some of those unfinished projects, you'll be taking another step toward tying up the loose ends in your life, which always feels righteously good!

Top Priorities

Here's a simple system for determining which things to finish first. Make an extensive To-Do list. Rate every item from one to three, according to time required: Ones are quick fixes, an hour or less; twos need moderate amounts of time; threes call for a major commitment—more than a day or many hours, in stages. Add a second number to indicate importance: Ones are urgent, twos are important but not critical, threes can be done anytime. Tackle the items with two ones first; they are both urgent and quick. Schedule time for the remaining ones; put them on your calendar. Then, see what's left and make some decisions. Doesn't that feel *good*?

Chapter 79

Try Trust

Building and maintaining networks of people to whom you can turn when you need support is one way to keep the blues at bay. The most basic element in relationships is trust. When I facilitate a teambuilding or personal growth workshop, trust is the first thing with which we deal. People want to feel sure that they'll be heard, included and told the truth. They also want to know that others won't try to hurt them, talk about them behind their backs, fail to support them or be unfair to them. This is as true in life as it is in workshops. We all want the people we trust to care about our well-being.

One of the best ways to develop trusting relationships is to trust first. That means taking the risk of trusting others and letting them know it. We're more likely to trust those who trust us, so start by assuming positive intent. When someone does something nice, accept and appreciate it at face value. Don't look for hidden motives or underlying designs. This doesn't mean blindly trusting everyone. The old saying applies: If it looks like a snake, sounds like a snake and moves like a snake, it's probably a snake. Pay attention, but don't automatically assume the worst.

Most importantly, be worthy of trust yourself. Tell the truth. If you have a problem with a family member, lover, friend or colleague, tell them. Be both honest and kind. Take responsibility for your feelings and check out your story (See chapter 80, "A is for Awareness"). Listen to what the other person has to say with an open mind and without interrupting. If you're concerned that telling the truth will make things worse, begin with this first truth. "I want to talk something over with you, but I'm afraid you'll think I'm being critical." Then, clarify your intent and share it. "I'm upset, it's true, but I think I'll feel better if we talk about it and I also think it'll help our relationship."

The Ultimate Trust

The most important person you need to trust is you. When you trust your own word and honor your commitments to others and to yourself, life gets easier. Here's how that works. You're probably afraid of sharks and would refuse to swim in shark-infested waters. If you were outfitted with a shark-proof suit, shark repellent and were inside a shark-proof cage, you still might not like the idea much and you still wouldn't trust the sharks, but you'd feel a lot better. Similarly, when you keep your word to others and to yourself, you're equipped to go through life feeling more relaxed and confident, no matter what happens. Even if you can't always count on others, you'll be able to count on yourself to cope, survive and thrive. That's a tremendous advantage. Of course, that doesn't mean you'll always be happy. You may still have to swim with sharks once in a while, but you'll be more likely to come out of the water smiling.

Don't use your truth to beat up on others. Before you bring up the problem, check your own motivation. Do you want to be right or solve the problem? Do you want to improve the relationship or make someone hurt the way you hurt? Of course, you probably believe you're right, but it's likely that the other person believes he or she is right, too. There's more than one way to see a situation and more than one way to improve things. Needing to prove you're right is often the way to stay locked in the problem.

Start thinking about solutions instead. Wait until your emotions have cooled and rethink the situation. See if you can put yourself in the other person's place. How might he or she have experienced what happened? How might they be feeling? Then, when you talk, ask for that person's truth and listen to the answers.

It's okay to be vulnerable and to show it. Let the people to whom you feel close know when you're confused, worried or uncertain. When you make a mistake, say so. We're all human and, therefore, imperfect. Letting others into your not-so-flawless life helps strengthen connections and encourages them to be open with you about their own imperfections.

Finally, to build trust, honor your commitments. If you say you'll pick someone up at seven o'clock, do it. If you say you'll call, call. If you're unable to keep your word, say so as soon as possible and apologize. Keeping your word is one of the most important ways you earn the respect and trust of others.

BLUES
FLASH!

Don't Have a Blue Christmas

You may feel more depressed, irritable or anxious during the holiday season, especially at Christmas or Hanukkah, gift-giving and supposed-to-be joyous occasions. Plus, winter's short days can sap your spirit and lack of sun may bring on S.A.D. (Seasonal Affective Disorder).

From now on, make this your mantra: Anticipate the best, plan for the worst. Prepare in advance for negative things (family conflicts, loneliness, yearning for a mate, dreary weather) and come up with ways to cope.

Ask a friend to help you brainstorm ideas or list potential problems and solutions in your journal.

Chapter 80

A Is for Awareness

When you're feeling down, your blue mood may be a reaction to the behavior of others. You feel hurt, angry, sad, lonely and so on, because of something someone else has or hasn't done. Often, if you look a little deeper at the situation, you'll find it's the story you told yourself about what's happened that's really the cause of your upset. If you're extremely distressed, it's likely the triggering event has touched upon fears concerning your own significance, competence or lovability.

Using your blues as a tool can help you get to know yourself at a deeper level, improve your relationships and prevent the occurrence of similar blue moods in the future. Here's a simple process to use whenever your reaction to another person's behavior causes distress.

Step One: Look carefully at the situation that triggered your troubled response. Be specific about the circumstances and the other person's behavior. What did he or she do or say? What did the person leave undone? Focus on observable behavior. "Tom didn't call on my birthday." "Jane was two hours late to my dinner party."

Step Two: Consider what you were feeling and try to express it in words. Begin your sentence with "I am" or "I was," then add a specific feeling: sad, angry, frustrated, hurt. In this way, you'll be sure that you're getting at your feelings, not your thoughts or beliefs about the other person. "I was disappointed and hurt when Tom didn't call." "I was angry and embarrassed when Jane didn't show up until dinner was over."

Step Three: Connect your feelings to the situation, as you understand it. Look at what you expected or believed should have happened. "If Tom loved me, he would have called to wish me happy birthday." "I expected Jane to do as she said and arrive on time."

Step Four: Discover your story about the situation. To feel safe and comfortable in a world of ambiguity, you may tend to fill in the blanks and connect the dots. Whenever something unexpected happens, you probably look for a reason. Often the way you find this reason is to make up a story to explain the incident. This usually happens so quickly, you don't even know you've done it. Your story becomes your truth.

It is this new truth, rather than the event itself, that creates your bad feelings. When Tom didn't call as you expected, your story might have been something like "Tom doesn't really love me. He knew it was my birthday, but didn't bother to call. Tom is a liar." When Jane showed up late, perhaps your story was "Jane is always on time when she thinks something is important. Obviously, keeping her word to me and arriving on time meant nothing to her. She's a self-centered jerk." Once you think you know what's going on, you can blame others for your blues. When you do that, you feel helpless, a victim of someone else's behavior.

Step Five: Explore the self-concept issues that may be generating your story. When your feelings run especially deep or are overwhelming, the bottom line is probably fear of your own inadequacies. "Tom doesn't love me, because I'm unlovable." "Jane thinks I'm unimportant. I guess I *am* unimportant."

Realizing that your blues are the result of the stories you tell yourself can help you recognize that you don't really know "why" people do the things they do. You only know "what" they do. Someone else's bad behavior doesn't reflect on you, but rather on them. This knowledge can become the ladder you use to climb out of your low mood.

Open Up

Once you know what your story is, you can take this awareness and your relationships to new and deeper levels. Begin by checking out your story. It may be inaccurate. In the Tom example, you could say, "Tom, what happened? I thought that if you loved me, you'd certainly call on my birthday." Tom's response might range from: "I do love you, but when I'm into a project, sometimes I forget everything else" to "I'd never forget your birthday! I tried to phone all day, but got no answer, so I came by to make sure you're okay." Whatever the response, you now have more accurate information and can decide how you want to handle the situation. If you're feeling trusting, you might share your fear. "Thanks for setting me straight. You know what? I was afraid you didn't love me and it triggered some old fears." When the relationship is important, try opening up. The result can be greater closeness and intimacy.

Chapter 81

Positively Speaking

Here's a radical-sounding idea that really isn't: Your thoughts and beliefs create your life. This is true whether you believe in God, gods, goddesses, your own higher power or nothing at all. This concept isn't about religion or divine creativity, but rather creativity on a scale much closer to home. Even if it sounds New Age, it's also behavioral science: Changing your thinking changes your life.

Consider this for a moment: What you think and believe determines how you behave and what can happen in your life. The way you explain your life is the way you experience it. In fact, you're inventing your own future right now, moment by moment, day by day, even if you're unaware of it. You even may be creating problems for yourself as a result of negative thoughts and beliefs.

One way to consciously invent the life you most want is by changing the way you think with the help of affirmations. To affirm something is to declare it to be true. An affirmation, then, is a description of how you want to behave, think or feel in the future—an articulation of a new belief or the strengthening of an old one. Here's how they work to create change: When you affirm the way you want to see yourself and the world around you in the future, your expectations change and so does your behavior. Then, of course, the results you get change, too. To create powerful affirmations, make sure they are:

- **In Writing:** Writing gives substance to thought and gives you a document as a reminder of the way you want your life to be. Writing also helps you clarify what you want and revise your words until they are exactly right.

- **Stated Positively:** When you affirm what you don't want, you give energy and power to the negative belief: "I won't gain weight." "I won't lose my temper." Instead, describe the outcome you desire: "I'm proud of my slim, healthy body." "I'm calm and considerate under pressure."
- **Short and to the Point:** You are not writing an essay, although it may start that way. A succinct affirmation is easier to focus on. Keep whittling your complex ideas down until you have a single key thought.
- **Specific:** Exact results come from specific thoughts; vague results come from unclear thoughts. Being specific can be scary; you may be disappointed, make mistakes or fail to achieve your desire. But remember, you create your life with every thought. The only difference now is that you are doing it on purpose.
- **Exciting and Emotionally Charged:** Use language that evokes strong feelings and enlivens your spirit. Your emotional involvement adds energy to affirmations and increases their power.
- **Present Tense:** If your affirmation describes something in the future, you'll maintain it as a dormant possibility. See the future as if it has already happened and describe it: "I am, I have, I know."
- **About You:** Use your name or say "I." "The universe is abundant" won't do much, if anything. "I have an abundance of love, money and good health" is more like it. You can't affirm for others, either; the only person you can control is you.
- **A Bit of a Stretch:** Expand your boundaries, but don't push them so far that they seem out of reach. Build your scope of possibilities gradually.
- **Repeated Daily:** Say each affirmation, with all the emotion you can muster, ten times in a row, three or four times a day. For how long? As long as it takes.

Give It Wheels

To get your new life rolling, come up with a visualization to match your affirmation. A visualization is a vivid mental representation of what you want to create. Close your eyes and imagine it, using as many of your senses as possible. Visualize what you'd see if it were happening right here, right now. Hear what you'd hear, feel what you'd feel and so on. Use a single image, like a snapshot, or run it like a video. Always include yourself in the picture; after all, you're the star! You also might want to create a physical representation of your visualization—a drawing, painting, sculpture or collage. This will add excitement and power. Hang your depictions and affirmations where you'll see them daily. The more focused attention you give them, the faster they'll become real to your subconscious and the faster your life will change!

Chapter 82

Fire the Captain

Ever feel like Captain of the World? So much responsibility, so much important work, so little time. You have to make sure your career is on track, your home runs smoothly and that your kids (and spouse) behave well, get enough attention and look like they live in Ralph Lauren country. You have to see that your own wardrobe is fashionable and fitting, your nails and yard perfectly manicured, your knowledge of world affairs current, your ability to ace a Pop Culture quiz assured, the cookies for the Cub Scout bake sale appropriately delectable and, of course, homemade. It makes me tired just reading that list of requirements and it's only a small part of your eternal To-Do list.

No wonder you're so stressed. If only you had a first mate and crew who would listen, pay attention, do things your way—the right way!— your life would be so much better, so much easier. It's a tough job, trying to keep yourself and everyone else shaped up to your exacting standards. Thankless, too, most days. And you know what else? It's a recipe for meltdown as well as relationship disaster.

You're familiar, of course, with the term "control freak" and have no doubt used it to describe other people. As Captain, you have no idea how many of them use these words to describe you! If this shoe fits, it's probably killing your ability to enjoy life, so why not wise up? Retire the Captain. Better yet, fire yourself. Try letting your spouse, kids and others in your world do things their way. Stop taking responsibility for everybody else's behavior for a change and focus on your own.

Yes, I know. If you step back and shut up, they're going to make mistakes. Embarrassing mistakes. Inefficient mistakes. They'll take up the bassoon instead of tootling the flute, wear brown shoes with white socks and black pants, put the silverware in the dishwasher wrong side up, use the gravy boat for mixing green hair dye, undercook the chicken and befriend people who make you wonder if there's too much chlorine in the gene pool. They'll make an ungodly mess in the kitchen instead of cleaning up as they go, file CDs by how much they like them instead of artist or title, wash the dog in the hot tub, get parking and speeding tickets, lose their debit cards. At the office, peers and even bosses will make stupid decisions about how to handle clients, prioritize their workloads, how the new brochure should look. And worse. Believe me, much worse.

You'll survive. So will they. And it's worth giving up all that awesome responsibility. It will remind you what really matters and teach you to let go of unrealistic expectations for yourself and for others. As a realtor friend of mine is fond of saying, we are all fixer-uppers. When you fire the captain, the people in your life will get invaluable experience that comes only from attempting new things, making honest mistakes and learning from them. They'll also get a spouse, mom or dad, friend, co-worker or boss who trusts and approves of them—messy or tidy, right or wrong, efficient or stumbling, on target or off the mark. And what you'll get is the life-giving freedom that comes from letting people be who they are, not who you think they ought to be.

Remember When?

Sit down for fifteen minutes or so. Open a computer file or just grab a pen and some paper. Now think back. Remember the mistakes in your past that taught you something you needed to know. Remember the times someone told you not to do something and you did it anyway. Remember how you felt when they told you, in no uncertain terms, what you "should" do. Remember how it felt living or working with someone who was constantly critical of your behavior (of course you have; haven't we all?). Remember what being around them did to your spirit, your sense of adventure and your self-esteem. Write it all down. Keep it handy while you're nudging the Captain out of the chair that looks so much like a throne. And hang on to your sense of humor. Old habits die hard, but they'll eventually stop if you persist.

One final thought, which comes from my daughter: no one likes to be told what to do. I'm not saying you should never offer opinions, guidance, coaching or mentoring, especially when requested or truly needed and most especially when children are involved. Relax and stop trying to run the world. Stop over-controlling your children. You'll be surprised how much lighter your own burdens will feel.

Chapter 83

Help Yourself

A visit to the self-help section of a large bookstore can be confusing, even overwhelming. The shelves are filled with eye-catching tomes and titles that promise everything from fabulous wealth to effortless weight loss. Many aren't worth your time or money. Some actually deliver.

How to tell gold from lead? Here's my Top Ten Really Helpful Self-Help Books list. They are beloved by many of my clients and by me, too. Some are fun to read, some are enlightening, some are comforting, some are all three. A short review accompanies each, to help you choose. They're listed alphabetically by title, not in order of preference or importance.

Coach Yourself to Success: 101 Tips from a Personal Coach for Reaching Your Goals at Work and in Life by Talane Miedaner. In an easy-to-follow program, this book helps you discover what's really important to you and offers a blueprint for living the life of which you've always dreamed.

Crucial Conversations: Tools for Talking When Stakes are High by Kerry Patterson, et al. A great course in communication skills. The book tells how to defuse explosive situations and get what you really want. Equally useful at work or at home.

The Four Agreements: A Practical Guide to Personal Freedom by Don Miguel Ruiz. Based on ancient Toltec teachings, this book spells out a simple code of conduct that can transform your restricted life into one of true freedom, happiness and love.

Loving What Is by Byron Katie. This eye-opening handbook contains dialogues between Katie and people doing The Work, a process that helps people find ways out of their emotional, spiritual and physical problems by asking four critical questions.

The Nine Fantasies That Will Ruin Your Life (and the eight realities that will save you) by Dr. Joy Browne, a reality-loving, witty, wise psychologist. Written in the form of questions and answers, it's fun to read and easy to pick up, put down and learn from.

Optimal Thinking: How to Be Your Best Self by Rosalene Glickman. Glickman goes one step beyond positive thinking. This revolutionary book shows you how to move past the commonplace and access your extraordinary, highest and best self.

The Road Less Traveled by M. Scott Peck. This is the clipper ship of self-help books. Written by a generous-spirited psychiatrist, it has become a modern classic. It's about love and serenity, reality and spirituality, growth and grace.

The 7 Habits of Highly Effective People: Powerful Lessons in Personal Change by Stephen R. Covey. This enlightening book is as useful today as when it was first published. It offers step-by-step guidelines for living with fairness, integrity, honesty and dignity; Covey's seven habits provide the security needed to adapt to change and take advantage of its opportunities.

Something More: Excavating Your Authentic Self by Sarah Ban Breathnach, author of *Simple Abundance*. This wonderful collection of 366 essays that merge spirit and style shows you how your daily life can be an expression of your authentic self.

The World According to Mister Rogers: Important Things to Remember by Fred Rogers. An intelligent and inspiring collection of stories and insights about friendship, love, respect, individuality and honesty from one of the world's most beloved television personalities and a truly gifted educator. Rogers reminds us that there is more in life to unite us than there is to divide us.

Fictional Shrinks

After a few self-help books, you may crave a little change of pace. These novels, which focus on the relationships between shrinks and clients, will entertain you and you may even recognize your own problems or solutions in them: *I Never Promised You a Rose Garden* by Joanne Greenberg, a great story about a warmly competent shrink and one patient; *Mount Misery* by Samuel Shem, a very funny book about the world of psychiatric hospitals; *Lying on the Couch* by Irvin D. Yalom, written by a terrific real-life shrink who has also written a great deal about the art and science of psychotherapy; *Free Association* by Paul Buttenwieser tells the story of a psychiatrist who discovers that his own problems are a lot like those he hears about from his patients.

PART SEVEN

Heart and Soul

If love really is the answer to most of our important queries, then the question "How do I break out of a blue mood?" is no exception. And if soul is the everlasting part of us that transcends earthbound misery, then this section is a great place to explore. Gratitude, goddesses, meditation, dreams, intuition; ritual, Zen, sex, sanctuary, love sweet love and the astonishing power of being truly present—we'll look at all these qualities and more.

Chapter 84

Sweet Sanctuary

Sometimes the blues descend because you're doing too much for others and not enough for you. When you keep pouring yourself out for everyone else, you need a way to refill your own vessel, otherwise you'll run dry.

Elizabeth came to see me because she felt overwhelmed and empty. She had three young children, a full-time job, a demanding husband and an ailing mother who needed lots of her time. On top of all that, she was committed to volunteer work at her church's soup kitchen. She managed to take care of all of this, barely. But guess who got left out of the equation? Bursting into tears one day, she wailed, "I wish there were a me for me!"

Exactly. Elizabeth needed to be there for herself. We came up with the idea of creating a personal sanctuary—a place of refuge and protection, or a sacred space. Chapter 86, "Stage a Great Escape," is about creating such a place in your imagination. But first let's talk about putting together the real thing, an actual sanctuary to which you can escape whenever possible.

You'll need to find a private space, a place where you can be alone, let go of your pressures and tensions, nurture yourself and feed your spirit. Size is unimportant. It can be an entire room, a tiny closet (emptied of clothes, of course) or even a corner of a room defined by a curtain or screen. Make it as comforting and attractive as possible. Here are a few suggestions:

Bring the outdoors in. Use green and flowering plants, cut flowers, pretty rocks, driftwood and other outdoor elements to create a sense of nature. This is especially important if your space doesn't have any windows. Posters of forests, gardens, glades or seascapes are also great additions and you might even play one of those audio tapes of twittery birds, babbling brooks or ocean waves breaking on the shore.

Create beauty at every level. Bring in your favorite prints, paintings or sculptures. Add soft, gentle textures—silk scarves, sheer draperies, velvet pillows. Soothing sounds are wonderful, especially watery ones. Buy an indoor waterfall or just play some special, relaxing music you love.

Make the colors speak to you. Colors affect feelings. Blue and green tend to be cool and relaxing; peach and pink are soft and nurturing; yellow, orange and gold offer the warmth of the sun and are upbeat and energizing. Paint and furnish the room correspondingly.

Be sure it's quiet. You'll want this to be a place of peace and calm, a place where you can meditate, reflect, write in your journal or just sit quietly and zone out. As much as possible, shelter yourself from the jarring distraction of noise. If that can't be done, try earplugs for at least part of the time you're there.

Avoid Clutter. You've heard this before: less is more. A low-maintenance area is refreshing after a demanding day. Fewer things equal less to worry about and a feeling of order and open space is good for the soul. Think of the simplicity of a Buddhist temple.

Design a closed-door atmosphere. Keep interruptions to a minimum. Hang a *Do Not Disturb* sign. Talk with your family members or housemates about your need for privacy. Keep the space loving by bringing in meaningful mementos, symbols and pictures of friends, family and places that make you feel connected and cared for.

Make it sacred. Create an altar. Place it on a windowsill, shelf, small table or in a corner of the floor. Start with an altar cloth—a scarf or covering that adds beauty and meaning. Decorate it with crystals, candles, statues, talismans, pictures and any other spiritual/religious items you wish.

Use your sanctuary whenever you need it, but try to schedule some time there each day for solitude and renewal.

More than Moments

Sometimes a few minutes or hours alone isn't enough. If you need more time to heal, rest your spirit or reflect on your life, see if you can take sanctuary for a week, a month, even six months or a year. Go to a retreat—religious, meditative or otherwise. Rent a cabin in the woods, a cottage by the sea, or a hotel/motel room with a view. Go alone. Bring the same kinds of items you have in your home sanctuary. You might also bring books, music and videos to enhance your spiritual quest. Keep a record of your thoughts and feelings. If you can't spare the time for a full-blown retreat, read some of the modern spiritual classics like *Gift From the Sea* and *Wisdom From Gift From the Sea* by Ann Morrow Lindberg. For an updated view of Lindberg's wisdom, read *Return to the Sea: Reflections on Anne Morrow Lindberg's Gift From the Sea* by Anne M. Johnson. Bring these books into your sanctuary and read a little every day. Again, record your responses in a journal.

Chapter 85

No Place Like "Om"

When I was growing up, no one taught me to control my thoughts. Behavior, yes and emotions, to some extent. But not my mind. Besides, why bother? Wasn't it already under my control? After all, it was *mine*.

Then, when I was in my late thirties, I was introduced to meditation in a stress management seminar. I was pretty sure that meditating would waste my time. After all, I already have a natural talent for doing nothing, which is what meditating seemed like to me and I wanted to accomplish more, not less. I also thought that the very idea of "mind control" sounded strange, like something that paranoid schizophrenics and people who claim to have been abducted by aliens rant about. But I was wrong on both counts.

Even though it's been around for a long time, there's still a lot of confusion about what meditation is, what it does and how it works. In a nutshell, it's a gentle, effective way to slow down the random, fragmented chitchat of your brain. It acts on both body and mind like a good night's sleep, promoting renewal, healing and clarity. But instead of seven or eight hours, it takes fifteen or twenty minutes and you don't have to lose consciousness to do it—both big pluses in my book.

Meditating is easy. To begin, sit comfortably in a quiet place. Support your spine so that it's straight but not stiff and rest your open palms on your thighs. Take a few full breaths and let them out all the way. The goal is to clear your mind of its nonstop chatter by focusing all of your attention on one simple thing. This, as I discovered, takes some practice.

Some people like to use a word or phrase as a mantra—a single sound to repeat and return to until their minds become still and receptive. To create your own mantra, try this: Imagine yourself in a wonderful, peaceful place—real or imaginary. Picture it clearly in your mind. See what you'd see, hear what you'd hear and feel what you'd feel. Now, think of one or two words that describe the experience and trigger those pictures. This is your mantra. Repeat the word or phrase over and over in a rhythm, silently or aloud. After a bit, it may begin to seem like a meaningless sound and that's fine. When you find your mind wandering (believe me, you will), gently bring it back and start the mantra again. And relax, because there's no wrong way to do this.

If using a mantra doesn't appeal to you, try to focus on your breathing. Count your breaths, each as one, one, one, or slowly repeat the words "in" and "out" as you inhale and exhale. Don't try to change your normal breathing; just allow it to be what it is and observe it. Or try focusing on a candle flame, crystal or other object. Again, when your attention wanders, don't judge your performance. Just quietly refocus.

People who meditate regularly are enthusiastic about the benefits, including better health, less stress and a sense of connection, confidence and calm energy. When I pray/meditate (I often combine them), I go to the same place at about the same time of day. I express thanks and request deeper clarity. Then I begin repeating my mantra. One twenty-minute session a day works wonders, especially when I'm blue or harried. Two sessions would be better, but, despite good intentions, I don't usually get around to the second.

Mini Meditation

This clarity-enhancing, focusing shortcut takes two minutes instead of twenty. Before you get out of bed in the morning, relax by breathing slowly and deeply several times. Now, take a minute or two to tell yourself how you intend to feel and behave during the day. Say it aloud, using words such as, "Today I intend... Today I feel... Today, I remember...Today I am," and complete the sentences any way you like, as long as they are phrased positively and in the present tense. If you can, do it again around lunchtime. If others are nearby and you don't want to say anything out loud, just repeat the words in your mind. These affirmations remind you of what you truly want and help set your internal rudder or guidance system.

Try any of these meditation techniques every day for a week. You may decide that meditation is not only a quick fix for a blue mood, it's also a wonderful inoculation against getting the blues in the first place.

Chapter 86

Stage a
Great Escape

What if I told you there was a place you could go where you would feel completely in harmony with the environment and yourself? A place where you would feel centered, relaxed, calm, whole and safe. What if I said that you could go when you want, stay as long as you want and when you decide to leave, you could take many of those wonderful feelings with you? Not bad, huh? There *is* a place like that and if you have any experience with guided meditation, you know what I mean. If you don't, I'll explain.

During a guided meditation, you close your eyes, sit or lie down in a comfortable place and follow audible instructions, sometimes from a live facilitator, often on a CD or audiotape. The instructions ask you to relax and imagine doing or feeling various things. When it's over, usually somewhere between ten and twenty minutes later, open your eyes and get up. That's all there is to it.

Except that the things you've been imagining have changed the way you feel. As far as your body and your subconscious mind are concerned, there isn't a significant difference between something you vividly imagine and something you actually experience. Guided meditation helps you to have a vivid imaginary experience that is very positive and, in many respects, as good as the real thing. No wonder you feel better!

Guided meditation audio tapes are readily available and inexpensively priced. All major bookstores carry them. Many natural/health food stores and mail-order catalogs have them, too. You'll probably find some in your public library. Some will be general and others designed to assist with special issues, such as healing illness, combating depression, building self-esteem, weight loss, stopping smoking, etcetera. Check with the clerk and read the labels and instructions to make sure you're getting an actual guided meditation, not simply a lecture. If you can, listen to a portion of the tape before you buy; some voices are better than others. My favorite is Belleruth Naparstek, whose Web site www.healthjourneys.com is a treasure trove of healing information.

You can also create a special place to visit in your imagination, without audio assistance. Close your eyes, sit comfortably or lie down and take slow, deep breaths for a couple of minutes. Focus your mind on your breathing. Then, either recall a place from your past where you felt at peace, safe, centered and very much alive or create one in your imagination. Make your mental picture as vivid and detailed as possible. See the colors. Smell the smells. Feel the sunlight, mist or breeze on your skin. Hear the sounds. Feel the feelings you experience as you explore this wonderful place or simply sit quietly and take it all in. Be there as fully as possible in mind, body and spirit.

When you're almost ready to leave, think of something you can do that will help you recall this place, these feelings later. Maybe a gesture: "When I touch my hand to my heart, it will remind me of this." Maybe a single word: "When I say *serenity*, out loud or silently, this place will come back to me." This will be your symbolic key. In computer jargon, it's a hyperlink, making it easy for you to jump from one place to another.

The next time you're feeling stressed, bummed out or not sure where you belong in the scheme of things, close your eyes and take a quick trip back to your special place. Just do what you did last time, only now you have a device that helps you access it more quickly. After you're relaxed and breathing deeply, just repeat the word, make the gesture, activate your key. It's not quite like clicking your computer's mouse, but it makes returning faster and easier. Bon voyage!

Group Getaway

Start (or join) a guided meditation group. All it takes is two or more people and a quiet place. Allow fifteen to twenty minutes for the meditation audio, then share some tea and conversation. It's a wonderful way to get to know people better. If a different audio is played each week, you get to experience several voices and techniques. Staying with a group favorite can also be nice; each time you listen, you find something new. Once in a while, skip the instructions and go unguided; just sit with eyes closed and listen to music designed to soothe and heal. I highly recommend *Gaia Mama*, an astonishingly beautiful CD of Tibetan singing bowls, gongs, chimes and improvisational vocals, available at www.gaiamama.com.

BLUES
FLASH!

Give a Little, Get a Lot

A University of Massachusetts Medical School study has shown that altruism may be its own best reward.

Not only does it help others, it can also counter the negative effects of stressful life events.

Researchers studied a group of churchgoers. Results indicated that people who give help and support to others are generally more resilient and feel better than people who just receive help.

No surprise, huh? Haven't you always known that it *feels* good to *do* good?

Chapter 87

Dream a
Little Dream

Experts describe dreams in a variety of ways: as messages from a guiding spirit or divinity; communications from your own "higher power," what Jung called the collective unconscious; or information from your own unconscious mind. The jury's not in and probably never will be on a definite answer, but that doesn't matter. Wherever they come from, some of the amazing experiences that happen when your conscious mind shuts down can serve you well, if you're open to them.

Studies show that dreams may help you learn new skills, sort and consolidate memories and even boost your creativity. When you're blue, stressed or anxious, they can help change your perspective, sometimes profoundly. Dreams may allow you to become aware of previously submerged feelings or invite you to accept disowned parts of yourself. In many dreams, there often is a nugget of truth that can bring a joyful insight, offer consolation, reveal a dilemma or maybe even suggest a path to a problem's solution.

To unlock this intriguing source of information, you'll first need to remember and record your dreams. If you think you don't dream, it's because you don't remember them. Everyone dreams. In fact, most of us have four to seven dreams a night. A good way to begin to remember your dreams is to program yourself. Before you go to sleep, tell yourself that you'll awaken immediately after a dream. Keep paper and pen on a bedside table and record the dream while it's fresh in your mind. Then go back to sleep. Don't just tell yourself you'll remember it in the morning; that seldom works.

The next day, close your eyes and reimmerse yourself in the dream. Pay attention to the emotions and physical feelings you experienced. Remember the details—colors, textures, sounds, smells. Consider how you felt when you woke up and how you feel as you rework the dream. Relax. Be open to whatever comes. Think of your dream as a puzzle and play with the pieces. How might they fit together? What might they mean? Choose one character or object that draws your attention and investigate it. Pretend you are that person or thing and describe yourself. Trust your instincts, go with your first reaction and don't censor yourself. Then, work with the other characters and objects in the dream. Become the voice for each. Have them talk to each other. What are they experiencing? What do they want? What do they feel? Do they speak for parts of you?

Waking Dreams

If you absolutely can't remember or make sense of your dreams, try a guided fantasy. Here's a simple one that works well. For best results, record the instructions and play them back. Sit comfortably, take a few deep breaths and relax. Let your waking world float away. Imagine you're on a journey. Notice your surroundings, mode of travel and how you feel. Suddenly, your trip is interrupted. What's happened? What's your reaction? What do you do about it? Your journey continues, but now you see someone coming toward you. What does this person look like? Do you know him or her? What's your reaction? How does meeting this person make you feel? Next, the person gives you a message. What is it? How does it make you feel? Does this change your journey? Do you do anything as a result? Finally, you arrive at your destination. What does it look like? Who else is there? How do you feel now? When you're finished, write it down and reflect on it using the same process you'd use to understand a dream.

A client once told me she dreamed of a copper teapot filled with boiling water on a red-hot stove. There was nobody around to turn off the stove. She said she woke up feeling very tense. In her reimmersion, she chose to be the teapot: "I'm screaming for attention! I have to let off some steam. Too much is bubbling up. If someone doesn't turn off the heat, I'll burn up!" When she went to the next level, she described the physical qualities of the teapot: "I'm attractive and valuable. I can take a lot of heat, but sometimes it can be too much. When I overheat, I let off steam and scream, because I need to stop." We talked about the fact that her therapy sessions had been "heating up" lately, because she had been making some important emotional breakthroughs. After a few minutes, she asked if we could pull back a little for a while. When I said, "Sure thing," she breathed a sigh of relief. Her dream helped her ask for and get what she needed.

When you're done analyzing and re-experiencing the dream from several perspectives, reflect on what you've learned. Ask yourself, "How am I like this person/object?" Which of the words you've used to describe it also could be used to describe you? Don't jump to conclusions. Explore your ideas until the message in your dream rings true.

Chapter 88

Right It
with Ritual

Is "Life sucks and then you die" your motto when you feel blue? When you're trying to manage a complex, compartmentalized, demanding life, it's easy to get lost and become spiritually paralyzed for a while.

Time for a bluesbusting ritual! The right ritual can help you change your mood and raise your spirits. It can expand your consciousness and make it easier to connect with your higher self. It can bring a sacred feeling to ordinary experiences, help you celebrate significant events, ease transitions and give you more structure and stability. It can even add meaning to your life and provide a sense of purpose. The ancient art of ritual endures because it works: Your subconscious mind doesn't differentiate between a symbolic ritual experience and an ordinary event. When you participate in a cleansing ceremony to rid yourself of bad feelings, you come away feeling clear and ready to start over with a clean slate.

Burning the Blues

Go to a special space, alone or with friends. Bring pencils, paper and a small fireproof container. Sit comfortably, take a deep breath and announce the beginning of a ritual to let go of the negative and invite positive possibilities. Sit quietly for a minute or two, mentally reviewing the things that are getting you down. When you're ready, write out each concern. Be clear and concise. After you finish, tear the paper into tiny pieces, place them in the container, light the paper on fire and stir until all the pieces are ash. Discuss or write about the experience or simply end by thinking of one word that describes how you feel now, then sharing or writing it.

Rituals can be simple or complex, done alone or with others, traditionally prescribed or created in the moment to meet a specific need. There are, however, a few basic considerations that should be included in every ritual.

Clarify the Purpose. Why are you doing it? The form of a ritual grows directly from its purpose. It can be anything from celebration to problem solving. Your bath could become a ritual cleansing, in which you let go of negativity and make room for creativity and pleasure. The evening meal might include a family ritual to acknowledge one another after a busy day. For example, a child might say, "Mom's hug felt good when I got home from school." Parents can reinforce desired behavior: "Jane did a good job cleaning her room." Or, "I'm happy that Dad could take Jason to soccer practice."

Gather the Ingredients. Choose the things to include in your ritual carefully; they'll help make the experience extraordinary and add to its meaning. Consider candles, crystals, art supplies, paper, pen, seashells, stones, wood, incense, food, drink, religious objects and any other items that have special importance to you. You might also want to wear special clothes.

Start with Style. A good beginning gets you engaged and says something special is about to happen. Start with a sacred space, one in which you won't be interrupted. Spread a beautiful cloth, burn incense, go to your special chair. Any place can become sacred if that's your intention. It can be as simple as lighting a candle, forming a circle, listening to music, meditating and saying a few carefully chosen words or as complex as going to a special place (beach, mountain, desert) at a special time (sunrise, sunset, midnight), building a fire, making an altar or constructing a sweat lodge (a native American steam bath used for spiritual cleansing). As you begin the ritual, announce your intention. If others are participating, describe what will happen so they know what to expect.

Make Your Actions Speak. What you do during your ritual means as much as what you say. Simple actions can create profound meaning. Use the four elements (earth, water, air, fire) to focus your actions. To let go of certain feelings or attachments, you can bury (earth), wash/float (water), blow away/set free (air), burn (fire). To gain insight, focus on a flame, breathe deeply, drink from a special cup, touch the earth, eat special food, sing, dance, speak or record your innermost thoughts. Be creative and be sure the actions touch your spirit.

End with Heart. Rituals need closure, something specific to end the experience. Common ways to close include a few moments of silence, the sharing or speaking of a single word to sum up the experience, special food or drink, a bow, a prayer or, if you're with others, a big hug.

BLUES
FLASH!

Finding Balance

According to Buddhist psychology, the blues can be a consequence of seeking stimulation.

What goes up must come down. When you keep striving for highs, you'll end up feeling low when the exhilaration wears off.

This Buddhist view counsels us to seek balance in our emotional lives.

One way to find that balance is through the daily practice of meditation. It helps you to create a feeling of inner peace, no matter what highs and lows life sends your way.

Chapter 89

The Pow!
of Now

One of the most inspiring and useful books I've read lately is Eckhart Tolle's *The Power of Now: A Guide to Spiritual Enlightenment*. It made me aware once again, in a fresh and immediate way, that every moment of life is a miracle. It's not a religious book, in that it embraces all traditions and contradicts none, but it does what all great spiritual teachings do: it reveals by example and in clear, straightforward language that the way, the truth and the light are within us.

The book's message is both simple and profound: When we can get beyond our bodies and our minds, we're in for a pleasant surprise. Of course, what's happening in our bodies and minds tends to dominate our daily lives and perhaps that's as it should be. But there's also a spiritual dimension to being human—an aspect of ourselves that is timeless, boundless and quite wonderful. Tolle calls this spiritual dimension *being* and he says that it's always waiting in the wings—waiting for us to stop thinking, stop doing and just be. When we do, we experience our true nature, which is one of deep peace and pure love.

This isn't an easy concept to grasp. The way to do it, explains Tolle, is not to try and understand it with the mind, but rather to make an attempt to be present, fully and intensely present, in the *now*. One of the biggest obstacles to being fully present is our hyper-busy "monkey minds." If you've ever tried to meditate, you know how hard it can be to stop the incessant chatter going on in your brain. Like a monkey swinging from branch to branch, noisy and easily distracted, your mind swings from thought to thought, sometimes purposefully, sometimes without any sense of direction. When you try to stop it, more thoughts rush in. Experienced meditators have learned that "allowing" the mind to become still is more effective than trying to force it to become quiet (see Chapter 85, "No Place Like Om").

A part of this concept I really like is the idea that the journey matters more than the destination. In fact, the journey *is* the destination. While it's helpful to know where you want to go, or at least the general direction, the only thing that's ultimately real about your journey is the step that you're taking at this immediate moment. Your life's journey has both outer and inner purposes. The outer purpose is to arrive at your goal or destination, accomplish what you set out to do and achieve this or that at some point in the future. But if what's going to happen in the future takes up so much of your attention that it becomes more important than the step you're taking now, you'll miss your journey's inner purpose, which has nothing to do with *where* you're going or *what* you're doing, and everything to do with *how* you're doing it. It's not about the future. It's about you and your awareness, right now, this very moment.

Think about it. How much of your blue-mood distress is coming from the past (What did I do? What was done to me? What went right/wrong? What should/shouldn't I/they have done?)? How much is coming from the future (What will happen? What should/shouldn't I/they do? Will I be okay? Will I be happy again?)?

It may help to remember that neither past nor future is real; the only place you can truly be alive or feel anything is in the present. What if, just for today, you conducted a little experiment? What if you focused your attention, not on past or future, but on what's happening in the present? Don't criticize or analyze. Just watch, notice, feel and be. See what happens when you meet yourself where you are right here, right now.

Stop Killing Time

How much of your time do you spend waiting, both small- and big-time? Small-time waiting: in line at supermarket or post office, in traffic, in an airport, in waiting rooms, for five o'clock to roll around, for your nails to dry. Big-time waiting: for your kids to be older, for your soul mate to show up, for the job where you'll make big bucks, for your dad to stop being a jerk. Waiting is a state of mind: You want the future to hurry up, because you're not happy with the present. Sure, it's fine to strive for better things, but stop "killing time" by waiting. Instead, make time come alive. When you catch yourself waiting, come into the present moment and find something to notice or enjoy. And the next time someone says, "Sorry to keep you waiting," say, "I wasn't waiting. I was having a great time!"

Chapter 90

Gratitude:
More than an Attitude

Gratitude is the operative word of the new millennium. Everyone from Oprah to the Dalai Lama has been touting its value. Of course, when you're mired in the blues, it may seem that there's nothing much to be grateful for, but a broader perspective may change your outlook.

When I first heard someone mention the Japanese word naikan, I thought they were talking about a camera. It's actually a system of self-reflection and introspection developed by a devout Buddhist who wanted to make the process available to more people. Dr. David Reynolds introduced it in the United States in the 1970s. Naikan can help you master the attitude of gratitude and make it a way of life. Its techniques allow you to open up the way you experience the world, as if you've gone from a small-screen black-and-white television to a larger-than-life, panoramic view. While not exactly a quick fix, there are multiple, long-term benefits from seeing the world from this expanded point of view.

Naikan asks you to take a fresh look at your life, based on three questions that you reflect upon daily: What have I received from _____? What have I given to _____? What troubles and difficulties have I caused? You use these questions to see yourself in relationship to others: people, animals, growing things, even inanimate objects. In each case, they help you evaluate how your world works in terms of the give and take in every relationship. As you think about each question, make a list of your responses.

Your "What have I received?" list might include: My cat purred, nudged my face and woke me up just before the alarm. My partner made breakfast. The gas station attendant put gas in my car and it worked perfectly as I drove to work. These are clear, simple descriptions of reality—

attitude and motivation are unimportant, as you benefit regardless. They're small things that might ordinarily go unnoticed, because they support you while your attention is elsewhere. On the other hand, if your car breaks down, you don't get breakfast or your cat goes missing, you realize how important these seemingly insignificant things are. Try to remember everything you've received. When your consciousness shifts to the many ways the world supports you, you're no longer trapped by a focus on problems and obstacles and you deepen your sense of appreciation and gratitude.

Taking the efforts of others for granted, as if you feel entitled to what they give, can make you begin to resent it when your expectations aren't met. When you answer the second question, "What do I give?", your perspective shifts from collecting what is owed you to noticing what you receive and wanting to give back. It helps you, not only to feel grateful, but also to consciously maintain more balanced relationships.

The third question may be the most difficult. We're usually aware of how circumstances and people hassle us and cause problems. We're annoyed when someone cuts us off, when the grocery checker keeps us waiting or when we can't find our keys. Yet, when *we* are the source of inconvenience or aggravation for others, we seldom notice. If we do, we're likely to say, "It was an accident," "I made a mistake," "It's no big deal," or even, "They're being too sensitive." If we avoid knowing how we are a source of suffering or trouble, we won't really know ourselves or learn the grace by which we want to live.

By reflecting on all three questions, your view of life can make a radical shift. You'll stop experiencing your world as one of frustration and irritation and begin to feel grateful for what you get, pleased by what you give and more forgiving and tolerant of inconveniences.

Make It Work

Naikan is a process through which you may be able to bring your world view into better balance. Without practice, though, it remains an elegant theory. The simplest way to develop the Naikan attitude of gratitude is to spend twenty to thirty minutes before you go to bed each night reviewing your day. Find a quiet spot, get a pen and paper or open a computer file and reflect on the three questions. Be specific with your answers. For example, rather than writing that you ate at a friend's house today, record what you ate and who provided the food. Don't leave anything out, because you do it every day or because it seems trivial. The more you notice what you get, what you give and in what ways you cause difficulties for others, the more your perspective will shift and the better you'll feel.

Chapter 91

Zap Your Mood
with Zen

When you take a Zen approach to a blue mood, you won't be doing anything nearly as aggressive or forceful as a "zap," although that may be the eventual result. At first, what you'll do is nothing.

Often, when we feel lost, frightened or required to face something new, our first impulse is to either run or fight. Sometimes fight or flight is a good choice. Other times it just increases our pain and sense of being trapped. Instead of frantically looking for a way to make yourself feel better, what if you simply sat down, allowed your body and mind to become still and listened? Perhaps your blue mood has something to tell you. If you're willing to be still and feel what you feel—to bring both attention and compassion to your emotional state—you may discover what it is.

This might seem scary, but when you sit quietly and patiently with your feelings, you'll have an opportunity to notice how they present themselves in your body. You'll be able to see how you respond to them, too. If you can be present with your fear and meet it with compassionate attention, you may discover its opposite—a place of peace and fearlessness inside you.

Of course, it's natural to avoid painful feelings. Avoiding pain keeps us alive. Where we sometimes go wrong, though, is in believing that we should never feel pain, that something outside ourselves is to blame for our suffering or that there is something wrong with us for feeling the way we do. None of these things is true.

Buddhism teaches that pain can't be avoided, but suffering is optional. Suffering comes, Buddhist teachers say, from our attempts to avoid pain; all that is needed is to stand up straight in the midst of your pain.

"Easy for her to say," you may be thinking. "I feel too helpless and hopeless to stand up to anything right now." So don't stand up. Just sit for a while and reflect. Your blue mood may be bringing you face-to-face with the fact that there are many things, both outside and inside yourself, that you can't control, no matter how hard you try. In a culture that seems to prize control over all things (wealth and success are forms of control), admitting you aren't completely in control may feel frightening, but it can also be a relief. Take comfort in this: often, deepening spirituality is not the result of greater control, but of a greater acceptance of your inherent powerlessness.

Another Buddhist practice involves letting go of the desire to blame self or others for painful feelings. Looking for places to lay blame distracts us from what's really happening and serves as a barrier to true understanding of and intimacy with our own lives. When you feel the impulse to blame others or yourself for your discomfort, is it possible to simply notice the impulse, setting aside the need to follow it? How do you feel when you do this? Can you give up trying to explain your situation or find a solution to it, if only for a few minutes? Do you feel some relief during this time?

When you honor your own feelings, no matter what they are, you move toward a place of compassion within yourself. Compassion starts with self, then spreads to encompass those around you and the entire world. In this compassionate place, if you want to cry, cry. If you want to laugh, laugh. Maybe what you feel is a frozen sea inside you, beginning to melt. Perhaps it's the courage to listen to your own heart.

Find Your Inner Parent

A great deal has been written about finding your "inner child." When you're blue, that usually isn't hard: You don't want to take care of yourself. You want to sleep late, eat ice cream for breakfast, avoid responsibility and play games that make you forget your woes. Nothing wrong with that—not for a while, anyway. But maybe what you really need to find is your inner adult, or, better yet, your inner parent. Your ideal inner parent, not the critical one who often pops up when you're down. Ideal parents are patient and see progress in small steps. They know results don't always come right away. They love and accept you just as you are. They are attentive and willing to take a back seat. They speak gently and calmly, even when angry. They admit their mistakes and have faith that you will turn out well. And they are ready to learn from whatever happens and teach their kids what's really important. Deliberately adopting this state of mind can be a great help when you're blue. Give it a try.

Chapter 92

Small Voice, Big Rewards

Your blue mood may be a wake-up call reminding you to pay attention to something you've been ignoring: your intuition. The psychologist Carl Jung described intuition as the ability to see around corners. For most of us, it feels like a small inner voice or feeling that comes from the gut, heart or out of thin air. Some folks think that immediate perception of this kind, without rhyme or reason, is too irrational to be trusted. Many others, including me, believe intuition is as real and as valuable as intellect. It's our sixth sense, enabling us to live larger, more conscious lives in every dimension.

We acknowledge the ability of animals to understand and react to things that are beyond their normal brainpower, calling it instinct. Although it defies logic, we accept it as real and valuable, yet we tend to ignore our own illogical feelings and hunches. While your intellect is an important and powerful tool, it's finite, limited to logic, reason, facts and data.

Your intuition, on the other hand, appears to have access to endless amounts of information. It provides insight and guidance you simply can't get any other way. I think of it as being like the nifty GPS (Global Positioning System) that some new cars come with. You may not always know where you are, but, once you learn how to use it, the GPS sure does. Nevertheless, many of us have been taught to mistrust our feelings. Instead, we suppress them and depend on our intellect. If this sounds like you, maybe it's time to re-educate yourself to hear and trust the truths that come to you intuitively.

The first step is to develop the habit of tuning in to your feelings. Quiet your mind and ask yourself, as many times a day as you can, "How does this make me feel?" Notice uneasiness, excitement, attraction, repulsion and so on. How do these feelings show up in your body? Listen to your inner dialogue, too. Does one part of you say, "Yes, go ahead!" while another says, "No, hold off, this isn't safe"? Cultivate a habit of talking and listening to your inner self or selves. When you're feeling low, ask for guidance and stay alert for answers, which may come in many forms: words, images, flashes of insight, or sudden awareness.

At first, this may cause you to feel uncomfortable or vulnerable, maybe even a little scared. You may hesitate to change your plans or course of direction in case your intuition is wrong. Learning to trust your intuitive sense is a slow process. It takes practice and a willingness to make mistakes.

As with so many other steps toward change, it's a good idea to start small. You'll need to learn to distinguish your intuition from all your other internal voices — critical parent, anxious child, rebellious adolescent — telling you to depend only on facts and reason. With practice, you'll learn to recognize which voice is intuition and be able to move forward.

Give it a Face

For many of us, it's easier to connect with someone we've met in person than someone to whom we've only spoken. This may be true for your inner voices, as well. If so, it helps if you personify them. Before you go to sleep at night, invent a little fantasy. Ask to meet your inner guides. Imagine yourself in a beautiful, comfortable, safe space. Look around and enjoy this wonderful place while you wait and watch for your guides. Imagine them coming through a door to your right. Notice their gender, how they look and what they're wearing. Allow them to introduce themselves and introduce yourself to them. Talk for a while and get to know each other a little. Then, invite them to be the faces of your intuition. If you wish, ask for advice. The next time you check in with yourself, imagine these guides and ask for their counsel.

Notice what happens when you follow intuitive feelings and what happens when you doubt, suppress or ignore them. Remember, sad or bad feelings may be an indication that you have ignored your intuitive knowledge. Use discomfort as a signal that it's time to tune in to your inner GPS for guidance. When you do, you may improve your mood and boost your energy.

Chapter 93

Spirited Sex

Ever feel like sex between you and your sweetie has shifted from "making love" to "doing it?" That shift is almost inevitable in a world that encourages sex as a contact sport and portrays both men and women as objects to use for personal gratification. Ever feel like you've lost touch with yourself and others? It's easy to do in a world of information overload, quantum change and services delivered by machines instead of real people. When the loss is extreme, it can lead to a crushing sense of isolation and sadness.

Tantra, an ancient mystical teaching originating in India, can put the love back into having sex and bring you back to yourself and the world. It can help you reconnect with your loving spirit and live your life to the fullest, without guilt or fear. Tantra teaches a sacred way to make love, harmonizing the male and female aspects of your nature into one balanced, blissful self. It also teaches the art of paying 100 percent attention to whatever it is you're experiencing, so that your body isn't busy with one thing, while your mind is someplace else. Tantra can teach you how to find exhilaration in the everyday sensual experiences of eating, drinking, tasting, smelling and touching.

Tantric theory, refined by western psychology, promotes daily spiritual growth. Practicing Tantra means practicing forgiveness and unconditional love, as well as learning how to balance mind and heart. It encourages the discipline of both physical and spiritual practices to help you be more fully present in every moment of your life. These practices may include yoga, meditation, journal writing, bodywork, whole-body health, focused sexual behavior or the worship of a higher power.

Couples who want to increase their harmony, intimacy and sexual pleasure need to learn about things they can do to transform the act of love into one with an even higher purpose. To enrich the relationship with yourself or another person, be willing to risk vulnerability. It's okay to do it wrong, (whatever "it" may be) to look bad or to feel emotionally stuck. It's an act of courage and love to face your demons. Tantra teaches you to honor, trust and be open with yourself and your partner. This alone greatly improves your ability to please your lover.

Become Each Other's Guru

For a taste of Tantric sex, try this exercise with your partner. It can help you connect your body's experience to your heart's experience, bringing you both immense pleasure and healing. Focus your mind on your heart and on your partner's heart. Imagine them connected by waves of love. At some point, while looking into each other's eyes and stimulating each other's bodies, reach out and rest one hand on the other's heart. This serves as a message and reminder: We are connected in spirit, as well as in a physical sense. Imagine breathing love deeply into your partner. Imagine your own heart opening like a flower and receiving love. Continue this loving meditation for as long as you wish. When you're both ready—don't rush; go slowly—you may or may not choose to complete your lovemaking by bringing each other to orgasm. If, on your first try, you don't have an orgasm that creates a glow in your heart as well as bliss in your body, don't worry. Making love is about the entire process, not just a few seconds at the end. And, like most things, Tantric skills improve with practice.

Tantric sex can become a path to ecstasy and spiritual enlightenment. Tantric practices can transform sexuality from doing to being and turn the act of sex into a sacrament of love. Through lovemaking with your partner, you can find union with the divine, move closer to your own soul and access the power that resides in self-realization. The ultimate goal is to dissolve the ego and join two opposites that, when united, become one with the universe. Tantra enables you to slow down love's dance and make the instant of orgasm a moment of affirmation and empowerment.

Tantric sex brings seemingly contradictory aspects of the self into harmony: masculine/feminine, dark/light, spirit/matter, most experiential/most holy. It helps you create a balanced blend of these opposites and, in so doing, you become whole. With Tantra as your vehicle, sex becomes a metaphor for life. The more you are able to remove your blockages, focus your attention on what you're doing and open your heart, the more joy and love you'll experience.

Two books that explain more about this extraordinary practice are *Sexual Secrets* by Nik Douglas and Penny Slinger and *Tantra: The Art of Conscious Loving* by Charles and Caroline Muir.

Chapter 94

Negotiation 101

Unless you're still in the honeymoon phase of couplehood, you probably know that conflict is part of the deal. I don't know any couples who don't fight from time to time, no matter how happy they are. No big deal. Conflict is healthy. Conflict is simply the expression of differences and, unless you've found a clone to mate with, there are going to be differences. Some of those differences will be big.

What's not healthy is fighting all the time. Or fighting that escalates to violence. Or fights that leave one or both of you feeling abused. You can't expect to be disagreement-free. However, happy couples learn, sometimes the hard way, how to fight fair and, even better, how to avoid many fights in the first place. Here are some guidelines for resolving conflict before it reaches the point of hard feelings.

If you have a gripe, start by describing the *behavior* that's bothering you. Begin with the word "When." For example, if you're not feeling loved these days, what are the behaviors that are causing it? Does your partner fail to express physical affection except when you're between the sheets? Does she read the newspaper or watch television while you're trying to talk to her? Does he fail to express appreciation for the things you do for him? What things? When? How often? Stick to the facts. "When the only time you touch me is in bed…" "When you don't look at me while I'm talking to you…" "When you don't thank me for ironing your shirt…"

Finish the sentence with an "I" statement about how the behavior makes you feel. I statements help you take responsibility for your feelings and avoid blaming them on your partner. "When the only time you touch me is in bed, I feel like something you use for sex." "When you don't look at me while I'm talking to you, I feel unimportant to you." "When you don't thank me for ironing your shirt, I feel taken for granted and unappreciated."

In the next sentence, make a specific, respectful request for change. What behavior do you want? Why do you want it? "I'd love it if you would snuggle with me sometimes while we're watching television, or just give me a little hug and kiss for no reason." "I'd feel happier if you looked at me when I have something to say. I want to matter to you and that would help me know that I do." "I'd like you to express appreciation when I iron a shirt for you. I take care to do it well and it'd be worth the effort if you notice and say thanks."

If you want to be really persuasive, add a few words about how the new behavior you're asking for will benefit, not just you, but also your partner. "You know, when I'm getting lots of affection from you away from the bedroom, it makes me a lot more interested in going there." "When you're interested in what I have to say, I feel ten times more interested in you." "Honey, when you thank me sincerely when I do things for you, I want to do even more!"

At this point, it's a good idea to add a few more words, requesting confirmation of cooperation. "Would you be willing to do that?" If you get a yes answer, express appreciation. Whenever you ask for and get what you want, you want to reinforce it. Smile. Show some affection. "Thanks, darling. You're the best. I really appreciate your hearing me like this." If your partner needs to air some feelings, be willing to listen.

Before you go into the discussion, you might want to think about how you contribute to the problem. Perhaps you've brushed off a few too many kisses in the kitchen. Maybe you've ignored talk about her less-than-fascinating book discussion group. Possibly you've taken the times he's washed the car or fixed the garbage disposal for granted.

Chapter 95

Level Three Living

Centuries ago, Plato talked about four levels of happiness. Level One happiness, he said, is all about immediate gratification leading to physical or sensual enjoyment. For example, you can get Level One happiness from a gourmet dinner or great sex with your sweetie. Level One happiness can be intense, but it doesn't last long.

There's nothing wrong with Level One happiness, except when it's overemphasized or misused. When physical pleasure or gratifying the senses becomes more important than other, deeper kinds of happiness, you're in for trouble. That's when all kinds of addictive behaviors pop up—drug abuse, alcohol abuse, people who put their lives at risk for powerful but short-lived pleasure. It's not a pretty picture and it leads to a world of grief.

Level Two happiness isn't concerned with physical pleasure at all. Instead of being about gratifying the senses, it's about gratifying the ego. Level Two happiness depends mainly on achievement and it comes from things we do to strengthen our self-esteem and compete successfully in the world. For instance, you get Level Two happiness if you beat out the competition for a promotion or take a class and come away from it feeling smarter and better off. We all like to win. We like to grow. We like to feel Level Two good.

There's also a negative, compulsive side to Level Two happiness. If your ego takes over, if you have to win because you need to feel superior, if you get pleasure from feeling smarter or more competent or better than other people, then Level Two turns ugly. You may become the kind of person who can't admit a mistake and has to criticize other people in order to feel good.

We've all known people like that. They're not happy unless they're in the one-up position and someone else is one-down. So, if you're looking for happiness that lasts—a deep kind of happiness that really makes a difference in your life—Level Three is where it's at. At this level, your happiness comes from using your talents, skills and energy for something bigger than yourself. You care about making other people happy, about contributing something, about giving back and the happiness you get from these things fills you with energy, creativity and deep contentment. You make a difference in your own life by making a difference in other people's lives.

Can you imagine giving without expecting anything in return? Can you imagine being generous with your appreciation, praise, information, time, energy and—yes—money, without expecting anything back, not even gratitude? If you can, hold that thought, because you're imagining yourself as a Level Three person!

Level Four happiness takes place on a spiritual plane. It's an ultimate happiness that can only come from an ultimate source. Level Four is about your relationship with a higher power. It's at level four that your conception of God—whatever that may be—comes into play. This is a personal matter and we'll leave it at that.

If your life is lived mainly at Level One and Level Two, it's a safe bet that you'll have a more than passing acquaintance with the blues. The more you shift your thinking to Level Three, the better the likelihood that you'll go around with "a smile on your face and a glow in your heart," as my friend Jim Madrid likes to say. Jim teaches Plato's Levels of Happiness as part of a terrific personal development seminar called *The Ten Principles of Entelechy.* Entelechy is a word coined by Aristotle that means the vital force urging an organism to self-fulfillment. It's in you. It's in me. You're most likely to feel the vital force when you're making a good-faith effort to get your pleasures at Level Three.

Letting Go

To grow toward your vision and become a whole, happy person, you must strive for what you most want. You must also let go of what doesn't fit. To let go is not to regret the past, but to grow and live for the future. To let go is to fear less and love more. To let go is to take each day as it comes and cherish yourself in it. To let go is not to deny, but to accept. To let go is not to nag, scold or argue, but instead search out your own shortcomings and work to correct them. To let go is not to fix, but to be supportive. To let go is to say "no" when that is what needs to be said and "yes" when yes is the truth. To let go is to realize that you can't control anyone else and to refuse to allow them to control you. To let go is to go forward with faith.

Chapter 96

Friends:
First, Last and Always

As you've read this book, you may have noticed how often friendship is mentioned as an uplifting source of support when you have the blues. Of course, if you can develop an abiding friendship with your mate, the relationship is more likely to last and satisfy you both. Friendship is often the prelude to love and many people believe that friendship itself may be the strongest kind of love.

Friends help you celebrate your successes and mourn your losses. They bear witness to your life transitions, support your hopes and dreams unconditionally and bring light to your darkest times. They're the ones who love and accept you, no matter what, and stand by you through thick and thin.

Without my friend and co-author I couldn't have written this book. Friends have helped me see things I didn't want to see but needed to face. They have encouraged me to stretch and grow, leave bad relationships and take better care of my health. Once, after what seemed like an unbearable betrayal, I dove into a deep depression. I wasn't even sure I wanted to go on living. My friends saw what was happening and gently, persistently pushed until I agreed to get help.

Friends can help you put your life in order, let go of the past and move toward the future. I can't think of a better antidote to the blues. Good friends will put their lives on hold to listen, sympathize and advise when you need it. They'll let you rage or cry or just sit quietly with you, holding your hand. Friends help you grieve and fill the emptiness when you suffer the loss of a loved one, whether human or pet. They will bear witness, stay with you through your long night of pain and help you greet the morning with renewed hope.

Friends are there when you need them and when you know that, it makes life easier. Epicurus, a philosopher living in Greece about three hundred years before the birth of Christ said it perfectly: "It is not so much our friends' help that helps us as the confident knowledge that they will help us." Exactly.

Kids know as much about true camaraderie as any adult. In interviews conducted at an elementary school, children were asked about the nature of friends and friendship. Here's how they answered the question:

- What is the main problem in friendship? *Leaving someone out.*
- What is a good friend? *Somebody you can depend on.*
- What if your friend said they wouldn't be your friend if you were another person's friend? *That friend wouldn't mind if she or he were really your friend.*

When asked about the secrets of having a good friendship, here are the behaviors they listed:

- Treat your friends the way you want to be treated.
- Keep secrets that are told to you.
- Pay attention when your friend is talking.
- Keep your promises.
- Share things with your friend.
- Tell your friend the truth.
- Stick up for your friend.
- Take turns.

If your supply of friends seems scant, think about what you might do to make new ones. The best place to find friends, of course, is close to home and in real life. Join a group of people who share one of your interests—church, hobbies, sports, politics, the environment, reading, dancing, fitness, pets—doesn't matter what. Get to know them slowly and see which ones you genuinely like. Then smile, chat and express interest in them. If you get a positive response, make a casual invitation: Would you like to (go to a movie, have a cup of coffee, join me for lunch, go hiking) some time? The rest is will follow naturally.

Friends on Film

Rent one of these first-rate friendship movies, invite one of your best friends (or a person you'd like to become a best friend) over:

Beaches (Bette Midler and Barbara Hershey); *Boys on the Side* (Drew Barrymore, Whoopi Goldberg, Mary Louise Parker); *Circle of Friends* (Minnie Driver, Colin Firth, Saffron Burows); *Enchanted April* (Miranda Richardson, Joan Plowright, Polly Walker); *First Wives Club* (Diane Keaton, Goldie Hawn, Bette Midler); *Waiting to Exhale* (Whitney Houston, Angela Bassett, Loretta Devine); *Now and Then* (Christina Ricci, Melanie Griffith, Demi Moore, Rosie O'Donnell).

Chapter 97

Love, Love, Love!

The opposite of love, someone once said, isn't hate but fear. That sounds true to me and here's something that sounds even truer: When your heart is full of love, it's almost impossible to feel anything negative—fear, anger, apathy, sadness, anxiety, boredom, blue, you name it. There are, of course, a great many shades and flavors of love, but three stand out as primary: love of self; love in relationships with others; and the biggest love of all—the spiritual kind of love that reaches far beyond the self and the people and things you know to touch the whole world. Three kinds of love, three ways to keep the blues at bay.

Love of self. It all starts here. You can't love anyone better than you love yourself and I'm not talking about selfishness or self-absorbed narcissism. Loving yourself means treating yourself as if you have value (you do!) and are worthy of respect (you are!). It means caring for every aspect of yourself—mind, body, heart and spirit—thoughtfully and gently. You don't do things that demean you, you don't sacrifice your self-respect to please others or gain their approval and you certainly don't allow others to abuse you.

Self-love means you try to eat right, steer clear of things that harm you, get enough rest and exercise, don't ignore signs of trouble and get help when you need it. It also means you don't beat yourself up if you're not doing all those things perfectly. You make every attempt to enjoy life, develop a career that suits you and keep growing in skills, understanding, compassion and wisdom. None of this is beyond you. It's a portrait of who you were meant to be or, if you prefer, of who you are capable of being.

Love in relationships. Even if you don't have a sweetheart right now, you have plenty of relationships: family, friends, kids, coworkers, people you interact with every day. When you bring a loving spirit to these relationships, they become more loving and when they become more loving, you get happier and your loving spirit expands. It's the opposite of a vicious circle—an expanding spiral of love, sweet love! It's not complicated if you just practice the old Golden Rule: Treat others as you wish to be treated, with respect, kindness, honesty and compassion. Pay attention to them, listen more than you talk, put yourself in their shoes and smile at them a lot.

The big love. The spirit knows no bounds. If you love all life, you know that an African child orphaned as a result of AIDS is your concern, as is the inner city kid whose father isn't in the picture and whose mother smokes crack. People going to bed hungry are your concern. The degradation of the planet is your concern. The way animals and livestock are cared for is your concern. So is the waging of war, the treatment of women and minorities and the ever-increasing numbers of those who live in poverty.

I'm not suggesting that you try to shape up the planet single-handedly or worry yourself into an even darker mood. But if you love, you care and if you care, find a little corner of the world where you can make a difference and do something. Write a check to Oprah's African Relief Fund, Habitat for Humanity, Doctors Without Borders or another worthy cause. Recycle and support "green" businesses. Contact your senators and representatives about issues that touch your heart and outrage your sense of decency and fairness. Educate yourself so that you can persuade others to care and get involved, too. That's all. That's a lot.

A Loving Kick in the Butt

You are running out of time. I don't want to alarm you, but I do want to get your rear in gear when it comes to this loving stuff. Even if you had all the time in the world, I'd be on your case. The time to love is now. The place to love is here. The people to love are you, first, then everyone else. The excuses (refuse to call them reasons) that keep you from loving are holding your spirit hostage. Stop resenting and start forgiving. Stop taking and start giving. Stop letting your emotions rule you and start choosing the way you feel. Stop being afraid to live and love fully and start taking a few risks. Heal the wounded parts of yourself (get help from a pro to speed things up) and get on with it. Today. Right now. You'll love, love, love what happens next!

:60 Second Bluesbusters Quiz:
Are You Dealing with the Big D?

Mood swings come and go; everybody gets them. According to a University of Michigan study, most of us spend nearly three days out of ten trying to shake off low moods. With an array of :60 Second Bluesbusters tips and strategies, you can recover in a lot less time. However, if your moods become too dark or lengthy, you may be dealing with more than the blues. Ask yourself if you've experienced any of these symptoms of clinical depression for two weeks or more:

- Constant sadness: feeling down in the dumps
- Little or no interest in things you usually enjoy, including sex
- Feeling guilty, hopeless, helpless and/or worthless
- Changes in appetite; weight gain or loss
- Change in sleep patterns; too much or too little; restless waking
- Constant fatigue and/or low energy
- Difficulty concentrating
- Persistent thoughts of death and/or suicide

Other symptoms may include:

- Frequent headaches or bouts of weeping
- General aches and pains for no clear reason
- Digestive/bowel problems or trouble swallowing
- Sexual problems, loss of interest or excessive activity
- Feeling anxious or worried without knowing why
- Increasing reluctance to leave the house

What to Do If You're More than Blue

If you have experienced two or more of these symptoms for two weeks or longer, visit the National Mental Health Association's Web site *www.depressionscreening.org* and take their online test (it's free and confidential) or talk with a mental health professional.

Clinical depression is a treatable illness, so don't wait another minute. Educate yourself so you can make informed decisions. If you don't know of one, ask your family doctor to recommend a good therapist or call your local crisis hotline; they have an extensive list. Call the crisis line immediately if you're planning or even fantasizing about suicide. And remember: You will feel like yourself again. Help is within reach.